Faith in Schools?

Faith in Schools?

AUTONOMY, CITIZENSHIP, AND
RELIGIOUS EDUCATION IN
THE LIBERAL STATE

Ian MacMullen

PRINCETON UNIVERSITY PRESS

PRINCETON AND OXFORD

Library of Congress Cataloging-in-Publication Data

MacMullen, Ian, 1976–
Faith in schools? : autonomy, citizenship, and religious education
in the liberal state / Ian MacMullen.
p.   cm.
Originally presented as the author's thesis (doctoral)—Harvard University.
Includes bibliographical references and index.
ISBN-13: 978-0-691-13091-0 (hardcover : alk. paper)
ISBN-10: 0-691-13091-4 (hardcover : alk. paper)
1. Church schools—Government policy. 2. Church and education—
Philosophy. 3. Education and state—Philosophy. I. Title.
LC368.M32 2007
371.071—dc22   2006039724

British Library Cataloging-in-Publication Data is available

This book has been composed in Palatino

Printed on acid-free paper. ∞

press.princeton.edu

Printed in the United States of America

1   3   5   7   9   10   8   6   4   2

To Lola

———————————

CONTENTS

Acknowledgments ix

Introduction 1

PART I: *Civic Education and Religious Schools* 13

CHAPTER 1
The Civic Case against Religious Schools 15

The Civic Goals of Education 16
Civic Goals as the Only Goals of Public Education Policy 21
Do Religious Schools Make Good Citizens? 29
The Civic Value of Religious Schools 35
Responses and Conclusions 37

CHAPTER 2
Civic Education and the Autonomy Problem in
Political Liberalism 41

Conflicting Educational Goals: Three Approaches to Resolution 41
Liberalism without Political Primacy 49
Is Autonomy a "Cost" of Civic Education? 54
Liberal Democratic Principles Presuppose the Value of Autonomy 60
Conclusion 62

PART II: *Autonomy as a Public Value* 65

CHAPTER 3
Autonomy, Identity, and Choice 67

Autonomy as Ongoing Rational Reflection 69
Caricatures of Rational Autonomy 73
The Nature of Autonomous Reflection 81
Conclusion 86

CHAPTER 4
The Value of Autonomy in a Pluralist World 88

John Stuart Mill, Joseph Raz, and the Intrinsic Value of Autonomy 88
Contemporary Liberal Responses to Mill: The Neutrality Condition 92
Autonomy and Moral Responsibility 93
Arguments for the Instrumental Value of Autonomy 96
The Instrumental Value of Autonomy and the Neutrality Principle 103
Conclusion 111

CHAPTER 5
Autonomy as a Goal of Education Policy:
Objections and Responses ... 113

Parental Rights and Interests ... 113
"Parents Are People Too" ... 119
The Death Knell for Traditional Ways of Life? ... 124
Other Objections and Responses ... 129
Conclusion ... 136

PART III: *Religious Schools and
Education for Autonomy* ... 137

CHAPTER 6
Secular Public Schools: Critiques and Responses ... 139

What's Wrong with Secular Education? ... 141
Public Control of Schools ... 147
Authority and Autonomy ... 151
Conclusion ... 155

CHAPTER 7
Religious Secondary Schools as Threat to Autonomy? ... 157

The Development of Autonomy Cannot Be Taken for Granted ... 157
The Autonomy Case against Religious Schools ... 162
Hallmarks of Permissible Religious Secondary Schools ... 169
Regulation and Entanglement ... 175
Conclusions and Policy Implications ... 179

CHAPTER 8
The Role of Religious Primary Schools ... 182

Age-Sensitive Education ... 182
Primary Culture and Identity ... 184
Reasoning within an Ethical Framework ... 188
Cognitive Development and Autonomous Reflection ... 190
Maintaining the Option of Autonomous Religious Belief ... 193
Hallmarks of Permissible Religious Primary Schools ... 197
Conclusion ... 202

Conclusion ... 205

Bibliography ... 221

Index ... 227

ACKNOWLEDGMENTS

I WAS INSPIRED to write this book by the experience of leaving my native Britain—where various Christian schools had long been supported by the state and the same status was gradually being offered to schools affiliated with other faiths—and wondering why so many members of the American Civil Liberties Union were so fervently committed to the principle that not one cent of the government's money should find its way into the coffers of a religious school. I already had a keen interest in the politics and political philosophy of multicultural and multi-religious societies; questions about public funding and regulation of religious schools seemed to me to offer a revealing window onto those fundamental normative issues. My conclusions in this book are, it must be conceded, broadly critical of American education policy toward religious schools, but I should like to put on record that my stance does not reflect any lack of warmth in the welcome I received in this country. Indeed, I am deeply appreciative of the support provided by many American institutions, colleagues, and friends during the last seven years.

A Frank Knox Memorial Fellowship enabled me to spend five wonderful years at Harvard, during which time my project was conceived and a doctoral dissertation written that served as the first draft of this book. Lowell House was my home for four of those years: I am grateful to Dorothy Austin and Diana Eck, co-masters of the house, and to the students and tutors who made Lowell such a stimulating and pleasant place to live and work. During my final year at Harvard, the Edmond J. Safra Foundation Center for Ethics gave me additional financial support and, more importantly, the most engaging intellectual community I found at Harvard. I was fortunate to have a seat at the table each week with Arthur Applbaum, Frances Kamm, Michael Blake, Sandra Badin, Noah Dauber, Kyla Ebels-Duggan, and Waheed Hussain.

My advisors at Harvard—Nancy Rosenblum, Dennis Thompson, and Glyn Morgan—were exemplary. Few graduate students enjoy the level of attention that was lavished on me by three such accomplished scholars. I also gained a great deal from conversations with fellow graduate students Carla Marie, Bryan McGraw, and Debbie Sorensen, and from meetings with two visiting fellows at Harvard whose scholarship addresses many of the same themes as my own: Stephen Macedo and Meira Levinson.

Versions of my argument were presented at the 2003 meeting of the New England Political Science Association, at Harvard University's Political Theory Colloquium, and at Washington University's Political and Social Theory Workshop. I am grateful for all the questions and comments raised at those forums, at least some of which I hope to have addressed in this book. I am especially grateful to my Washington University colleagues Marilyn Friedman, Larry May, and Andrew Rehfeld for their probing scrutiny as I prepared the final version of the manuscript.

A shorter version of chapter 8 was published as "Education for Autonomy: The Role of Religious Elementary Schools" in the *Journal of Philosophy of Education*, vol. 38, no. 4 (2004). I thank Blackwell Publishing for permission to reproduce that work.

Ian Malcolm of Princeton University Press has been a fine editor, guiding me through this process with a judicious blend of encouragement, strategic advice, and gentle exhortations to learn from the constructive and insightful criticism offered by three anonymous readers, to whom I am also deeply grateful. Anita O'Brien's meticulous and thoughtful copyediting taught me a thing or two and significantly enhanced the readability of the final text.

Finally, and most importantly, I should like to thank my wife, Lola, who so rashly agreed to share her life with a political philosopher, and the two people who raised me as one: my father, Andrew, whose philosophic temperament I have inherited, and my mother, Linda, without whose influence I might never have communicated my philosophy to others. With the love of Lola and my parents, I know that I shall have the emotional support, even if I lack the intellectual capacity, to cope with the critical response I gladly invite by sending my thoughts into the world.

Introduction

How SHOULD a liberal democratic state respond to parents who want their children to attend a religious school, preferably at public expense? What principles should govern public regulation and funding of religious schools? One cannot adequately answer these questions without inquiring into the proper goals of liberal education policy and, more generally, into the principles that underlie liberal democracy: in other words, to settle these important practical policy questions we must first engage in normative political philosophy. When the state makes education policy, what are its responsibilities to parents, children, religious communities, and the citizenry at large? What values may reasonably be invoked to justify and guide public policy in a pluralist state where few if any values are universally accepted among citizens? What are the limits of the state's legitimate authority over children's education? In the pages that follow, I seek both to identify the legitimate and proper goals of public education policy in liberal democratic states and to explore the implications of these goals for arguments about public funding and regulation of religious schools.

In most liberal democratic societies today, a significant minority of parents desire a religious school education for their children. But different states respond in very different ways to these desires. In the Netherlands, the state undertakes to provide a publicly funded school affiliated with almost any religious tradition as long as local parents support the project in sufficient numbers to make it economically and educationally viable. Families in Great Britain are increasingly likely to be able to access free education with their preferred religious orientation as the government continues its controversial policy of expanding both the number and the range of faith schools funded by the public purse. Since the Islamia Primary School opened in London in 1998, several Muslim schools have joined the list of Anglican, Catholic, Methodist, Jewish, and Sikh schools that are funded by the British state. In France, all publicly managed schools are secular, but nonetheless, large amounts of public money flow to privately managed religious, predominantly Catholic, schools. In the United States, the established principle has long been that children go to religious schools only if their family (or some other private body) is willing and able to pay, but there is a powerful movement in favor of "voucher" schemes that would enable parents to send their children to private religious schools at public expense. Trial voucher schemes have been implemented in Milwaukee and Cleveland; since the U.S. Supreme Court upheld the constitutionality of the Cleveland program in 2002,[1] proponents of "school choice" have stepped up the pressure for widespread adoption of such voucher schemes across the country. But, at the other extreme, some academic writers argue that even the option of a privately funded religious education should be legally curtailed or regulated virtually to the point of nonexistence. These differences and disagreements—in theory and in practice, within and between countries—suggest the need for careful consideration of the proper goals of public education policy and their implications for religious schools.

Why do I focus on religious schools[2] to the exclusion of the many other types of schools that parents might desire for their children: military schools, schools for Democrats, etc.? Arguments about public policy toward religious schools are of special interest because all sides of the debate perceive the stakes to be so high: religious parents may believe that their deepest values and their children's souls are on the line; the state may worry that schools that are segregated along such fundamental lines of difference will undermine the foundations for mutual understanding, respect, and appropriate cooperation between citizens; liberals may fear that religious education is a form of indoctrination that leaves its victims unable to rationally endorse, revise, or reject the way of life they have been taught. Religious schools are central to the upbringing certain parents seek to give their children, but they may also pose a threat both to the civic health of the state and to the embryonic autonomy of children. If we are to find a just and principled solution to this controversy, rather than merely deferring in each country to the most powerful political lobby or to the uncertain authority of historical precedent, we shall need reasoned answers to some fundamental questions in political and educational theory.

Do liberal democratic states have any legitimate grounds for concern about religious schools, or are all such concerns ultimately rooted in

[1] *Zelman v. Simmons-Harris* (2002).

[2] Nothing in the argument of this book hinges on the special nature of religion vis-à-vis other nonreligious comprehensive doctrines: when I refer to religious schools, I should be understood to reference all schools that seek to educate children within a comprehensive system of values and beliefs. Here, I follow John Rawls (1993/1996, p. 13) by calling a system comprehensive if "it includes conceptions of what is of value in human life, and ideals of personal character, as well as ideals of friendship and of familial and associational relationships, and much else that is to inform our conduct, and in the limit to our life as a whole." In contemporary liberal democratic states, most schools that endorse and promote a comprehensive conception of the good life are religious schools, but my arguments apply equally to parents who want their children to attend a school that teaches a particular secular philosophy of the good life.

an illiberal intolerance of and disrespect for citizens of faith? If the liberal state does have good reasons to worry about religious schools, what are those reasons and what public policies do they warrant? Is there sufficient justification for policies, such as we find in America, whereby rich parents are virtually unconstrained in choosing a religious school for their child while poor families are stuck with the state-funded secular schools? And how should the important differences between primary and secondary education be recognized in public policy toward religious schools?

I shall focus my attention on two educational goals that have often been thought to justify some degree of state opposition to religious schools: civic education (teaching students the virtues and capacities of the good citizen) and education for autonomy (teaching students to think critically and reflectively about their ethical commitments). We need to establish four things about each of these goals in turn. First, what the goal really amounts to: what it means to be a good citizen or an autonomous person. Second, whether and how the goal can justifiably be adopted as a universal goal of education policy in a liberal state that is committed to respecting the plurality of religious, cultural, and other ethical views held by its citizens. Third, what implications the goal would have for religious schools, assuming that we designed our schools to realize that single goal. Fourth, what degree of normative force the goal has and how it should be balanced against other educational goals and broader liberal values in cases of conflict.

As we work our way through this agenda of inquiry, we shall confront two of the most important questions in contemporary liberal political theory. Does the importance of reproducing and improving our liberal democratic political community take priority over the private interests of individuals and families? Can the liberal state legitimately appeal to the contested value of individual autonomy to justify its use of coercive power? In the process of identifying the principles that should govern liberal education policy toward religious schools, I shall propose and defend answers to both of these questions.

The first question arises when we ask whether a general refusal to provide public funding for certain types of religious school would be sufficiently justified if it could be shown that such schools do a poor job at preparing children for their role as citizens of a multicultural, multireligious state. Should the political goals of education enjoy primacy in the policy process or should they be weighed against the private values of parents and religious communities in cases of conflict? Evidently this is only a particular application of a much more general question for liberal politics. Laws that serve important liberal public purposes may nonetheless impose significant burdens on certain citizens' pursuit of the good life as they understand it: how should the liberal state respond to such conflicts? According to one influential view, advanced by so-called political liberals, the goals of the state take priority as long as they are suitably circumscribed to include no more than the preservation of the liberal democratic regime upon which all citizens depend for the protection of their rights and freedoms. In chapter 2, I argue that the case for this kind of political primacy collapses once we recognize that it is only the degree of flourishing and not the continued existence of the liberal democratic regime that is at stake in most conflicts between civic values and private interests.

The second question introduces a cross-cutting cleavage as we seek to decide which noncivic values are legitimate goals for the liberal state or parents to pursue through children's education. Can the liberal state legitimately claim that religious education is objectionable to the extent that it amounts to indoctrination, that religious schools do a disservice to children to the extent that they resemble cocoons? Or, conversely, are religious parents entitled to have their (sometimes deeply held) opposition to autonomy counted in the decisions that shape their child's schooling? In short, does the liberal state have to remain neutral in the controversy about the value for individual lives of reflecting autonomously on one's conception of the good, or does the value of autonomy necessarily underpin the principles of a liberal regime? Even if the concept of autonomy is coherent and plausibly attractive, which several skeptics have doubted, is it any more suitable than religious doctrine for adoption as a public value in the liberal state? In chapters 3 through 5, I aim to rehabilitate and defend the autonomy liberal position both by rejecting a number of influential caricatures of autonomy and by grounding public justification in the instrumental rather than the intrinsic value of autonomy to individuals seeking to live a good life. Although civic values are insufficient to settle disputed questions of public policy, it does not follow that the liberal state must permit citizens' opposition to autonomy to weigh against these civic values.

It should be clear, therefore, that although my primary focus is on one particularly contentious issue in education policy, I hope through my arguments to improve our understanding of liberal political philosophy more generally. This should come as no surprise: issues concerning children, especially those characterized by a conflict of authority between parents and the state, often serve both to illustrate and to illuminate broader controversies in liberal political theory. We cannot decide how liberal education policy should balance, protect, and promote the potentially conflicting freedoms of children, parents, and other citizens without developing a general account of the distinctive meaning and value of the liberal freedoms, but consideration of the policy dilemma may nonetheless guide our inquiry into the abstract principles. Similarly, the liberal state's proper response to religious parents' desires to transmit their values and beliefs to their children is bound up with the general question of how and why such states should respect ethical pluralism, but we may find it easier to answer the general question if we simultaneously interrogate its implications for education policy. In short, my argument oscillates between abstract questions in liberal political philosophy and more concrete questions in education policy because of my conviction that such an approach is the best way to answer both types of question: in the methodological spirit of Rawls (1971/1999, pp. 18–19), we should seek a kind of "reflective equilibrium" in our considered judgments about political principles at different levels of generality.

Besides addressing these general questions of liberal political philosophy, I also take aim at the particular shape of established American public policy toward religious schools. On pain of inconsistency and unfairness, governments cannot justify the general policy of permitting the operation of a wide range of private religious schools while refusing to fund a similar education in the faith for those who cannot afford it. There is simply no principled justification for privileging the wealthy in this fashion. Whether the goals of public education policy are mistakenly believed to be merely civic in nature or are acknowledged to include the cultivation of children's autonomy, the availability of religious schooling should be determined by the balance of legitimate educational values in each particular case, not by the size of the parents' bank balance: it is arbitrary and indefensible for religious schools to be available only and always to those who can afford private education. All too many liberal theorists of education believe that wealth brings with it the privilege to buy one's way out of the educational principles that are thought proper to govern children educated at the state's expense; I argue that there should be no such possibility of opting out from regulations designed to strike the appropriate balance between the legitimate interests of children, parents, and the state.

While the first two parts of this book engage respectively with the aforementioned two major issues in liberal *political* theory, the third part primarily addresses a central question in liberal *educational* theory: do religious schools pose a threat to children's future autonomy? In chapters 7 and 8, I argue that the extensive debate on this issue in the last twenty years has become unnecessarily polarized, in large part because of the tendency to overgeneralize about "religious schools" as if there were no important differences between the many institutions that belong to this broad category. The suitability of religious schools to cultivate children's autonomy is a more complex and nuanced matter than most liberal theorists of education have realized: progress on this question depends upon making a number of key distinctions, especially between primary and secondary education and between pedagogical and curricular features of religious schools. The autonomy goal does not warrant prohibition of or a general refusal to fund religious schools, but there should be an extensive scheme of public regulation, especially to ensure that religious secondary schools expose children to and encourage open-minded, rational engagement with significant ethical diversity. Primary schools, however, should be treated quite differently: the developmental needs and capacities of preadolescents suggest that primary schools most effectively lay the foundations for children's future autonomy not by exposing them to diversity but rather by consolidating their grasp of their primary culture and encouraging a limited form of ethical reasoning within that framework.

My argument proceeds mainly at the level of theory and philosophy. While this is obviously appropriate to address the normative issues of principle in chapters 2 through 5, some readers may feel that the questions I pose about the relative effectiveness of religious schools to achieve certain educational goals are empirical questions that should be answered using the methods of social science. As I shall explain, however, the prospects for successful empirical work in these fields look bleak because the "dependent variables" are exceptionally difficult to operationalize and quantify. Good citizenship cannot simply be measured by counting acts of political participation, and autonomy cannot be gauged by observing the rate at which children defect from the doctrine in which they were raised. Education for autonomy and citizenship aims to give a certain form and character to a person's ethical reflection and political participation, but these qualities are scarcely amenable to measurement by social scientists. Fortunately, and as I hope to show, we can make considerable progress in identifying the types of educational institutions that are likely to foster the virtues and capacities of citizens and autonomous persons via a careful and nuanced analysis of the concepts involved, with a little help along the way from developmental psychology and a few uncontroversial empirical observations about the social conditions of contemporary liberal democracies. It should also be emphasized that I do not address the specific constitutional issues that surround government policy toward religious schools in America. My purpose in parts 1 and 3 is to scrutinize the implications for policy toward religious schools of the state's adopting certain goals, assuming that the only constraints on public policy are those given by the correct normative theoretical account of liberal democratic politics.

In chapter 1, I begin by identifying the distinctive civic goals of education in a liberal democratic state and defending the legitimacy of pursuing these goals through public education policy. I then consider the political liberal view that the state's legitimate interest in and authority over children's education is exhausted by the pursuit of these civic goals and, in particular, that the state may not act paternalistically by invoking the noncivic value of autonomy as a justification for education policy. After noting the covert ways in which this kind of paternalistic reasoning has nonetheless been used to smuggle autonomy into influential accounts of the civic goals of education, I conclude the chapter by examining and tentatively endorsing the view that religious schools, at least of a certain sort, are inferior instruments of civic education in a multireligious liberal democracy.

In chapter 2, I consider and reject the political primacist's view that important civic goals and values presumptively outweigh all other concerns in policy-making and therefore that the inferiority of narrowly religious schools to realize civic educational goals would suffice to justify liberal states in a general refusal to fund these types of school. An important premise of my argument is that the reproduction and flourishing of the liberal democratic state is a matter of degree. Both in an individual citizen and in the citizenry as a whole, the possession of civic virtues and capacities is a matter of more or less, not all or nothing. The extent to which a particular level and distribution of civic virtue sustains a *liberal democratic* state, not just a functional and stable set of political institutions, is a matter for normative evaluation. Arguments for the trumping status of civic educational goals based on assigning priority to the survival of the liberal democratic state are therefore rarely appropriate: survival is not really the issue. A more flourishing liberal democracy is certainly to be preferred, and the state quite rightly takes this as one important consideration in setting education policy, but there is no reason to accept that this civic goal should always prevail over reasonable private values in cases of conflict. Indeed, this argument need not be limited to questions of education policy, which leads me to propose the more general rejection of political primacy, a move that would have broad implications for liberal theory and practice.

Conflicts between civic educational goals and parental preferences will arise systematically because a robust civic education inevitably encourages the development of children's autonomy against the wishes of some religious parents. States that take no position on the value of autonomy must balance their civic grounds for opposing narrowly religious schools against their responsibilities to religious parents who want to send their children to such schools in order to prevent them from developing autonomy. Without making claim to the justificatory resources that might entitle one to deny that children are less well off as a result of developing autonomy, one cannot assert that the public values of a liberal democracy always trump the autonomy concerns of religious families. But, at the end of the second chapter, I argue that the normative force of liberal democratic principles actually presupposes the noncivic value of autonomy, and therefore that it is incoherent to value the reproduction of a specifically liberal democratic state without taking a stand on the value of autonomy.

In the second part (chapters 3 through 5), I develop a conception of ethical autonomy and argue for its adoption as a public value and, specifically, as a goal of public education policy. In chapter 3, I offer a more sophisticated and nuanced conception of autonomy than the ones that often underlie discussions of public policy. I argue that ethical autonomy involves both the capacity for and the commitment to ongoing, distinctively rational reflection about one's beliefs and values. Several influential critiques of autonomy should be rejected as caricatures of the ideal: rational autonomy is not incompatible with having meaningful commitments; it does not depend on an incoherent notion of radically free, criterionless choice; it does not require that people reject the values and beliefs with which they were raised. But nor is autonomous reflection in an ethically pluralist world simply a matter of auditing and weighing pre-existing values and desires: drawing on a hermeneutic tradition that is often used to attack caricatured conceptions of autonomy, I argue that autonomous reflection is actually a creative process of self-interpretation wherein reason plays a vital, liberating role.

Chapter 4 presents my positive argument for adopting autonomy as a public value in a liberal, pluralist state. I begin by distinguishing claims about the *intrinsic* worth of an autonomous life from the very different claim that the practice of autonomous reflection is *instrumentally* valuable to persons seeking to find and lead a good life for themselves. Political and civic liberals are right to insist that appeals to autonomy's supposed intrinsic value have no place in liberal politics, but they fail to see that appeals to its instrumental value are not similarly prohibited. Rational reflection is a demonstrably reliable way to evaluate and improve one's conception of the good, especially because it enables one to root out false beliefs and resolve inconsistent values within one's conception. Of course, claims about autonomy's instrumental value are not uncontroversial, but the liberal state is not barred from acting on controversial epistemological premises of this sort; we must insist upon the distinction between the substantive content of reasonable ethical values and beliefs, about which the liberal state must remain neutral, and the manner in which such beliefs and values are best reached and held, which is a matter on which the state quite rightly makes a judgment. The correct judgment—that rational reflection is valuable for individuals seeking to identify and lead a good life—does not warrant paternalizing adults by forcing them to attend autonomy boot camps, but it does appear to provide a legitimate basis on which to override parents' claims that the development of autonomy is contrary to the best interests of their children.

In chapter 5, to defend the legitimacy of adopting autonomy as a goal of public education policy, I argue against a series of objections, most notably those grounded in claims about parental rights and the liberal state's obligation to respect traditional ways of life. The independent interests of parents and children must be considered and balanced as we distribute educational authority and design educational institutions; in cases of conflict, it is sometimes legitimate for parents to act in ways that do not best serve their children's interests. But this does not imply that parents have the right to deny their children a formal education for autonomy. Given the dangers associated with authorizing routine public intervention in domestic life, liberal states should seek to preserve a balance between the interests of parents and children by permitting parents broad discretion to direct the upbringing of their children at home while insisting that children's independent interests be the first priority at school. (This distinction will be hard to draw in the difficult case of home schools, but the imperative that all children be educated for autonomy suggests the need for significantly greater regulation of home schooling arrangements than is seen in most liberal democratic states.) In response to the charge that mandatory education for autonomy is unfair to certain traditional ways of life that are incompatible with autonomy, liberals must insist that the inability to make rational judgments about one's way of life is simply too high a cost to allow parents to impose on a child in order that she should be raised in the traditional culture, especially when one remembers that autonomous persons can and often will exercise their autonomy to endorse the substantive values and beliefs with which they were raised.

In the third part (chapters 6 through 8), I venture into educational theory to explore the implications of the autonomy goal for public policy toward religious schools. But before we contemplate regulation or prohibition of religious schools on grounds of autonomy, we need to ask both whether secular schools can reasonably be expected to advance children's autonomy and whether public regulation of education might actually be inimical to the autonomy goal. If the alternatives to largely unregulated religious education are themselves ill-suited to promote autonomy, religious schools have no serious case to answer; so, in chapter 6, I review a number of prominent autonomy-based criticisms of secular education, public control of schools, and the institutional form of the school. Critics of secular education have variously charged that it amounts to promotion of a comprehensive secular philosophy, or that it aspires to a chimerical neutrality, or that the effect of neutrality is to encourage children to be relativists or subjectivists about ethics. Following John Stuart Mill, critics of public management and regulation fear that schools will simply become conduits for transmitting to children the beliefs and values of the (local) adult majority. And radical critics like Ivan Illich suggest that all schools, as sites of compulsory education, are inherently authoritarian institutions that cannot be expected to encourage children's autonomy. In responding to these diverse concerns, I argue that many of them are well-founded but none is insurmountable: suitably designed secular public schools supported by a vigilant citizenry can reasonably be expected to be effective in cultivating children's autonomy.

In chapter 7, I assess the autonomy case against religious secondary schools. Since autonomy is a cognitive ideal, mere exposure to ethical diversity outside of and after school cannot be relied upon to develop children's autonomy—secondary schools need to teach and model the appropriate methods of rational deliberation and inquiry. Some religious secondary schools are poor instruments of education for autonomy because they provide children with inadequate exposure to and rational engagement with ethical diversity: a degree of separation is needed between the ethical environments at home and school, but this requirement does not justify prohibiting or even presumptively denying public funding to religious secondary schools. Rather, a scheme of extensive public regulation should be implemented, enforcing curricular and pedagogical standards designed to ensure that all secondary schools effectively cultivate children's autonomy. The interpretation and application of these regulations may lead to some undesirable entanglements between religious groups and the state, but this is a price worth paying to secure the best interests of children without unfairly prohibiting religious schools whose educational methods are perfectly compatible with the autonomy goal.

In chapter 8, I argue that religious primary schools should be treated differently from secondary schools because of the particular developmental needs and capacities of preadolescents. Our conception of autonomy, coupled with observations of contemporary liberal democratic societies and insights from developmental psychology, suggests treating primary and secondary education as two distinct stages on the path to autonomy. Religious schools may often be desirable at the first stage, providing young children of religious parents with the opportunity to consolidate and begin reasoning within a framework of values that they are not yet cognitively equipped to challenge. The curriculum of these schools need not expose students to ethical views other than those found within their own religion, but some regulation of pedagogical methods is still appropriate and necessary to ensure that children develop the primitive ethical reasoning skills and instincts that can later be expanded into full-blown autonomy. Religious primary schools that meet these pedagogical standards are the best educational institutions to lay the foundations for autonomy in young children from religious families.

Liberals have been too easily dissuaded from placing the ideal of individual autonomy at the heart of their political philosophy: properly understood, autonomy has an important instrumental value for individuals that can be demonstrated without illicitly appealing to substantive ethical principles. Rawlsian political liberals wrongly maintain that the claims of liberalism lose none of their normative force when appeals to the value of autonomy are eschewed. The political liberal position relies on two false notions: first, that liberal democratic civic values enjoy priority over all competing claims of value, and second, that liberal political principles can be detached from claims about the importance of autonomy to individuals seeking to lead a good life. Liberalism will look very different, in theory and in practice, when we dispense with these two false notions: in the conclusion of this work, I sketch some of the broader implications for liberal politics of adopting autonomy as a public value and of rejecting the principle of political primacy. But my central purpose in the chapters that follow is to explore these issues in liberal political philosophy as they appear in the politics of religious schooling.

A robust liberal political philosophy must include education policies that aim to cultivate the virtues and capacities of both citizenship and autonomy, but the implications of this statement for religious schools are far less stark and clear than both liberals and nonliberals have commonly assumed. There are good reasons to believe that narrowly religious schools are poor instruments of civic education in a pluralist society, and secondary schools of this sort are definitely at odds with the goal of cultivating children's autonomy: the combined force of civic and autonomy-based reasons is sufficient to justify more stringent public regulation of religious secondary schools than we see in most liberal democracies today. But a general prohibition of religious schools is unwarranted, and therefore, more controversially, the liberal state cannot justify presumptively denying public funding to religious schools without doing an injustice to poor parents who wish to send their children to a moderate religious school. In particular, religious primary schools have some distinctive advantages as sites of the first stage in education for autonomy for the children of religious parents, and therefore, subject to certain pedagogical regulations and any concerns about the civic educational pedigree of such schools, the state should be willing to fund a wide range of religious primary schools.

PART I

Civic Education and Religious Schools

Chapter 1

THE CIVIC CASE AGAINST

RELIGIOUS SCHOOLS

ON WHAT GROUNDS, if any, should a liberal democratic state discriminate against religious primary and secondary education in its policies on school funding and regulation? It has been suggested that a sufficient reason, perhaps even the only legitimate reason, for the state to discriminate against religious education derives from a consideration of the civic educational role our schools should play. This suggestion raises a host of questions, three of which I hope to address in this chapter. First, what are the legitimate civic goals of education policy in a liberal democratic state? Second, how and why does so much recent liberal democratic theory assign these civic goals a special status? In particular, I explore the claim of Stephen Macedo (2000) and John Rawls (1993/1996) that civic goals are the only *permissible* goals of liberal democratic public education policy, and the related but different argument by Amy Gutmann (1999) that they are the only *required* goals of such a policy. Third, is it the case that religious schools—at least those of a certain type—are inferior to common, secular schools for the purpose of advancing the civic goals of education?

I should say something immediately to clarify the relationship between the contents of this chapter and the shape of my larger argument. I think Macedo and Rawls are wrong to argue that the state *must* limit itself to pursuing civic goals, and I think Gutmann is wrong to say that a liberal state *may* limit itself in this way: toward the end of the next chapter and throughout part 2, I shall argue that the cultivation of individual ethical autonomy must lie at the heart of liberal education policy. But for the moment, I am interested in the internal logic of those, like Gutmann and Macedo, who mistakenly believe that liberal states can do without a commitment to the value of individual autonomy. In the next chapter, I shall argue that the policies they advocate toward religious schools cannot be justified if we limit ourselves to the narrow, merely civic view of the goals of public education policy. But first we need to understand the claim that religious schools have a civic case to answer.

The Civic Goals of Education

When the state undertakes to provide free primary and secondary schooling, it is not simply offering a private benefit to children and their parents. Similarly, the state does not regulate private schools merely to ensure that children and their parents should be able more reliably and effectively to satisfy their narrowly defined self-interest. The consumerist model of education characteristic of libertarian treatments of schools (Friedman, 1955, 1962) neglects the civic function of schooling by assuming that education is rightly understood as being merely a private good, whose form and distribution are properly responsive only to the preferences of individual consumers, that is, parents (and perhaps their children). The fact that the political community might undertake to finance provision of this good for all those who are unwilling or unable to buy it in the private sector does not, for libertarians, change the fact that its value is properly understood as purely private. This analysis either overlooks or denies the legitimacy of the idea that the political community has its own collective goals to pursue through the education system as it seeks to defend, propagate, and reproduce its institutions, principles, and values.

But how can the pursuit of these collective goals justifiably be imposed on individual children and their parents in liberal democratic states, grounded as such states are in respect for individual rights and freedoms? The answer, of course, flows from the fact that liberal democratic states can and should view themselves as providing, by their continued existence and flourishing, a very great good to each individual citizen, a good that consists precisely in securing his or her fundamental rights and freedoms against encroachment by other private persons or by the state. If civic education is necessary for the reproduction and improvement of the liberal democratic state, then the general project of civic education is justified by reference to the vital interests of citizens. But, as we shall see, it is characteristic of civic education in a liberal democratic state that its delivery to one child is primarily a boon not to the individual recipient but rather to all other persons in the state: the existence of an appropriately educated citizenry is a kind of public good, which is of value to all, but whose realization is not without cost to certain individuals. In the next chapter, we shall need to examine more deeply the nature and distribution of these costs because the ultimate purpose of this first part is precisely to inquire into the limits of state authority to impose civic education on a child in the name of the public good, against the objections of the family that such civic education is inimical to the individual good of the child.

The civic goals of liberal democratic education policy might seem to consist merely in securing the conditions necessary for ongoing peaceful social cooperation, including widespread law-abidingness among citizens, but this would be to overemphasize the values of peace and social stability and to miss the distinctive ideals of liberal democracy. As Aristotle (1984, ch. 8) rightly observed, the civic goals of education are relative to the nature of the regime: so, for example, oligarchical states will typically try to use education policy to minimize the power and aspirations of the poor majority in order to shore up the position of the ruling elite. Analogously, liberal democratic regimes need a particular type of civic education. When Amy Gutmann (1999, p. 14) describes the primary goal of education in a democratic state as securing the conditions for "conscious social reproduction," she draws our attention to the important idea that the way in which a regime perpetuates itself is partly constitutive of the nature of the regime. Democrats are not committed to reproducing just any peaceful society, or to buying peace at any price. If social reproduction is to be *conscious*, and the regime we create is to count as a democracy, we must not "undermine the intellectual foundations of future democratic deliberations by implementing educational policies that either repress unpopular (but rational) ways of thinking or exclude some future citizens from an education adequate for participating in democratic politics" (p. 14). Similarly, we might add, if civic education aims at reproducing a *liberal* democratic state, it will seek to ensure that each new generation of citizens is committed to respecting the individual rights and freedoms that should limit the scope of majority decision-making power in the political sphere.

The key point here is that liberal democratic states, committed as they are to the moral and political equality of citizens, can only achieve their goal of self-reproduction through the great majority of children who will one day jointly exercise the power of the state over one another. There is no option to follow Plato's model in the Republic, whereby the ideals of the regime are upheld by careful attention to the education of a select few future rulers. In liberal democratic societies, we are all rulers, present or future. McConnell (1991a, p. 131) is misguided in his belief, following in the tradition of Kant and Hume, that a suitable set of political and social institutions will suffice to secure the conditions for a good liberal democratic state, regardless of the capacities and values of the citizenry. Laws and constitutions are not self-enforcing, liberal democratic institutions and minority protections are not self-sustaining in the face of widespread public opposition, and no set of formal mechanisms, checks, and balances can safeguard liberal democratic principles to which private citizens and public officials attach insufficient value. "Democratic institutions do not work by default. Their operations require a citizenry with particular habits of mind and particular commitments" (Fullinwider, 1996, p. 16). If we are to understand the particular demands of civic education in the liberal democratic state, we need to take a closer look at these habits and commitments.

Good liberal democratic citizens possess both a distinctive set of character virtues and an equally important set of intellectual capacities. The central virtues are toleration, mutual respect, and a commitment to reciprocity: the principle that "political power will be exercised on the basis of reasons that we can share, for purposes that we can hold and justify in common, notwithstanding our religious [or other reasonable] differences" (Macedo, 2000, p. 136). These virtues must form part of a positive civic spirit—the willingness and enthusiasm to exercise one's virtues through participation in the core activities of citizenship—which typically relies upon a sense of attachment to the particular political community of which one is a citizen. As Callan argues (1997, pp. 100–31), liberal democratic citizens need a degree of patriotism, but it should not be of the excessively sentimental type. Liberal patriots partially identify their individual good with the good of the state, but they maintain that "their community's flourishing depends on its justice" (p. 175), by contrast with sentimental patriots, who subscribe to the illiberal doctrine of "my country, right or wrong."

The intellectual capacities required of citizens are primarily those necessary for them to adequately discharge their responsibilities in the process of political deliberation and decision making, including voting. Liberal democratic states are committed to free public discourse and deliberative procedures, both formal and informal, as means to discovering and making wise and just public policy. Deliberative competence entails the ability reliably to identify irrational and unreasonable arguments made by oneself and by others in public debate. This competence is required not only of active participants in the discussions that precede political decisions, but also of those who simply watch and listen with a view to judging the active participants and their claims by the standards of rationality and reasonableness. As Galston observes (1989, p. 94), citizens of modern liberal democratic states are far more likely to play a role in deliberative politics by evaluating candidates for elected office than by actually participating in the debates themselves. But he is wrong to imply that we should therefore significantly revise our account of the intellectual capacities required of citizens in a modern liberal democratic state with the usual institutions of representative government. The intellectual capacities one needs to be a critical observer of televised presidential debates or a discerning reader of newspapers and campaign materials are substantially similar to those one would need to be a more active participant in electoral or legislative politics.[1]

As Gutmann observes (1999, pp. 50–51), a virtuous character and the capacity for rational deliberation are individually necessary, and only jointly sufficient, for good liberal democratic citizenship. An impeccable commitment to the reciprocity principle has little value if one cannot distinguish reasonable from unreasonable arguments; the well-meaning but intellectually deficient citizen is unable to recognize when his ideals of public justification are being violated. He is also vulnerable to manipulation, especially if he knows that his deliberative capacities are lacking and therefore lacks confidence in his independent judgments of reasonableness. And he will be manipulated, of course, by his inverse, the dastardly clever debater who recognizes no obligation to respect the reasonable ways of life pursued by others and specializes in misleading fellow citizens by painting the reasonable as unreasonable and vice versa.

Once we recognize the truth that liberal democracy depends upon citizens' virtues and capacities, we must beware of complacency, of taking for granted that citizens will develop the requisite abilities and commitments outside of the institutions of formal schooling. Primary and secondary schools are not the only social institutions through which civic educational goals can be pursued, but they have certain important advantages for this purpose. Few people would deny that the intellectual capacities necessary for deliberative competence are best learned through instruction, example, and practice in institutions of formal education. It would be foolish to assume either that parents will always be willing and able to teach their children these intellectual capacities (Gutmann, 1999, p. 29) or that children can be expected to develop them elsewhere and/or later in civil society through institutions, such as the workplace or the media, whose educative effects are not their primary purpose. Of course, civic education must focus as much on developing character virtues as on equipping children with the intellectual acuity to participate in democratic politics, and here too schools have a distinctive role to play. As Aristotle (1985) clearly saw, virtues must at first be taught nonrationally, as habits learned by practice, before they can

---

[1] There are, of course, conceptions of democracy that do not require of citizens even the intellectual capacity for deliberative competence in the fairly weak sense that I describe. Schumpeter's (1950) minimalist conception of democracy as elite electoral competition is an example. I do not think such a conception could be normatively appealing, but it is true that a Schumpeterian might see little value in the civic education I describe. My general point is that one need not be committed to a full-blown conception of deliberative democracy to accept my account of the intellectual capacities needed by citizens.

be endorsed by critical reflection. "Children are not taught that bigotry is bad . . . by offering it as one among many competing conceptions of the good life, and then subjecting it to criticism" (Gutmann, 1999, p. 43). Schools, as the only communities amenable to direct political control that almost all children will inhabit at substantial length, offer a unique opportunity to ensure that citizens are engaged in sustained practice of the civic virtues during their most formative years.

Even if the principles of liberal democracy are uniquely justifiable among political theories, Aristotle's observation reminds us that we still need to teach them, and their corresponding citizen virtues, to children who are not yet capable of rationally apprehending their decisive superiority. Of course, our eventual goal must always be to secure citizens' rational endorsement of the principles of liberal democratic government; it would be utopian to believe that this reflective assent will actually be forthcoming from all persons, but we need not be as pessimistic as Galston (1989, p. 91) is on this matter when he writes that "it is unrealistic to believe that more than a few adult citizens of liberal societies will ever move beyond the kind of civic commitment engendered by [a pedagogy that is far more rhetorical than rational]." In short, liberal democratic states need their schools to pursue civic educational goals almost as much as do the most authoritarian and repressive regimes. "There is no reason to think that the dispositions that characterize good liberal citizens come about naturally: good citizens are not simply born that way, they must be educated by schools and a variety of other social and political institutions" (Macedo, 2000, p. 16). This observation rings especially true in the multicultural, multireligious conditions that characterize many contemporary liberal democratic states, where intolerance and failure to observe political reciprocity are regularly to be seen. In light of these dangers, Appiah (1996, p. 84) argues, it must be "a central part of our educational system to equip all of us to share the public space with people of multiple identities and distinct subcultures."

As we shall see, liberal regimes do have a special reason to be cautious about civic education, lest the shaping of young minds become so comprehensive that we lose the authentically free consent that is supposed to ground the legitimacy of liberal political authority (Brighouse, 1998). The ideal of conscious social reproduction is not satisfied by a society where each generation's commitment to liberal democratic principles is simply manufactured by the preceding generation through public education policy. And yet we have excellent reason to believe that the requisite virtues will not arise spontaneously and that the cultivation of good civic character is a legitimate and indispensable role of the political community. The balance between cultivation and indoctrination may be difficult to define, but we must seek it if we believe in liberal democracy and want it to endure across generations. "To an extent difficult to measure but impossible to ignore, the viability of liberal society depends upon its ability effectively to conduct civic education" (Galston, 1989, p. 92).

CIVIC GOALS AS THE ONLY GOALS OF PUBLIC EDUCATION POLICY

A distinctive feature of several recent influential theories of education in the liberal democratic state is the claim that the civic goals I have been discussing—securing the conditions for conscious social reproduction by ensuring that the next generation of full citizens has the requisite virtues and capacities—are the *only* legitimate goals of public education policy (Rawls, 1993/1996; Macedo, 2000; Galston, 1989). It is important to pause and consider what exactly is meant by this claim. Obviously, liberal democratic authorities can and must still intervene in schools that inflict wanton physical cruelty on their students; such interventions are justified not by anything particular to the educational mission of the state but rather by appeal to a set of human rights enjoyed by all persons at all times, not simply by children in schools. What is meant by the claim that the state may not pursue noncivic goals through its education policy is specifically that liberal democratic states cannot justify imposing an educational goal on all schools by appealing to conceptions of the good life about which there is reasonable disagreement. This constraint on the grounds of legitimate public justification is, of course, a hallmark of the later theory of John Rawls. "We try, so far as we can, not to assert nor to deny any particular comprehensive religious, philosophical, or moral view, or its associated theory of truth and the status of values" (Rawls, 1993/1996, p. 150).

Limiting the legitimate goals of public education policy to those civic imperatives that are dictated by the political values internal to liberal democracy turns out to be an application of the reciprocity principle. Reasonable persons recognize the burdens of judgment: "the sources, or causes, of disagreement between reasonable persons" understood as "the many hazards involved in the correct (and conscientious) exercise of our powers of reason and judgment in the ordinary course of political life" (Rawls, 1993/1996, pp. 55–56). The burdens of judgment mean that free societies are and will continue to be characterized by a reasonable pluralism of comprehensive value and belief systems. Reasonable people see that it would be disrespectful and therefore illegitimate to employ the coercive power of the state to impose elements of one of these systems on all citizens, unless such an imposition can be sufficiently justified purely by reference to civic values. Those who accept the reciprocity principle—the obligation to support only those exercises of state power that can be justified by appeal to reasons that are accessible to all—will reject the idea that schools might be required to cultivate in children values whose justification can only be found by taking sides in the competition among equally reasonable ways of life. "We try to answer the question of children's education entirely within the political conception. Society's concern with their education lies in their role as future citizens" (Rawls, 1993/1996, p. 200).

This political liberal strategy of denying that reasons drawn from comprehensive doctrines can serve as public justifications is often described as remaining *neutral* among reasonable conceptions of the good, but one should immediately dispense with some of the more misleading implications of such a description. As Rawls (p. 195) says: "The principles of any reasonable political conception . . . and the basic institutions those principles require inevitably encourage some ways of life and discourage others, or even exclude them altogether." Neutrality of effect is not and could not be guaranteed in the pursuit of any substantive set of political and civic goals. The neutrality involved in saying that states may pursue only civic goals through their public education policies is in the sphere of *justification* to one's fellow citizens and not at the level of effects on them: laws that pass the political liberal's test of public justification may still tilt the playing field significantly in favor of certain ways of life. Neutrality of justification is ensured by adhering to the standards of public reason in the political realm, according to which arguments (and votes) grounded in comprehensive doctrines are not permitted.[2]

The nonneutral effects of policies that nonetheless pass the political liberal's test of public justification are immediately apparent when we consider schools as the primary institutions of civic education in the liberal democratic state. As Macedo (2000, p. 179) observes, schools that are engaged in "promoting . . . core liberal virtues—such as the importance of a critical attitude toward contending political claims—will probably have the effect of encouraging critical thinking in general" even though the politically liberal state of Rawls and Macedo supposedly does not make any judgment about the value of such an autonomous approach to life outside the political sphere.[3] Much

---

[2] I shall argue in chapter 2 against the primacy of political values that underpins the standards for public justification and the requirements of public reason in political liberal theory.

[3] Rawls (1993/1996, p. xlv) writes that "while autonomy as a moral value has had an importance [sic] place in the history of democratic thought, it fails to satisfy the criterion of reciprocity required of reasonable political principles and cannot be part of a political

heat and some light have been generated in recent scholarly disputes about the nature of autonomy and its proper relationship to liberal political theory. Chapters 2 through 5 of this book are a contribution to that important debate: I shall argue that a certain conception of autonomy, albeit one that differs greatly from the various unappealing and unrealistic caricatures that have distorted the debate, can and must lie at the heart of any coherent liberalism. Chapter 3 will develop such a conception of autonomy at some length. But for our purposes in chapters 1 and 2, a more succinct, working definition of the term will be sufficient to understand the implications of and critique the aspiration to a liberal theory that avowedly takes no position on the value of autonomy.

Autonomy is the capacity for critical-rational reflection about one's ethical beliefs and values, including those that are foundational, and the commitment to practice this reflection on an ongoing basis. This bald statement raises many questions and invites a variety of important challenges to both the feasibility and the desirability of achieving autonomy understood in this way. I anticipate and respond to many of these concerns in chapter 3. For the moment, I just want to emphasize and explain three key elements of the definition. First, the autonomous person engages periodically and voluntarily in a certain type of activity, therefore autonomy requires not only the capacity for but also the *commitment* to rational reflection. Second, the autonomous person must engage in *ongoing* reflection, not in the sense that she must necessarily exercise her autonomy every hour, day, or week, but rather in the sense that she must remain perpetually open to reevaluating her ethical commitments in the light of significant new experiences, evidence, and arguments. The status of being an autonomous person is not one of those things that, once achieved, can never be lost. Third, although one cannot simultaneously question all of one's ethical commitments, none of them is immune to autonomous reflection and *all* must periodically be reviewed. Autonomous reflection may often take the form of asking whether one's actions and particular judgments are proper applications of temporarily unquestioned higher-level commitments, but an autonomous person will also rationally scrutinize her foundational beliefs and values on occasion. This working definition of autonomy will suffice for our present purpose, which is to identify the particular approach to one's ethical commitments that, according

conception of justice." I consider and reject this view in chapters 4 and 5, but for the moment I explore the possibilities of a liberal theory that does not appeal to the value of autonomy.

to Rawls and Macedo, the liberal state may not endorse. On their political liberal view, the realization of civic values is the only permissible goal of education policy.

Amy Gutmann (1999) offers an argument that is very different from, but nonetheless importantly related to, the view of Macedo and Rawls. She argues that the pursuit of civic goals is the primary, and the only indispensable, function of education in a liberal democratic state. Therefore, liberal democracies *may* legitimately limit themselves to the pursuit of civic goals through education, although Gutmann (pp. 292–303) does not defend or require such a limit. In what follows, I explore the implications and coherence of her theory on the assumption that democratic citizens do indeed choose to adopt this minimal conception of the goals of public education policy. Why do I assume this, given that Gutmann neither requires nor urges such a choice? Gutmann thinks that the civic goals of education are *sufficient* by themselves to justify her twin principles of nonrepression and nondiscrimination (1999, pp. 44–45) in a form that is strong enough to entail the general refusal to provide public funding for religious schools. The obvious way to test such a claim of sufficiency is to examine the case where there are indeed no other public policy goals to support the prohibition on public funding. Macedo and Gutmann have in common the claim that civic goals alone justify a certain conclusion: since I am interested in scrutinizing that claim, I treat their two theories together in spite of the fact that civic goals are the only *permissible* goals for Macedo as opposed to the only *required* goals for Gutmann.

It might be suggested that Macedo does not limit himself strictly to advocating civic goals, and that Gutmann does not really permit states to pursue only civic goals, because both writers end up endorsing the cultivation of individual autonomy as a universal goal of public education policy. If this is the case, and Macedo and Gutmann are not in fact making claims about states in which civic objectives are the only goals of public education policy, then the next chapter may seem like an elaborate attack on a straw man. I must therefore take a moment to justify my reading of their theories. This may seem unnecessary to some people who are familiar with the texts. After all, Macedo (2000, p. 207) says explicitly that liberal democratic states may not adopt the autonomy goal. And the essence of Gutmann's theory (1999, p. 39) is that the only required goal of a democratic education system is to secure the conditions for conscious social reproduction. Yet there are passages in the work of both Macedo and Gutmann that might seem indistinguishable from an endorsement of the autonomy goal for education policy in all liberal democratic states. How can we reconcile these passages with the explicit claims of the authors?

Macedo proposes that "All children should have an education that provides them with the ability to make *informed* and *independent* decisions about how they want to lead their lives in the modern world. Liberal freedom to choose is the birthright of every child" (p. 207, emphasis in original). What is the difference between autonomy and Macedo's "liberal freedom to choose," when this latter concept is understood in such an expansive way, going far beyond the mere absence of external constraints to include conditions on information and independence? To make sense of Macedo's insistence that he is not permitting states to promote the value of autonomy, one must understand his conditions on information and independence to be minimal—no more than is required to make the concept of free choice intelligible. "Liberal freedom to choose" presumably need not have all, and perhaps need not have any, of the three hallmarks of autonomy I just discussed: the *commitment* to *ongoing* reflection on *all* of one's ethical commitments. Perhaps there is a thin theory of the good embedded in Macedo's defense of this minimal freedom to choose, just as there is in a right not to be physically abused, but it is sufficiently uncontroversial to belong to the "overlapping consensus" of reasonable comprehensive doctrines (Rawls, 1993/1996, p. 15). But we must always remember that Macedo cannot have it both ways: he cannot support the autonomy ideal in everything but name while continuing to claim that liberal states may not legitimately impose such a value on all children. In light of this tension, it remains hard to know what to make of Macedo's (p. 124) apparently bold statement that "critical thinking about one's own convictions is an important part of moral education."

At times, Gutmann goes even further than Macedo in seeming to require the state to teach children to be autonomous. Perhaps she only commits to the same minimal standards discussed above when she says: "The same principle that requires a state to grant adults personal and political freedom also commits it to assuring children an education that makes those freedoms ... meaningful in the future ... by equipping children with the intellectual skills necessary to evaluate ways of life different from that of their parents" (1999, p. 30). "Meaningful" here would have to be interpreted as "coherent" or "intelligible" if Gutmann is to be acquitted, along with Macedo, of requiring public policy to promote autonomy. But to reconcile Gutmann's apparent enthusiasm for education for autonomy with her defense of the view that democratic citizens may legitimately adopt a narrowly civic view of the goals of public education policy, we must remember Gutmann's basic philosophy that democratic decisions must be respected even if they are wrong, so long as they do not undercut the values of democracy itself.

Gutmann believes that educational authority should be shared among parents, the state, and professional educators (as guardians of the child's independent interests), and she periodically adopts the perspective of each of these groups to press their respective claims. When she argues for children's interests in autonomy, Gutmann should be understood as arguing in the voice of professional educators, or of citizens (like herself?) who are comprehensive liberals, but she is not proposing that the liberal democratic state *must* impose the autonomy goal on all schools. If this reading is right, Gutmann can evade Barry's (2001, p. 224) charge that she smuggles the autonomy goal into civic education by presenting it, implausibly, as a precondition of democratic citizenship.[4] When she supports education for autonomy, Gutmann is offering examples of the kind of arguments that should animate deliberative democracies, but she does not wish to bypass democratic institutions by establishing any principles as beyond the reach of review and repeal by citizens, unless those principles are fundamental to democracy. It seems clear that, according to Gutmann, the only principles that schools *must* respect are Gutmann's nonrepression and nondiscrimination principles because these are the only principles that are justified in the name of democracy itself, as the necessary conditions for conscious social reproduction. Gutmann may personally believe in, and she may hope that like-minded citizens and professional educators will advocate for, children's interests in developing as autonomous persons, but she cannot argue that the satisfaction of these interests *must* be recognized as a goal of public education policy. Civic goals do not include the requirement that children be taught to think skeptically about their parents' values (Galston, 1989, p. 99).

When theorists of liberal democratic civic education say that the goals of public education policy must not (or need not) be justified by appeal to values within a particular comprehensive doctrine, they should not be understood as saying something quite different and altogether stronger, namely, that the goals of public education policy do not include equipping children to pursue their conceptions of the good, *whatever those conceptions may be*.[5] To make this latter claim would

---

[4] In chapter 2, we shall consider Callan's (1996, 1997) view that ethical autonomy is indeed the mark of a good liberal democratic citizen.

[5] Here I rely upon the idea that children should be treated as sharing their parents' conception of the good, at least in the sense that parents have the right to raise them in that conception and that the politically liberal state is not entitled to assert the counterpoising need of children to develop the autonomy to make their own choice of ethical doctrine. It is precisely this assumption that I shall argue forcefully against in part 2 of this work, but it is an assumption of the political liberal theories whose internal coherence I am currently investigating.

be to propose that the state takes no interest whatsoever in the noncivic value of schooling, its private value to individuals in helping to make their lives successful. As we shall see, there are times when Gutmann (1996, p. 164) appears to be making this radical claim, but I do not think that we should take her quite at her word. There are decisive reasons for thinking that a legitimate goal of public education policy, and indeed part of the reason why the liberal democratic state undertakes to provide and regulate schooling, is to help prepare children to live successful lives. So when it is said that the state has no view on questions of the individual good, this does not mean that the makers of public education policy either can or should be indifferent to the way that schooling affects individuals' capacities to pursue their own conceptions of the good. Instead, liberal democratic states should incorporate into education policy the goal of providing children with the means to live good lives. Schooling is treated in part as a primary good, in the Rawlsian sense of the term as something with which "men can generally be assured of greater success in carrying out their intentions and in advancing their ends, whatever these ends may be" (Rawls, 1971/1999, p. 79). But we do not make the assumption here that exactly the same form of schooling will serve as a primary good for all persons.

Two more issues need to be addressed to justify my claim that Macedo's theory requires, and that Gutmann's theory permits, public education policy to take no position on questions about the nature of the good life for individuals. It might be objected that the civic goals of education necessarily include cultivating in students a conception of the good life as engaged citizenship in the polity. This objection could be pressed on two grounds, one of which initially looks rather more promising than the other. The less promising option is to observe that citizenship brings with it a share of political power, and then to argue that the goal of education for citizenship is really some particular good for the individual, namely, political power. One might look for support for this argument in Gutmann's insistence that all children receive "an education adequate *to take advantage of* their political status as citizens" (1999, pp. 287–88, my emphasis).

In a model of democratic politics as self-interested bargaining, it would presumably be accurate to say that education for citizenship is primarily intended to equip individuals to advance their good and defend their private interests through participation in the political process. But Gutmann's vision of democratic politics is not a bargaining table, and liberal democratic citizens are not being taught to maximize the satisfaction of their private interests through politics. The capacity for democratic deliberation is not simply the ability to drive a hard bargain (p. xiii) because, as we have seen, the intellectual capacity must be allied with and tempered by the commitment to reciprocity. Gutmann's talk of citizens *taking advantage* of their status is surely not to be understood to refer to a private, nonmoral sense of advantage.

The second reason to think that the civic goals of education include cultivating in students a conception of the good life as engaged citizenship actually emerges from further consideration of the sense in which good citizens of a liberal democratic state can "take advantage of their status." Recall Callan's argument (1997, p. 175) that civic education must aim to create "liberal patriots"—it must move us to identify with our political community in a way that "makes the flourishing of the community a constituent of our own good." This looks like a contradiction of the thesis that merely civic education does not aim at promoting a particular conception of the good. If citizens are being taught to partially identify their own good with the good of the state, then surely education for citizenship does after all aim both to shape citizens' conception of the good and to promote the good of all those who hold such a conception (precisely by advancing the good of the state).

But we are in danger here of failing to see the wood for the trees. Callan's characterization of liberal patriots as adopting the goals of their state as ingredients of their private good threatens to obscure the fact that the goals in question do not extend beyond the maintenance of a fair scheme of social cooperation. A liberal patriot endorses the goal of perpetuating and improving the liberal democratic state of which she is a member, and she does not regard this political goal as a duty that potentially constrains her pursuit of the good life. Rather, the success of the liberal democratic enterprise is *integrated* into the patriot's conception of her individual good, such that "conflict is mitigated between the rational pursuit of good and reasonable deference to the claims of others" (p. 175). The civic goals of education therefore include the transformation of ways of life that have unreasonable elements (Macedo, 2000). But this account of liberal patriotism does not take a position on the nature of the good life for an individual, it just restates the demands that liberal justice makes on citizens.

As Rawls (1993/1996, p. 206) puts it, one can teach civic virtue without teaching "civic humanism: the view that man is a social, even a political, animal whose essential nature is most fully realized in a democratic society in which there is widespread and vigorous participation in public life." Gutmann (1999, pp. 314–15) makes much the same point when she insists that civic education does not require that children be taught to identify as "republican patriots," since this is only one among many reasonable ways in which to be a good citizen. The goal of teaching children to be liberal patriots flows simply from the fact that the unconstrained pursuit of certain conceptions of the good is incompatible with good citizenship, and from the observation that a sincere commitment to reproducing the liberal democratic state requires in practice that one identify one's good at least partially with that objective. The goal of creating liberal patriots does not endorse a comprehensive conception of the good any more than does the goal of teaching children the virtues and capacities of citizenship. In fact, the former goal, properly understood, is simply an expression of the latter in the context of a particular political community. "Since the ideals connected with the political virtues are tied to the principles of political justice and to the forms of judgment and conduct essential to sustain fair social cooperation over time, those ideals and virtues are compatible with political liberalism" (Rawls, 1993/1996, p. 194) because they are not drawn from a particular comprehensive doctrine. The goals of civic education do not amount to the promotion of a particular conception of the good.

Do Religious Schools Make Good Citizens?

So far, I have done three things. First, I have identified the civic functions of education in a liberal democracy and justified the corresponding civic goals of public education policy. Second, I have explained what it means for these civic objectives to be the only goals of public education policy. Third, I have explored the reasons of Rawls and Macedo for requiring such a limited conception of the goals of public education policy, and I have shown that Gutmann's theory permits citizens to adopt this limited conception. With this introductory exegesis completed, I now want to pose a new question: to what extent are religious schools suitable to deliver an education that achieves the civic educational goals of a liberal democratic state? To put matters even more bluntly: do religious schools make good citizens?

One perfectly natural response to this question would be that it all depends upon the particular school so there is nothing profitable to be said in trying to answer it generally, at the level of political philosophy. As Callan notes (1997, pp. 163–66), a significant number of Catholic high schools in the United States admit students and employ teachers of other faiths or of none, and these schools typically pursue an educational mission that is more focused on traditional academic instruction and the inculcation of basic, relatively uncontroversial moral values than it is on the cultivation of faith in God and obedience to the tenets and authorities of Roman Catholicism. In the same country, increasing numbers of private Christian fundamentalist schools provide students with an education in which all goals are subordinate to and/or infused with the cultivation of a faith in the literal truth of the contents of the

Bible. In short, the category of religious schools is broad, and its members may have little in common with each other.

Perhaps what is needed is an empirical study that would find a way to quantify or otherwise measure and compare the extent to which a school's religious affiliation affects the experience of students (along several, at least partially independent, dimensions) and seek to correlate these measures with assessments of the quality of the citizens emerging from such schools (standardized in some way, also on at least two dimensions, and controlling for omitted variables such as family environment). I mention this strategy only to say that it is not *my* strategy. Empirical work does need to be done in this area, although it would be a formidable task to find satisfactory quantitative measures of the independent, and especially the dependent, variables. Measuring the quality of liberal democratic citizens would be very different from measuring, say, the volume of their political participation—in terms of voting, attending meetings, giving time and money—as Verba, Schlozman, and Brady (1995) have done. Good liberal democratic citizenship is a normatively laden concept that can only be assessed by engaging with the substantive *content of* and *reasons behind* acts of political participation. As Gutmann (1999, p. 106) puts it, "the ability of students to reason, collectively and critically, about politics . . . is no less essential to democratic citizenship by virtue of being difficult to measure by survey research." Doubtless, careful qualitative case studies could shed light on the relation between religious schooling and the production of good citizens, in this sense. But there is also much to be learned by examining, at a philosophical level, the relationship between the virtues and capacities we want in good citizens and the educational practices and environments of religious schools.

In chapters 7 and 8, I shall seek to distinguish between narrow and more moderate types of religious school along various dimensions: curriculum, pedagogy, openness to those beyond the community of faith. But this recognition that religious schools cannot sensibly be treated as a homogeneous category is strangely absent from the theories of civic education developed by Gutmann and Macedo. Perhaps this is because they have other grounds for worrying about the prospect of liberal states drawing distinctions among religious schools: I address concerns of this type in chapter 7. But, for the purposes of this chapter, I want to consider the most straightforward and plausible version of Gutmann's and Macedo's views, and so I shall consider types of religious school that might most naturally be thought to be unsuitable for civic educational purposes. Therefore, in this chapter and the next, when I refer to a religious school, I have in mind a school that exemplifies both of the following features. First, the school's pedagogy, its rules and structures of authority, and large parts of its formal curriculum are designed to encourage children's belief in a particular religion. Second, the school is relatively closed to those outside its community of faith, with the results both that the body of students and faculty is drawn heavily from that community and that there are few efforts to encourage interaction with children at other schools that are secular or organized around other religious traditions. Schools that are run by religious organizations but that do not exemplify these features are not my subject here, although they would seem to pose the stiffest challenge to Gutmann's and Macedo's insistence on treating all religious schools alike. In any case, I think it is uncontroversially true that most if not all multicultural liberal democratic states contain significant numbers of parents who would want a religious school, in the sense just specified, for their children. In this chapter, I ask philosophical questions about the extent to which schools *of this type* are suitable instruments to advance the civic goals of public education policy; in chapters 7 and 8, I shall attend more carefully to the key dimensions along which religion may color a child's school experience.

There are important arguments in liberal democratic educational theory for the view that religious schools are ill-suited to educating future citizens and that, other things being roughly equal, secular schooling is to be preferred for these civic purposes. The civic case against religious schools focuses not only on the curriculum and academic instruction in such schools, but also on other features of the institutional environment. Critics of religious schools are concerned about the effects on children of their lacking adequate exposure to persons of other faiths and those who are nonreligious (Gutmann 1999, pp. 63, 66). And they point out the importance of the so-called hidden curriculum—institutional rules, structures of authority, and the justifications that are given for them—in shaping the moral character of students (Gutmann, 1999, p. 53). We need to examine both the charges against religious schools and the responses available to their defenders regarding their suitability to deliver civic education.

As we have seen, a key component of civic education is to teach children the virtues of liberal democratic citizenship. These virtues—toleration, mutual respect, reciprocity—are centrally concerned with the way we respond to differences, especially the kind of differences between comprehensive value systems that we find between members of different religious communities, and between those with faith and those who are nonreligious. How are these virtues to be promoted and learned in schools? If Aristotle's account of moral education is right on this point, virtues of character are acquired primarily by practice, rather than by abstract acceptance of the principles that underlie them.

"A state of character arises from the repetition of similar activities" (Aristotle, 1985, p. 35), which is to say that one becomes tolerant by practicing toleration, and so on. But schools where children from religious families do not routinely encounter persons of different faiths and of none, because the school's membership is religiously homogeneous and the school does not seek outside opportunities for its students to engage with ethical diversity, are not providing an educational environment in which students can practice the virtues of liberal democratic citizens toward those with profoundly different values and beliefs. As Appiah puts it (1996, p. 82), "what is ideal in a multicultural society, whose multicultural character is created outside the state in the sphere of civil society, is that the state should seek in its educational systems to make these multiple subcultures known to each other."

It is hoped that students will learn through their schooling not only to tolerate and respect members of other religions—important virtues to be sure, but ones that emphasize a kind of principled noninterference—but also to engage such people in an appropriate form of dialogue aimed at agreeing on fair terms of cooperation in spite of our differences. The commitment to reciprocity and the practical wisdom to apply that commitment in concrete circumstances of collective decision making are best learned by grappling with the ideas and arguments of those with different comprehensive worldviews in the context of an institution that supports and itself manifests the commitment to reciprocity. "The Aristotelian thesis would suggest that the growth of reasonableness requires at some stage that reciprocity be practiced in dialogical contexts that straddle our social cleavages" (Callan, 1997, p. 177). Common schools, populated by students and teachers of different faiths and of no faith, are the institutions that can best provide that context for every child on his or her path to full participation in the liberal democratic polity.[6]

It might be objected that this characterization of common schools as places where children can practice the virtues of reasonable collective decision making radically overstates the extent to which primary and secondary schools are, should be, or can be democratic institutions. Decisions about school rules and curriculum content are not made by deliberative assemblies of the student body, and rightfully so. But this

---

[6] The achievement of significant ethical diversity in schools may require compulsory bussing schemes if residential communities are de facto segregated along religious lines; alternatively, children's engagement with diversity may be promoted by collaboration between neighborhood schools, as I discuss in chapter 7. But, I shall argue, in ethically homogeneous regions neither of these strategies may be possible, so the most we can *require* of schools is a genuine *effort* to expose students to those outside their community of faith.

objection begins by caricaturing the civic case for common schools. Students do not need to run schools in order to have opportunities to practice the deliberative capacities and virtues (although, in the opinion of the author, many schools could benefit from a greater degree of student participation in institutional governance). There are at least three obvious contexts in which students in common schools will routinely interact with one another in ways that model the formal political sphere of liberal democratic society. Students engaged in group projects (for example, to make a presentation to the class about violence in the Middle East) must learn to make binding decisions about the division of responsibilities among members and about the content of their presentation. Students involved in classroom debates and discussions are practicing the virtues and skills of reasonable deliberation. And even in their informal interactions outside of lessons, children will frequently argue and make decisions in groups that contain representatives of different religious traditions. Common schools are ideally placed to guide children toward practicing liberal democratic virtues and developing deliberative capacities in their daily interactions with one another, inside and outside the classroom.

So, to fulfill their civic function, schools must "teach students how to engage together in respectful discussions in which they strive to understand, appreciate, and, if possible, resolve political disagreements that are partly rooted in cultural differences" (Gutmann, 1996, p. 160). Religious schools are not well equipped to serve this function because of the relative homogeneity of their membership and their failure to encourage routine educational interaction with those outside the community of faith. But they are also ill-suited to prepare students for democratic citizenship because they do not govern their internal affairs in accordance with the principles of public reason and justification that are required of participants in the political sphere of liberal democratic societies. It is important to be clear what this argument is not saying: it does not propose that all institutions in civil society should ideally operate as miniature liberal democratic states. It merely proposes that to the extent that institutions perform an educative function, particularly if their members are children, it will be desirable *from a civic perspective* that they instantiate liberal democratic norms in their rules and decision-making procedures. As we shall see in the next chapter, I do not think that this civic benefit is always sufficient to outweigh other values, especially if the state makes no judgments about the child's individual good, which religious parents may claim will be diminished in the pursuit of civic goals.

Secular schools, unlike religious schools, can and should be committed to the principles of public reason for governing their affairs, and this commitment sets an important example to students. "An educational establishment that teaches children that important public issues can be deliberated upon without considering religious questions is itself part of the education for liberal democratic citizenship properly understood" (Macedo, 2000, pp. 121–22). But students should learn the capacity for deliberation in accordance with the rules of public reason through the content of their formal studies as well as through their observations of and participation in the authority structures and decision-making procedures of the school. To the extent that a school's curriculum and pedagogy are infused with religiously based reasoning, students can be expected to emerge both less reliably capable of distinguishing religious from secular reasons and less competent in the exercise of the purely secular forms of argument expected and required in the public sphere of a liberal democratic state.[7]

Gutmann and others are right to worry about the civic implications of teaching creationism in public schools: "The rationale for teaching any particular religious doctrine in public schools—either as science or as a reasonable alternative to science—conflicts with the rationale for cultivating common, secular standards of reasoning among citizens" (Gutmann, 1999, p. 103–4). The same argument surely tells equally against using religious doctrine as a lens through which to study any issue that is liable to be the subject of public deliberation in a liberal state. But this is a statement with broad implications, since the only issues that are necessarily beyond the scope of liberal democratic deliberation and decision are those that concern only the truth or falsity of particular reasonable conceptions of the good, including religious doctrines. A school whose curriculum encourages religious reasoning about potential issues of public policy does a disservice to the liberal democratic state. And this is true whether the school is public or private—a point that I shall press in the next chapter.

Defenders of religious schools may be starting to think that this is all a little overblown. Even if a religious school education is not the optimal preparation for citizenship (and I consider objections to this claim shortly), it is hard to believe that the civic costs are really significant. Graduates of secular high schools may be slightly better versed in public reason, and they may have had more opportunities to practice liberal virtues in cases of concrete engagement with people who do not share their ethical beliefs and values, but many liberal democracies seemingly thrive despite the presence of religious schools, and the citizens who attended these schools do not appear to threaten the political

---

[7] When I refer to secular reasoning, I mean the use of reasons that are not grounded in a comprehensive doctrine, even a nonreligious comprehensive doctrine.

order. In response, democratic theorists who have examined the American case urge that we not take for granted the moral capital built up by decades during which the large majority of children have attended common public schools. If we want to see the civic risks associated with religious schools, we must consider the potential long-term effects in eroding that capital of greatly increasing the number of religious schools through, for example, the widespread implementation of school voucher schemes (Gutmann, 1999, p. 32). The goals of civic education are far more ambitious than merely maintaining a stable and peaceful society, the existence of which might indeed not be threatened by increased numbers of religious schools. Rather, we must remember "the degree of moral convergence it takes to sustain a constitutional order that is liberal, democratic, and characterized by widespread bonds of civic friendship and cooperation" (Macedo, 2000, p. 2).

The Civic Value of Religious Schools

But we should take some time to consider a more robust defense of the potential of religious schools to serve as instruments of civic education. It can be argued that religious schools have more resources than their secular counterparts with which to cultivate the virtues of liberal democratic citizenship (Strike, 1996, pp. 46–47). Many of the major religious traditions in the world are deeply committed, for reasons internal to their comprehensive doctrine, to the values of toleration, mutual respect, and reciprocity in the political sphere.[8] Religious schools can perhaps be more effective at civic education by drawing on the resources within their religious tradition, resources that are unavailable to common, secular schools that must make do with the more limited grounds available in the so-called public political culture (Rawls, 1993/1996). Children who are provided with reasons from within their comprehensive doctrine to respect the constraints of public reason in politics will have a more profound and reliable commitment to the principle of reciprocity than children who have been urged to accept reciprocity merely for those reasons that are acceptable to all. If liberal politics is built on an "overlapping consensus" of reasonable comprehensive doctrines (Rawls, 1993/1996, pp. 144–50), why should not civic education take advantage of this fact and avail itself of all the resources

[8] See, for example, the survey conducted by Alan Wolfe (1998), which suggests that all the major religious traditions represented in contemporary American society have valuable doctrinal resources that could buttress support for key liberal democratic political principles.

that are available to encourage particular communities in their support
for the liberal democratic state, rather than limiting itself to the more
sparse common justificatory resources?

Kenneth Strike (1996, p. 47) argues that we should welcome contributions to civic education from those religious groups "who find their
own reasons for reciprocity regardless of the standing of those reasons
in liberal thought." The *public* grounds for endorsing the reciprocity
principle are supposed to lie, as we have discussed, in recognition of
the burdens of judgment and the resulting fact of reasonable pluralism
in all free societies. But broad support for liberal democratic principles
is no less valuable if it stems from convergence (shared conclusion for
different reasons) than if we have achieved consensus (shared conclusion *and* reasons). "The heart of the tolerance a liberal society needs is
the refusal to use state power to impose one's way of life on others.
Such refusal need not be incompatible with an unreflective commitment to one's way of life" (Galston, 1995, p. 524). And, according to
this school of pluralist thought, it is unreasonable of the state to insist
upon consensus because it is a mistake to regard recognition of the
burdens of judgment as a publicly acceptable basis for reciprocity. "To
demand that every acceptable way of life reflect a conscious awareness
of value pluralism is to affirm what value pluralism denies—the existence of a universally dominant value" (Galston, 2002, p. 53). And
Strike agrees: "Reciprocity and tolerance among liberal citizens are
clear requirements, but people need not accept the burdens of judgment" (1996, p. 47). Why should the state be concerned about the religious believer who regards heretics as unreasonable as well as wrong,
but who nonetheless has a sincere *religious* belief that heretics must not
be coerced into right conduct?

Before responding to this important point, it is worth briefly noting
a different strategy for defending religious schools in the name of civic
education. It is sometimes suggested that, even if religious schools are
inferior for the purposes of cultivating the distinctive virtues and capacities of liberal democratic citizenship, they may be more effective
at instilling certain other character traits that are of value to any state.
What might these traits be? Galston (2002, p. 118) suggests a few: "law-
abidingness, personal responsibility, and the willingness to do one's
share (through taxes, jury duty, military service, etc.) to sustain a system of social cooperation." I cannot hope to evaluate this claim here.
There are no obvious reasons of principle to believe that religious
schools will be generally superior in these respects, but it is a matter
for empirical investigation and it could turn out to be true, at least in
particular societies and for certain religions. That I cannot perform the
necessary empirical investigation at this time should not unduly con-

cern us, for two reasons. First, my purpose in this chapter is not primarily to *vindicate* the civic case against religious schools but rather to *review* the case that has been made, before I argue in the next chapter that a purely civic case is not decisive for policy purposes when there is a conflict between civic goals and other educational values. Second, as I shall now explain, I am not convinced that Galston's claim about religious schools and the broader set of civic virtues is especially weighty even where it is true.

RESPONSES AND CONCLUSIONS

Even if it turns out that certain religious schools encourage the virtues of obedience and responsibility at some cost to the virtues of reasonableness and deliberation, I am not sure that the trade-off is one that liberal democrats should accept. I do not wish to underestimate the civic value of obedience and a sense of civic duty, but without being qualified by a strong dose of specifically liberal democratic virtues, such character traits may threaten the ideals of the state more than they advance them. Israel Scheffler (1973) emphasizes that obedience to authority all too quickly becomes the virtue of the good subject rather than the democratic citizen, unless it is tempered by a lively sense of oneself as author and critic of the laws and institutions of government. Civic education in a liberal democracy must "liberate the mind from dogmatic adherence to prevalent ideological fashions, as well as from the dictates of authority" (Scheffler, 1973, p. 142) if citizens are to learn "not just to behave in accordance with authority but to think critically about authority" in its various forms (Gutmann, 1999, p. 51).

Let us return now to Galston's and Strike's important claim that civic education has nothing to fear, and much to gain, from schools run by religious groups that support the principles of liberal democracy for reasons drawn from within their comprehensive doctrines. The challenge to opponents of religious schools seems to be to show that their opposition is not limited to intolerant religions, groups that would not hesitate to use political power to advance their sectarian goals at the expense of reasonable dissenters. Civic education aims at securing all future citizens' support for the regime and its values, but do we have any reasons to prefer that this support come in the form of consensus rather than convergence? I think we do. In a polity where deliberation will inevitably often be difficult and heated, even assuming that all citizens are reasonable and not merely self-interested, there are going to be moments of crisis. Deliberation will sometimes break down when some participants, especially those holding minority opinions that

seem likely to lose the day, lose confidence in the reasonableness and
sincerity of their opponents. Trust is a vital resource in liberal democratic deliberation, but it is a fragile commodity. When trust breaks
down, each side must try to demonstrate to the others that their mo-
tives and inclinations are honorable, that they maintain a sincere commitment to the virtues of toleration, mutual respect, and political reciprocity. But the prospects for rebuilding trust and reassuring one's
fellow citizens are much reduced if there is no common language adequate to articulate the grounds of one's allegiance to the goals and
norms of liberal democratic politics. Once I have begun to doubt your
commitment to reciprocity, I need to hear you reaffirm that commitment in terms that I can understand and share, not in terms of a set of
religious beliefs that cut no ice for me. When the virtues of citizens are
common by consensus rather than by convergence, trust is more easily
maintained and rebuilt.[9]

Callan (1997, pp. 27–33) also has an important argument to show
that one must accept the burdens of judgment if one's principles of
toleration and reciprocity are *necessarily* to function as liberal democratic virtues. Toleration is not without its limits in liberal democratic
states, and reciprocity does not require that we achieve the actual consent of all citizens for a law to be legitimate. In particular, good citizens
of liberal democracies mark a difference between reasonable and unreasonable disagreement, and they are only committed to respecting
the former type. But one cannot grasp the relevant distinction between
reasonable and unreasonable disagreement without first recognizing
the burdens of judgment. So toleration and reciprocity that are justified
merely from within a religious tradition, without acceptance of the
burdens of judgment, will only contingently have the same extension
as the toleration and reciprocity of a citizen who does accept the burdens. This is the problem with granting the status of good citizen to
the religious believer (discussed above) who regards heretics as unreasonable as well as wrong but who has a sincere *religious* belief that
heretics must not be coerced into right conduct. Such a believer may
also be inclined to accept genuinely unreasonable arguments in public
deliberation, and/or his toleration may run out before it should.

It must also be remembered that, although religious traditions may
contain reasons of principle to recognize toleration, respect, and reci-

---

[9] Rawls (1971/1999, p. 593) takes the opposite view, arguing that "it is wise . . . for all
sides to introduce their comprehensive doctrines, whether religious or secular, so as to
open the way for them to explain to one another how their views do indeed support
those basic political values." My concern about this view is that, when trust is breaking
down, it is unrealistically demanding to expect citizens to step into the shoes of others,

procity as virtues, regular instruction in these reasons may not be sufficient to cultivate the corresponding virtues in children. The Aristotelian view, discussed earlier, implies that virtues will only be effectively learned through practice, but opportunities to practice civic virtues in the face of deep disagreement will likely be lacking in a school whose membership is largely homogeneous around a set of religious values and beliefs. As Levinson (1999, p. 114) argues: "it is so hard for students to learn to be mutually tolerant and respectful of other people, traditions, and ways of life unless they are actually *exposed* to them." Common schools and religious schools may both espouse the virtue of reciprocity, albeit for different reasons that may translate into different practical applications, but only common schools concretely embody reciprocity in their daily institutional life.

When the children of religious parents attend a religious school, it is not just those children whose exposure to ethical diversity is diminished. Children who continue to attend supposedly common schools find that their schools are not so common after all (Macedo, 2000, pp. 160, 204). It is just as important for nonreligious citizens to respect and tolerate their religious compatriots as it is for liberal virtues to be exercised the other way round. Indeed, in contemporary liberal democratic societies, the members of any single religion often constitute a small minority, so it will frequently be more important to focus on the extent to which a religious believer will be *tolerated* than the extent to which he will be *tolerant*. If we argue thus on civic grounds for keeping religious children in common schools, we are not proposing to *use* them for the benefit of the majority, who need guinea pigs on whom to practice toleration. As we have seen, the development in one citizen of liberal virtues is primarily a benefit to *other* citizens: civic education and virtues are, in this sense, public goods. So we must not make the mistake of thinking that the civic implications of choosing a school for a particular child are manifested only in that child's development: advocates of civic education must be attuned to the externalities involved in religious parents' choice of a school for their child.

What conclusions can we draw from this debate about the suitability of religious schools to advance civic goals? Those who criticize religious schools as instruments of civic education in a multicultural society may not have as clear a case as they think they have, but there is definitely some force to the reasons they offer for preferring common schools for the task. Religious schools do not provide the ideal environment in which students may practice toleration, mutual respect, and

---

to grasp and be reassured by the reasons those others find within their comprehensive doctrines to support liberal democratic principles.

deliberation informed by the principle of reciprocity. Although many religious traditions have resources to support something like the virtues of liberal democratic citizenship, the state has an interest in promoting these virtues on common grounds that are acceptable to all reasonable people. And, contrary to the view of Galston, this interest in consensus is a legitimate one for the liberal democratic state to pursue, though, as I shall argue in the next chapter, it may not be a compelling interest in the sense that it necessarily trumps the objections of religious parents. Even Michael Walzer (1995, p. 27), in his defense of religious schools as *compatible* with a lively concern for civic education, concedes that common schools are *preferable* from the civic point of view. This is obviously a complex and difficult issue, but Walzer's conclusion looks about right.

It would be possible, and quite worthwhile, to write a whole book about the relative suitability of religious and common schools for the task of civic education. But that is not my project here. I am primarily interested in showing that, even if narrowly religious schools are inferior instruments of civic education, this fact does not suffice to justify liberal democratic states in a general refusal to fund such schools. Nor, I think, would the demonstrated civic superiority of common schools be compatible with an indefeasible parental right to send one's child to a narrowly religious school at private expense. So, having understood the nature of the civic goals of education in a liberal democratic state, the implications of saying that the achievement of these civic goals exhausts the state's (legitimate) interest in children's education, and the force of civic arguments against religious schools, I shall proceed somewhat hastily to consider the implications for policy. From now on, I assume that common schools are significantly preferable to narrowly religious schools from the perspective of civic educational goals. Readers who remain unconvinced by the civic case against religious schools will have to regard some of my policy recommendations in chapters 7 and 8 as hypothetical imperatives: *if* the civic concerns are well founded, *then* certain measures are justified. But those recommendations will also be grounded in the value of cultivating children's autonomy, which, I shall soon argue, we should adopt as an additional, noncivic goal of public education policy. By contrast, my purpose in chapter 2 is to show that the *merely civic* inferiority of narrowly religious schools would not warrant the conclusions that some prominent liberal democratic theorists have drawn from it.

Chapter 2

CIVIC EDUCATION AND THE AUTONOMY

PROBLEM IN POLITICAL LIBERALISM

IN THIS CHAPTER, I ask first whether the inferiority of religious schools for civic educational purposes would be sufficient to justify liberal democratic states in a general refusal to fund such schools, especially against the objections of religious parents that the alternatives—common, secular schools—tend to foster a kind of ethical autonomy that corrupts children and their religious faith. My answer is that civic goals alone cannot provide sufficient justification for such a policy. I reach that answer by rejecting the principle of political primacy, a move that has profound implications for liberal political theory and practice: once we reject political primacy, we shall have to think differently about all policy proposals that would advance the political values of the liberal state at the expense of the private values of certain citizens. But, returning to the particular case of religious education, some reflection on the relationship between the virtues and capacities of citizenship, on the one hand, and individual autonomy, on the other, will suggest that it is actually incoherent for liberal democratic theory to regard the development of autonomy as an unintended and undesirable cost of civic education. Indeed, our reasons for wanting to reproduce specifically liberal democratic political institutions depend importantly upon the noncivic value of individual autonomy, so we need to reconsider the legitimacy of using such a value to guide public policy in a multicultural state. This reconsideration will be the task of part 2 (chapters 3 through 5).

CONFLICTING EDUCATIONAL GOALS:
THREE APPROACHES TO RESOLUTION

What should liberal democratic states do if the pursuit of civic goals through public education turns out to be in tension with other values? Gutmann (1999, p. 287) has a simple response: "Political education—the cultivation of the virtues, knowledge, and skills necessary for political participation—has moral primacy over other purposes of public education in a democratic society." The good to all citizens of living in a healthy liberal democratic state is sufficiently great that we should assign priority to measures necessary to reproduce that good. As Rawls (1993/1996, p. 157) puts it, "the values that conflict with the political conception of justice and its sustaining virtues may be normally outweighed because they come into conflict with the very conditions that make fair social cooperation possible on a footing of mutual respect." I call this the *principle of political primacy*. The political liberal state, committed as it is to eschewing all substantive and sceptical positions on the good life for persons, cannot deny that something of genuine value may be lost when common schools are imposed on children against parental objections, but it can argue that the cost is reasonable given the overriding importance of sustaining the regime.

At times, supporters of the primacy of civic educational goals sound as if they are proposing an absolute priority, without exceptions. In this vein, Macedo (2000, p. 202) writes: "All of us must accept limits on our liberty designed to sustain a system of equal freedom for all. . . . There is no right to be exempted from measures necessary to secure the freedom of all." Perhaps not all civic goals automatically outweigh competing values, but "the most basic public purposes will routinely trump religious complaints and warrant intransigent support" (p. 203). But Macedo ultimately disclaims this extreme position—which he labels Hobbesian and ascribes to Justice Antonin Scalia of the U.S. Supreme Court—according to which no principled exceptions can be made to policies that advance the legitimate interests of the liberal democratic state. Likewise, Gutmann is willing to infer the possible legitimacy of exceptions to a general policy against religious schools from the fact that "the welfare of democracy does not depend on *all* schools teaching common democratic values" (1999, pp. 119–20, emphasis in original) although, as we shall see, she seems to think that these exceptions are satisfactorily distributed simply by permitting the operation of private religious schools. So there is some need to clarify the sense in which Macedo and Gutmann regard the civic goals of education as enjoying primacy, since this does not indicate a simple trumping relation over other competing values.

The stance of Macedo and Gutmann is best described as permitting only occasional exceptions to education policies that further important civic goals. We may contrast this view with its opposite, to be found in a certain school of thought in American constitutional law, namely, that burdens on the free exercise of religion can only be justified by a compelling state interest pursued by the least restrictive means available (Dent, 1988).[1] The real source of the difference between these views lies in the contrast between "important civic goals" and "a compelling state interest." Those who believe that only a compelling state interest can justify restricting parents' educational options typically hold that the legitimate civic goals of education are exhausted once we have secured the conditions necessary for the regime to survive and reproduce in a recognizable form. By contrast, Macedo and Gutmann rightly uphold the legitimacy of pursuing through education policy a vision of the flourishing liberal democracy that goes well beyond mere survival, but we shall see that their arguments fail to justify giving primacy to the pursuit of that vision.

It would be absurd to suggest that the existence of a liberal democratic regime is a simply binary question—either you have one, or you don't. There are degrees of flourishing of the liberal democratic state, whose principles express an aspiration that can never be fully realized. In this spirit, Gutmann (1996, p. 161) proposes: "By teaching the skills and virtues of deliberation, schools can contribute to bringing a democracy closer to its own ideal." We might assess the success of the education system in securing the conditions for conscious social reproduction along three different dimensions. First, we could gauge the aggregate or average impact of education on the level of civic virtues and capacities among citizens: taken as a whole, how *strong* is the citizenry in its commitment to political reciprocity and its capacity for democratic deliberation? Second, we might look to see what proportion of citizens is equipped by the education system to participate in liberal democratic public life at a decent level: how *many* citizens are capable of adequately discharging their civic responsibilities? Third, in view of our commitment to political equality, we might be concerned if our schools produce or perpetuate significant disparities among citizens in their capacity for political participation: to what extent are citizens equipped to take on the *equal* shares of political responsibility that they have been formally assigned?

The key point to realize is that the education system can succeed to a greater or lesser extent along each of these three independent dimensions. Gutmann (1999, pp. 13, 46) sometimes suggests that the second dimension is really an either/or criterion—conscious social reproduction requires that *all* educable children be given adequate preparation for citizenship—although she undermines this claim with her remarks about private schools (pp. 119–20). This seems excessive: surely we are

[1] This was the standard that the U.S. Congress sought to establish in its 1993 Religious Freedom Restoration Act and that was struck down by the Supreme Court in 1997.

willing to grant the existence of a liberal democracy even when the schools fall short of equipping 100 percent of educable children for citizenship: indeed, unless "educable" is defined to make the above standard tautologous, all actual educational systems must fall short of this goal. But, even more obviously and importantly, the first and third dimensions along which we might assess the success of civic education are obviously matters of degree, and we do not capture this complex reality by simply drawing a line and insisting that above that line we have a liberal democratic regime and below it we do not.

Dent's position fails to capture the normative aspirations of a liberal democratic regime: it seems clear that if we have reason to value liberal democracy over other stable political orders, then we must have reason to prefer a flourishing liberal democracy to one that barely clings to life. Macedo and Gutman rightly believe that this preference translates into a fully legitimate goal of public policy, but they fail to see that it is a goal that may sometimes have to be sacrificed where it conflicts with other values. Once we realize that reproduction of the liberal democratic state is a matter of more or less, not all or nothing, we no longer have an obvious reason to insist upon the general primacy of civic educational goals. Why is greater civic virtue always to be presumptively preferred to the other values with which it may conflict? Admittedly, if the choice were between Macedo's and Gutmann's approach of permitting only occasional exceptions to policies that advance important civic goals, and Dent's view that such policies are assumed to be illegitimate in the absence of a compelling state interest, we might well prefer the former. But there is a middle position, which I shall call the "balancing" position, and it is by comparison with this standard that I believe Macedo's and Gutmann's position can be shown to be inadequate.

The "balancing" position finds expression in Bill Galston's recent book, *Liberal Pluralism* (2002), although there are times in that book, as well as in other works by the same author (1989, 1995), when he seems committed to the Dent-like view that constraints on diversity can only be justified where necessary for the stability and unity of the regime.[2]

---

[2] For example, in "Two Concepts of Liberalism" (1995, p. 524), Galston defends the so-called diversity state, which has "public principles, institutions, and practices that afford maximum feasible space for the enactment of individual and group differences, constrained only by the requirements of liberal social unity." Of course, groups that want to suppress individual differences among their own members expose the tensions internal to this view. And, I argue, the principle of "maximum feasible accommodation" sits uncomfortably with any "multivalued pluralist perspective" (Galston, 2002, p. 96) that takes the reproduction and flourishing of the liberal democratic political community seriously as a good.

My task here is not, however, to figure out the most coherent reading of Galston's many contributions to the field, but rather to indicate how his work suggests a view of the justificatory force of civic goals that is more attractive than the Macedo/Gutmann view. Galston offers us what he calls the principle of political pluralism: "political goods do not enjoy a comprehensive priority over others in every circumstance" (2002, p. 38), and therefore the fact that a policy is the best way to pursue civic goals yields only a rebuttable presumption that we should adopt the policy (p. 81). So far, this might sound like a restatement of Macedo's and Gutmann's rule and exceptions approach, but Galston's distinctive claim is that civic goals are not to be privileged over other, competing values. Civic values do not, contra Gutmann, enjoy primacy and therefore they do not dictate the rules from which only occasional exceptions can be granted. Rather, civic goals must be balanced against noncivic values in the policy process. So, Galston goes beyond Macedo and Gutmann in acknowledging the limits of policy proposals based solely on civic goals, but he need not and should not go all the way to Dent's position that these proposals necessarily lose all justificatory force against the complaints of religious parents as soon as the conditions for a stable, recognizably liberal democratic regime have been secured. "Civic concerns do not function as trumps in discussions of education policy" (p. 94)—not even as *presumptive* trumps—but, I argue, nor are they automatically trumped when their aspirations rise above a minimal threshold.

The political liberal state will routinely encounter conflicting educational goals because common schools, although preferable for civic purposes, inevitably tend to foster in children a kind of ethical autonomy that many religious parents consider to be harmful.[3] An extreme example of the conflict arose in the case of *Wisconsin v. Yoder* (1972), in which Amish parents objected to the requirement that their children attend high school on the grounds that the public high schools available to help them meet this requirement would corrupt Amish children by exposing them to a "worldly" diversity of ideas and people. But the

---

[3] Of course, religious parents may well have reasons unrelated to autonomy to prefer that their children attend a religious school. Although the preceding discussion considers conflicts of educational goals quite generally, in what follows I focus on the conflicts generated by parental opposition to autonomy. I narrow the focus in this way for three reasons. First, I focus on concerns about autonomy because I think they underlie some of the deepest and most politically charged challenges to the pursuit of civic educational goals through common schools. Second, I want to highlight the distinctive problems and tensions that political liberals like Rawls and Macedo face in dealing with religious education. Third, I am trying to motivate my forthcoming argument (in chapters 3 to 5) for adopting the cultivation of ethical autonomy as a goal of liberal education policy.

conflict will arise in many less extreme cases. As we have seen, a robust and successful civic education will teach children the capacity for rational and reasonable deliberation and will instill in them the commitment to engage in this type of deliberation about matters of public concern. Inevitably, such an education will also have the effect of encouraging rational deliberation about personal ethical values, including those of a religious nature.

If parents regard this development of autonomy in their children as inimical to their individual and familial good, the political liberal state has no choice but to accept that judgment. Macedo, following in the footsteps of Rawls, deliberately eschews all claims to the kind of resources for argument that might justify discounting as irrational or wrong such parental hostility toward autonomy. And these theorists do indeed accept that the development of autonomy where it is unwanted is a cost: "The unavoidable consequences of reasonable requirements for children's education may have to be accepted, often with regret" (Rawls, 1993/1996, p. 200). But the political liberal's regret amounts to no more than crocodile tears unless he takes seriously the thought that the proposed educational requirements might be too costly to be justified on balance. Macedo and Gutmann would agree with this abstract claim, but their response is insufficient: one does not take the costs of a proposed policy seriously enough by demanding that the policy be adopted as a general rule but allowing for the possibility of a small number of exceptions if they can be shown to be warranted on a case-by-case basis. The anticipated costs of a policy might be sufficient to mandate rejection or significant redesign of the policy. For example, rather than having the Supreme Court grant the Yoder parents' request that their children be exempted from Wisconsin's compulsory high school attendance law, it might have been better for the state to divert public money earmarked for the education of Amish children from the large public high schools to specially created community schools that the Amish themselves would then run.[4]

The liberal democratic state's obligation to take seriously the implications of its actions for adherents of different conceptions of the good is especially stringent in the case of education policy. Whenever the state acts, it has a general obligation grounded in respect for its citizens to consider and try to avoid the burdens it may place on reasonable individual and familial ways of life. But, I argue, that obligation is especially weighty in the case of decisions regarding public funding of schools, and for two reasons. First, schooling is mandatory, and therefore any decision of the liberal state to limit the range of schools it will

---

[4] In Kansas, Reich (2002, p. 208) notes, there is now a "Yoder Charter School."

fund imposes a high cost on parents who object to the terms of public provision: such parents must either expend resources—money in most cases, but time where the parents undertake to home school their children—to secure a private alternative to public education or, if they are unwilling or unable to expend those resources, they are compelled to send their children to the public schools. There is no possibility for a costless opt-out from this public program. Second, liberal education policy is justified in part by the goal of assisting parents to prepare their children to lead successful lives. If the politically liberal state is to respect parents' legitimate interest in shaping the ethical development of their children while remaining agnostic on the value of autonomy for ethical development, then the state has a (defeasible) reason to provide access to schools that do not encourage autonomy for the children of parents who have ethical grounds to prefer such schools. To say this is not to contradict the premise that the only legitimate goals of liberal democratic education policy are civic in nature, because the goal of helping parents raise their children according to their conception of the good is not a goal with any determinate substance. As I explained in chapter 1, the reason invoked by Rawls and Macedo for restricting the state to civic goals is precisely that of avoiding taking sides in the competition between equally reasonable conceptions of the good life. The educational goal of assisting parents to prepare their children to live good lives is justified by the same basic Rawlsian logic that permits, and indeed requires, the state to maximize the holding of primary goods enjoyed by members of the least advantaged group in society (Rawls, 1971/1999, p. 266), even though these individuals will use those primary goods to pursue particular conceptions of the good that cannot be justified to all citizens.

Gutmann sometimes appears inclined to reject this goal of treating schooling as a kind of primary good. She asks pointedly: "Unless schools serve civic purposes that citizens can share, why should their support not be left at least primarily to parents and private associations?" (1996, p. 164). This seems odd. We might as well ask: unless welfare checks and state pensions will be spent exclusively on goods whose value can be seen by all citizens, how can the state justify its assistance of the poor and needy?[5] As Barry argues (2001, p. 209), the state involves itself in education partly out of a paternalistic interest in

---

[5] Of course, many welfare systems do provide some assistance in the form of vouchers or subsidies for specified goods that will meet uncontroversial human needs—food stamps, housing benefits, etc. But it would show scant respect for the recipients and the importance to their lives of being able to pursue their particular conception of the good if the state provided all welfare assistance in such a way, just to be sure that public money is not spent on Bibles.

the well-being of its citizens that is independent of its interest in promoting the skills and virtues required for regime reproduction. Even a state that passes no judgment on conceptions of the good can and should be moved by this paternalistic interest, which manifests itself through a concern that citizens have access to primary goods. In her *Democratic Education* (1999, p. 51), Gutmann herself appears to retreat from her earlier position when she writes that "Citizens value primary education for more than its moral and political purposes. They also value it for helping children learn how to live a good life in the nonmoral sense." Perhaps her position is that treating education as a primary good, just like adopting the cultivation of autonomy as a goal of public education policy, is permitted but not required in liberal democratic states. But, if the state takes no view on the value of autonomy, I can see no reason why one would not insist that public education policy adopt preparation for living the good life, as understood by the family, as one of its goals.

To recap, I hope to have shown the following three things. First, the civic goal of education—reproducing the liberal democratic state by teaching the requisite skills and commitments to the next generation of full citizens—is achieved by degree: one can be more or less a good citizen, and the state can be more or less a liberal democracy depending upon the distribution of civic virtues and capacities among its citizens. Second, civic education inevitably encourages children's ethical autonomy, and, when religious parents object, this byproduct must be regarded as a cost by states that take no position on the value of autonomy for the good life. Third, states must take seriously the impact of their education policies on the ability of individuals and families to pursue their reasonable conceptions of the good life, especially because schooling is mandatory and functions in part as a primary good. I contend that these three lemmas are sufficient to show that political liberals may not invoke a principle of political primacy to settle education policy questions when parental opposition to autonomy is at issue.

Macedo (2000, p. 38) briefly looks like reaching a similar conclusion when he observes that "we cannot show that political aims and values override competing religious imperatives on the basis of political argument alone." This observation would surely lead Macedo to endorse a balancing approach if he were not already committed to the conclusion that civic goals will serve as presumptive trumps. Instead, he argues that the potential for conflict between political and religious values—conflict that would seem to demand a trade-off—merely heightens the need for policies to shape and transform the religious doctrines in society in order that conflict can be averted. But this conclusion is a nonstarter because the type of transformative policies that are supposedly needed themselves stand in need of justification, and this justification must be valid before the fact of transformation. Many religious parents object to common schooling—the preferred instrument of civic education—because it fosters ethical autonomy, and it is no response to these parents to say that their objection will not seem salient to their children once these children have been educated as autonomous persons. Macedo recognizes that, for political liberals, "liberal transformative ambitions outrun liberal public reasons," but he refuses to draw the obvious inference, namely, that civic goals would have to be balanced against private values when the two conflict.

LIBERALISM WITHOUT POLITICAL PRIMACY

In response to parents who oppose common schooling because they are opposed to the autonomy it cultivates, the political liberal's strategy is to shift the debate, bypassing the question of autonomy's value by invoking the principle of political primacy to assert that the civic superiority of common schools suffices to settle the educational policy issue. But, I have argued, this strategy fails because political primacy is unwarranted in the sphere of education policy. In most of the rest of this book I shall develop and defend a better liberal response to opponents of autonomy, and I shall trace the implications of that better response for policy toward religious schools. But it is worth pausing for a moment to explore further my critique of the principle of political primacy, a principle that lies at the heart of political liberalism and whose implications extend far beyond education policy.

Although my argument in the preceding section is directed specifically at the appeal to political primacy in debates about education policy, much of my critique applies more generally to liberal politics. The realization of most liberal democratic goals is a matter of degree, and the liberal state always has an obligation to take seriously the impact of its proposed policies on citizens' ability to live in accordance with values about which the state takes no position. That obligation may be especially stringent in the case of education policies, as I argue above, but it exists in other domains as well. The fact that a proposed policy will best realize a legitimate public purpose counts strongly in favor of that policy's being justified, but it does not settle the question. Although I shall soon argue that political liberalism's agnosticism on the value of autonomy is a mistake, it is worth inquiring a little further into the educational policy implications of political liberalism without political primacy because we shall thereby glimpse some of the more general hallmarks of liberalism without political primacy. An extensive discussion would distract us from the urgent task of reconsidering the place of autonomy in liberal theory, but I shall pause just long enough to suggest how the rejection of political primacy might relate to two important issues in liberal theory: the distinction between funding and permitting, and the character of democratic discourse.

Some readers may think that the principle of political primacy can legitimately be retained if its application is restricted to cases where significant public funding is at stake. But, I argue, political values should not necessarily prevail in the design of publicly funded projects, and nor should citizens' private values be assigned primacy when the state decides whether to permit privately funded projects. Reliance on the distinction between funding and permitting breaks down most severely when either or both of the conditions I discussed above obtain: there is no costless opt-out from participation in a publicly funded project, and/or the project is publicly funded in part because it functions as a primary good for citizens. The political liberal state would not strike the correct balance between civic and noncivic values simply by saying, for example, that all private religious schools will be permitted, but no religious schools will receive public funds. The case for religious schooling depends on showing that the potential value of education as a primary good outweighs its potential civic value in particular circumstances, a matter unrelated to the size of the parents' bank balance. In the spirit of Michael Walzer (1983), we should be committed to distributing the good of religious schooling, and its attendant civic costs, in accordance with the meaning of the good, its significance and value to individuals, families, and the state. It is arbitrary and unjustifiable to say that religious schooling is to be provided always and only when the child's family (or some other nonstate party) is willing and able to pay. Coons and Sugarman (1999, pp. 2–3) call this "the American double standard. Among those who can afford private school, society leaves the goals and means of education to the family; for the rest of society, the informing principles are politically determined and implemented." This policy simply ignores the balance of civic and noncivic values in any particular case and substitutes as the decision rule a criterion—the availability of private financial means—that is entirely unrelated to the merits of the case.

Amy Gutmann (1999, p. 117) quite unjustifiably appeals to the distinction between funding and permitting to accommodate her theory of education to the fact that liberal democracy can achieve a high degree of flourishing even if a limited number of schools are permitted to provide an education at odds with the civic goal of conscious social reproduction. She argues against all public funding for religious schools but argues that private religious schools must be permitted as a concession to "the most strongly committed parents." It is absurd to imply, as this argument surely does, that "the most strongly committed parents" are one and the same group as the parents who have access to private education. Are there no devout poor people? Or do we just assume that there will always be enough private scholarships for the children of such families? Poor parents may be strongly religious but quite unable to afford a private school for their child, and, of course, rich parents with a far weaker faith may nonetheless choose to buy a private religious education for their children, since the cost of a private school is hardly a heavy burden for them. Gutmann's reasons manifestly fail to support her conclusion.

The unacceptable nature of allowing money to determine the distribution of religious schooling, as is proposed by those like Gutmann who would permit the operation of private religious schools but deny all public funding, may be illustrated by considering an analogous case. In this case, which I assume to be merely a thought experiment as I dread to think that anyone has ever actually proposed such a scheme, the good to be distributed is not religious schooling but exemption on religious grounds from parts of the curriculum of a common, secular school. How would Gutmann's logic apply to this case? Well, it is obviously true that liberal democratic states can prosper while still allowing a limited number of exemptions from an education designed to foster civic virtues and capacities. How should we distribute these exemptions? What better method, according to Gutmann's logic, than an auction?! We can start by fixing the number of lots up for sale, so as to guarantee that the civic costs are not too great. Then we rely on the principle that those parents who really care about the costs of civic education to their children will fork out in a competitive auction to be certain that they secure one of the scarce lots. The liberal democratic state does not have to make messy judgments about the relative extents to which different families need an exemption—the market will take care of everything. This would surely be an indefensible way of distributing the exemptions, and yet the same principle is at work in Gutmann's view that children can attend religious schools only when private funding is available.

The distinction between funding and permitting does not separate policy decisions neatly into two categories: those where political primacy applies and those where citizens' private values should hold sway. Not only should liberal democratic states be ready to fund religious schools when they are favored by the balance of educational values, they should also be ready to prohibit religious schools when the civic costs of their operation clearly outweigh the private benefits to families. To permit such schools to operate is to allow the very worst form of free-riding. Macedo (2000, p. 5) claims to support "a tough-minded liberalism," "a liberalism with spine," but his theory lacks the hallmark of such a liberalism, namely, the willingness to curtail parental freedoms when their exercise imposes unacceptable costs on society by undermining the future of the liberal democratic regime. Private schools are not somehow immune from public regulation under liberal regimes, and yet many liberals balk at the prospect of interfering for the sake of civic educational goals in the choices rich parents would make for their children. In this matter, we should side with Barry (2001, p. 205), who argues that "what goes on in private schools not in receipt of public funding is just as much a matter of legitimate public concern as what goes on in those that are." More generally, I suggest, liberalism without political primacy cannot assume either that civic values take priority in shaping publicly funded projects (especially those that lack costless opt-outs and/or are appropriately understood as providing primary goods to citizens) or that civic values are presumptively overridden by citizens' private concerns when public money is not being spent.

Liberalism without political primacy would have to depart significantly from the political liberal's standard of public reason, at least as this is commonly understood (Rawls, 1993/1996, pp. 212–54). Public reason is supposed to be a reasonable requirement for political deliberation because arguments grounded in religious or other comprehensive doctrines are inadequate to justify coercive impositions on fellow citizens, given the fact of reasonable pluralism. Public reason safeguards reciprocity by, for example, preventing citizens from using their religious values and reasons to justify the imposition of religious schools on the children of parents who do not want such a school. But it also seems to rule out the use of religious values by parents to argue for the opportunity for their own children to receive a publicly funded education at a religious school. As Galston (1995, p. 520) observes, these parents are not trying coercively to impose their values on other families: they just don't want their own family's private pursuit of those values to be burdened by a public policy that exclusively funds secular schools. The key distinction is between "defensive" public claims, made by citizens who want to escape the burdens imposed by laws grounded in civic concerns, and the "offensive" claims of those who wish to use political power to impose their comprehensive values on others (Galston, 2002, pp. 115–17). According to this powerful argument, the requirement of public reason should apply only to those making offensive claims. Rawls himself seems to recognize the force of this argument specifically on the issue of religious schools. He suggests, in a passage that interestingly appears to presuppose the suitability of religious schools to deliver satisfactory civic education (1993/1996, pp. 248–49), that citizens be allowed to invoke religious reasons in support of their claims for publicly funded faith schools precisely in order to demonstrate to fellow citizens that these claims are purely defensive in nature. But Rawls apparently did not see that these kinds of defensive claims might be appropriate in debates on a wide range of public policy proposals, and therefore that the account of public reason needs significant revision.

In the case of arguments over control of public funds, it might be argued that even supposedly defensive claims amount to an attempted imposition on fellow citizens. It is one thing for religious parents to argue that they should be left alone by the state to choose a private religious school for their child, but quite another to ask the state to pay for that education. This latter demand could be regarded as an attempted imposition of values on other citizens in two senses. First, the tax payments that the state coercively extracts from me are being used to finance an education whose basic values I do not, and cannot be expected to, share. Why should I be forced to spend my money to promote such values? Second, when the state of which I am a citizen supports, rather than merely permits, a religious school, it confers upon that school the approval of the political community. Why should my fellow citizens be allowed to hijack the prestige and authority of the state to pass such a sectarian judgment?

The answer to both these questions appeals again to the understanding of schooling as a primary good supplied by the liberal democratic state. Public funding of schools is justified not only by our shared civic purposes but also by our shared commitment to provide citizens with the means to pursue their conception of the good life, whatever that may be. If the balance of values favors public funding of a particular religious school, the state does not thereby declare its allegiance to that religion or even speculate about the truth or plausibility of claims made by that religion. Public funding of religious schools that are inferior vehicles of civic education will be justified in those cases where the state's obligation to help parents and families pursue their private values outweighs its obligation to pursue civic goals. And, of course, religious values must be admitted to public debate for defensive purposes in order to identify such cases in the sphere of education policy and beyond.

Once we reject the principle of political primacy, liberal politics must aim to strike an appropriate balance between civic and noncivic values in cases of conflict, but it is not clear that the theories of Rawls and Macedo have the resources to make meaningful comparisons between these different types of value. Raz (1994, pp. 61–62) observes that the "strong autonomy" of Rawls' political conception of justice—its independence from all comprehensive moral doctrines—rules out the possibility of principled adjudication of the competing demands of political values like civic education, on the one hand, and private values like unburdened pursuit of one's religion, on the other hand. This would be a problem even for those, like Macedo, who believe in political primacy but propose to grant occasional exceptions. Such exceptions are appropriate only in response to a coherent and publicly defensible claim that the importance of providing (or at least permitting) a religious education in a particular case outweighs the civic reasons to prefer common schools. But "strong autonomy" allows no basis for such a comparative claim. Once we reject the principle of political primacy the inadequacy of Rawls' conception becomes even more apparent because these types of comparisons will need to be made routinely in political deliberation. "Since a strongly autonomous political theory prevents us from considering its political values in the comprehensive context of a complete moral theory, it cannot yield practical conclusions. It can neither assure us that conflicts do not arise nor adjudicate when they do arise" (Raz, 1994, p. 62).

Liberalism without political primacy will look quite different from the political liberalism of Rawls and Macedo. When the pursuit of bona fide political values threatens to burden certain citizens in their pursuit of reasonable conceptions of the good, liberals must not shed mere crocodile tears: even if control of public funding is at stake, liberal politics must give weight to defensive claims grounded in comprehensive ethical doctrines. But, to return to my central theme, should liberals cry at all for those citizens whose claim to be burdened by a particular public policy is grounded in opposition to autonomy? Political liberalism's aspiration to sidestep these opponents of autonomy, to serenely override their objections without refuting them, is seductive but illegitimate. But the option of refutation may have been too quickly abandoned: we need to reexamine whether liberals can legitimately advocate public recognition of the value of autonomy.

Is Autonomy a "Cost" of Civic Education?

As discussed earlier, a major source of religious parents' objections to common schools is the fact that these institutions inevitably tend to encourage children to think autonomously about their own religious beliefs at the same time as teaching the virtues and capacities of liberal democratic citizenship. As Gutmann (1999, p. 40) puts it: "many if not all of the capacities necessary for choice among good lives are also necessary for choice among good societies," and so it may be difficult in practice to distinguish between civic education and education aimed at developing a child's personal autonomy. But for those who believe that the liberal democratic state should take no position on the good life, including the value of autonomy for such a life, this close connection between autonomy and good citizenship is one of the great tragedies of the liberal project. Civic education is important, but it has an inevitable and unintended by-product that burdens certain families. If this is one's position, I have argued so far, one should be committed to compromising on the pursuit of civic goals in order to mitigate the autonomy costs to those families.

Eamonn Callan (1996, 1997) proposes a different view of the relationship between civic education and autonomy. On this view, it is incoherent and normatively offensive to regard the development of personal autonomy as an unintended and unwanted effect of civic education because the conception of the good liberal democratic citizen encompasses personal autonomy, despite what Rawls and his followers would like to believe. Rawls tells us that good citizens are reasonable, and that reasonable persons are defined by their recognition of the burdens of judgment and their resulting commitment to the principle of political reciprocity. But how does one grasp the true significance of the burdens of judgment without simultaneously coming to question one's own beliefs and values? Callan (1996, p. 21) proposes that one cannot, because the virtue of reasonableness is conceptually inseparable from the quality of personal autonomy: "the psychological attributes that constitute an active acceptance of the burdens of reason, such as the capacity and inclination to subject received ethical ideas to critical scrutiny, also constitute a recognizable ideal of ethical autonomy."

The good citizen of a liberal democracy has to accept that many other citizens in his society have beliefs and values that are different from his own but no less rational or reasonable. What exactly does this mean? He may still believe that they are wrong, but he must recognize the real *possibility* that *he* is mistaken and that they are actually right, or that neither he nor they are wrong, because to do otherwise would be to deny what the burdens of judgment entail, namely, that some other beliefs and values are just as reasonable and rational as one's own. The good citizen must recognize that his own ethical position is not the uniquely rational one, and he must be able to distinguish among his own values and beliefs those that are merely personally justified and those that meet the more stringent test of public justification and are therefore appropriate guides for political acts like voting (Gaus, 1996; Nagel, 1987). And it is not enough for the good liberal democratic citizen merely to be able to articulate these implications of the burdens of judgment: he needs to understand the *force* of the idea that other people's doctrines are equally reasonable and rational in a way that will sustain a principled commitment to reciprocity. One cannot appreciate the force of this idea without either stepping into the shoes of others and attempting to follow their reasoning or at least contemplating what the value of such an exercise would be. But to do either of these things sincerely, as opposed to merely going through the motions, is precisely to adopt the mindset of the autonomous person. As Callan (1996, p. 17) puts it: "The attempt to understand the reasonableness of convictions that may be in deep conflict with doctrines learned in the family, say, cannot be carried through without inviting the disturbing question that these convictions might be the basis of a better way of life, or at least one that is just as good."

The Rawlsian response to this accusation is to point out that citizens are only required to think about *politics* in this way but are free to revert to less critical and reflective patterns of belief in their everyday lives. As Callan (1996, p. 12) observes, whether or not this is a psychological possibility, it is a profoundly unattractive picture of the relationship between citizens' public and private identities because it requires people "to oscillate between contradictory beliefs about the rational status of their ethical beliefs. . . . To retain a lively understanding of the burdens of judgment in political contexts while suppressing it everywhere else would require a feat of gross personal deception that cannot be squared with personal integrity." If the fact of reasonable pluralism really is a "fact" about our society[6]—a fact with profound implications for the limits of political legitimacy—then it is distasteful to suggest that people must know the fact *qua* citizens but can conveniently forget or ignore it *qua* private persons.

If Callan is right, and I think he is, then it is incoherent to say that the liberal democratic state aims to educate good citizens but regards the development of ethical autonomy as a regrettable by-product of that education: to be a good citizen is to be, among other things, an autonomous person. Unless I recognize that my own ethical doctrine is just one among many equally reasonable and rational doctrines, I lack principled commitment to reciprocity as a distinctively liberal democratic virtue. But I cannot see my own beliefs in this way without accepting the principle that beliefs can and should be assessed and re-

---

[6] Perhaps Rawls would wish to deny this, despite his choice of the word "fact," just as he wishes to deny that his conception of justice is true. But it is hard to see how he can do away with all such truth claims in a theory that is supposed to have normative bite (Raz, 1994).

vised by the standards of critical reason. At times, Macedo seems close to accepting this point, as when he writes: "All citizens should be capable of thinking critically about their private beliefs for the sake of honoring the demands of liberal justice" (2000, p. 240). But evidently he thinks it is both possible and normatively acceptable for people to restrict the use of this capacity to their behavior as citizens. We should reject this proposition: if people are to regard themselves as having good grounds for using the capacity for thinking critically about their private beliefs in their role as citizens, and for regarding other citizens who fail to exercise the same capacity as unreasonable, then they ought also to regard themselves as having grounds for using it in their lives as private persons.

What would be the implications of accepting that civic education really is education for autonomy because the good citizen is by definition an autonomous person? The liberal who claims that the only goals of public education policy are civic in nature is now committed to defending the value of autonomy, but not on the grounds that autonomy is either conducive to or constitutive of a good life. Rather, the political liberal must defend autonomy on the grounds that it is a political virtue. As Callan summarizes the position: "Rawls might be read as offering a distinctive and powerful argument for a partially comprehensive doctrine of ethical autonomy that derives not from speculative metaphysics or contestable intuitions about the good but from a principle of reciprocity and a shared recognition of the limits of the reason we must employ with each other when we try to live by that principle" (1996, p. 23). As we shall soon see, there is an important argument to suggest that the principle of reciprocity itself relies upon the nonpolitical value of autonomy, but for the time being I want to point out that Callan's reading of Rawls does *not* lend any additional weight to the claim that the civic goals of education should generally be presumed to trump the objections of religious parents who do not want their children to develop as autonomous persons. At first sight, this may seem strange. After all, we now have what we lacked before: an argument that can legitimately be deployed to show the value of autonomy to counter the objections of religious parents. But the crucial point is that we do not have any new justificatory resources, we have simply relabeled the resources we had before. We already knew that there were important civic reasons to support an education that has the effect of promoting autonomy, and those civic reasons have no more power to overcome parental objections if we say that personal autonomy is itself our civic goal than if we describe it as an unintended and unwanted but inevitable and foreseen by-product of the civic education process.

Callan's reinterpretation of Rawls tells us what we are really committed to when we support civic education, but he does not thereby enhance the normative force of the argument for treating civic goals as presumptive trumps (although it is arguable that the argument at least *looks* more attractive when one is clear about the status of autonomy within it). Callan explicitly recognizes the need for the defenders of merely civic education to weigh the possible private costs of an education for autonomy against its civic value: even if we rejected Callan's claim that the civic virtue of reasonableness encompasses an ethical doctrine of autonomy, his analysis would still remind us that we cannot invoke a principle of political primacy in this context. Callan is right to say that liberals need to take a position on the relationship between ethical autonomy and the good life in order to vindicate the claim that civic educational goals trump objections grounded in opposition to autonomy, but he is also right to insist that liberals do not need to demonstrate that ethical autonomy is either a necessary ingredient of or a useful means to the good life. There is already a powerful argument on the table for autonomy's positive value, namely, the civic argument (which, we should recall, is no more and no less than the old arguments for civic education, seen in light of Callan's claim that personal autonomy is itself a civic virtue). Therefore: "All that needs to be shown is that autonomy does not make our lives bad" (p. 24).

Having set himself this apparently modest task, Callan goes about it in a strange way. Let us first consider what Callan ought to do, according to his own logic. A robust civic education, as Callan repeatedly points out, will instill in children the commitment to and capacity for autonomous reflection at a fairly advanced level. What Callan, on behalf of Rawls and Macedo, therefore needs to show is that the future lives of these children will not be worse with a high degree of ethical autonomy than they would have been with the significantly lower levels of autonomy they would have developed if they had been exempted from many of the demands of civic education, perhaps by attending a religious school. And he needs to show that this is true for children, at least in the large majority of cases, regardless of their families' conception of the good. If this were the case, then liberal democratic states would be entitled to insist on pursuing civic educational goals, including the development of ethical autonomy, through common schools, responding to parental objections by saying both that an important civic good was thereby being served and that the children could be expected not to be harmed by the process.

But Callan never tries to make the case that a fairly high degree of ethical autonomy is not a harm relative to a much lower degree. Instead, he makes and defends the quite different claim that all children have an interest in developing their autonomy beyond "a primitive level of agency" that Callan calls "ethical servility," the condition of being unable to seriously consider alternatives to one's values and beliefs (1997, p. 152). The interest that is served in surpassing ethical servility is "the prospective interest in personal sovereignty our children have" (p. 152) because "to be made servile is effectively to forfeit one's sovereignty to another" (p. 156), and therefore: "To be reared in a manner that instills ethical servility . . . is to be denied one of the developmental preconditions of adult rights" (p. 155). There are two important senses in which Callan here fails to meet the burden of proof that he imposed upon himself. First, and most obviously, he defends only a minimal degree of autonomy, not the much higher level of critical reflection that will be encouraged by a civic education where children really grapple with the implications of the burdens of judgment. Religious parents might reasonably reply to Callan: "Yes, we agree that our children should not be left ethically servile by their education, and we are confident that our religious schools will not produce that result, but we still assert the dangers of developing a more thorough-going autonomy of the sort that you require of all citizens." Second, Callan fails to address directly the parents' concern that their children's lives will be less successful if they develop as autonomous persons: he focuses instead on the idea that autonomous persons are sovereign in their own lives. Religious parents might respond: "It would be better for our children to live lives of virtue at the direction of others than for them to utilize their personal sovereignty to pursue vice." As I shall argue in chapter 4, there is an important sense in which liberal democratic states should value personal autonomy as a condition of moral agency, but this sense needs to be bolstered by an assurance that autonomy has a positive, or at least a nonnegative, impact on the quality of an individual's life.

Callan does not answer his own question, and so he does not succeed in demonstrating that the civic goals of education can legitimately be pursued despite the objections of religious parents worried about the corrupting effect of autonomy. But it is important that he asks the right question—about the private (dis)value of autonomy to individuals and families—because he recognizes that we cannot appeal to the principle of political primacy in cases of conflict. If supporters of civic education want to avoid making major concessions to religious parents, they will have to engage with Callan's question and break the state's self-imposed silence on questions about the noncivic value of ethical autonomy. As I show in the next three chapters, I think liberal democratic states can and should endorse the noncivic value of individual autonomy because this value can be conclusively justified in ways that respect the fact of reasonable pluralism. Doubtless, some readers will be unconvinced by the particular arguments I offer and will continue to believe that the liberal democratic state cannot justify taking any position on the value of autonomy for individuals seeking to identify and lead a good life. But, I now want to argue, liberal democrats *need* a politically acceptable argument for the noncivic value of autonomy because it turns out that the civic goal of reproducing the liberal democratic regime only has principled force by virtue of an often covert appeal to the noncivic value of individual autonomy.

LIBERAL DEMOCRATIC PRINCIPLES PRESUPPOSE THE VALUE OF AUTONOMY

If reproduction of the liberal democratic state is to be understood as a goal of greater value than the mere preservation of peace and political order, it must be so by virtue of the special value of those features that are distinctive to the liberal democratic state. Rawls (1993/1996, p. 147) is certainly keen to insist that his political conception is no "mere *modus vivendi*," and supporters of liberal democratic civic education would not typically accept the more general claim that states should teach their citizens (or subjects) in whatever way best conduces to the preservation of the existing regime. Liberal democracy is supposed to be something special, the reproduction of which is preferable to the conversion of the state into a stable theocracy. But what is it about liberal democracy, with its distinctive commitment to individual rights and freedoms, that makes the mission of civic education on its behalf especially worthwhile? And can that value be specified without endorsing the value of autonomy for individual lives?

The first important thing to see is that the mere fact of reasonable pluralism is inadequate to justify the distinctive protections afforded to individuals by a liberal constitution. Rawls sometimes seems to deduce the principle of political reciprocity, which guarantees individual rights against government coercion and the rights of citizens against each other in civil society, directly from the burdens of judgment and the resulting fact of reasonable pluralism. But more needs to be said: the mere facts that you and I disagree and that neither of our views is irrational do not contain within themselves the normative conclusion that I may not force you to live according to my conception of the good. As many theorists have observed (Crowder, 1994; Gray, 1996; Newey, 1997; Galston, 1999a), even if we endorse the stronger thesis of metaphysical pluralism, rather than Rawls' weaker claim about the deficiencies of human reason on ethical questions, the move from pluralism to liberalism is not so simple, and indeed the two may not even be compatible. What is needed to arrive at the liberal conclusion is a principle "that coercion always stands exposed to a potential demand for justification" (Galston, 1999a), a demand that by definition could not be satisfactorily answered in cases of reasonable disagreement. But what is it about individuals that demands this kind of respect, according to which the burden of justification lies squarely on the agent who wishes to coerce another?

On some accounts of liberalism, respect is due to individuals because of their capacity to hold and pursue a determinate conception of their good. For Lomasky, persons enjoy a protected moral status because they are "independent project pursuers." "The ability to direct one's efforts toward certain ends that one has assumed as one's own and to value achievable outcomes in terms of the commitments that are central to one's identity as an active being are the essence of project pursuit" (1987, p. 181). But to qualify as an independent project pursuer, one need not assume one's ends by an act of choice or rational endorsement. On the contrary, projects may "instead be ingested with one's mother's milk, become by imperceptible degrees more firmly fixed over time within one's volitional makeup" (p. 44). Likewise, Tamir (1995, p. 10) argues for a conception of liberalism that "places at its core a commitment to equal concern and respect for individuals, their preferences and interests, regardless of the way these were formed." If these accounts are right, the value of liberal democratic institutions does not depend on an endorsement of the value of autonomy to individual lives.

But, as Kymlicka observes, it is far from clear that we capture the full sense of liberal freedom if we characterize the duty to respect persons as the duty to respect persons' pursuit of their existing conception of the good. Many key components of the familiar package of liberal rights, including freedom of speech and the right to exit one's religious community, do not seem to be necessary if we are only "committed to protecting a set of freedoms which were meant to allow individuals to pursue their preferences, desires, and interests," however these were formed (Tamir, 1995, p. 10). If liberal institutions are concerned only that people be free to do what they like, then why should we give special protection, in the form of free speech rights, to those who want to persuade others to change their preferences? And why should we respect an individual's right to change her preferences, instead of insisting that the way to respect a person is to help and require her to stay true to her (old) preferences? "Much of what is distinctive to a liberal state concerns the forming and revising of people's conceptions of the good, rather than the pursuit of those conceptions once chosen"

(Kymlicka, 1995, p. 82). If Kymlicka is right, the principles of liberal democracy are grounded in the special value of individual autonomy, whatever the source and nature of that value.

Levinson (1999, pp. 18–21) argues persuasively that Rawls himself is committed to the noncivic value of individual autonomy by the account he gives of the second moral power attributed to all persons under the political conception of justice. This power is called "the capacity for a conception of the good," but it extends far beyond Lomasky's notion of an independent project pursuer, and it effectively describes the capacity for individual autonomy. "The capacity for a conception of the good is the capacity to form, to revise, and rationally to pursue a conception of one's rational advantage or good" (Rawls, 1993/1996, p. 19). Why should the liberal democratic state be concerned to secure the conditions under which individuals can exercise this power, if not because of the value of autonomy to an individual life? Levinson (1999, p. 20) quite properly forces the issue: "we must have a further reason beyond the mere presence of this capacity to regard it as an important part of even the political conception of the person" rather than as a capacity that individuals would do better not to cultivate. As we shall see in chapter 4, Rawls himself offers reasons to believe that "the full and informed exercise of this capacity" is "a means to a person's good" or even "an essential part of a determinate conception of the good" (1993/1996, pp. 313–315). But whatever its exact relationship to the individual good, autonomy is clearly a foundational value for Rawls' political theory, albeit masquerading as "the second moral power" or "the capacity for a conception of the good."

Conclusion

Earlier in this chapter, I concluded that the civic goals of education, divorced from any view on the value of individual autonomy, are insufficient to justify the liberal democratic state in a general refusal to fund religious schools. Especially because the state should treat education as, in part, a kind of primary good, and because there is no costless opt-out for parents who object to common schools, the liberal state cannot appeal to the principle of political primacy to insist that its civic goals trump the private interests of families where religious parents oppose the development of autonomy that occurs in common schools. However difficult it might be, states with no position on the value of autonomy would need to consider the arguments for religious education on a case-by-case basis, rather than resorting to the simple but indefensible market solution of permitting religious schooling always and only when private funds are available.

However, I have gone on to argue that it is incoherent, in two quite different senses, to say that the liberal democratic state should in fact pursue through its education policy only the civic goal of conscious social reproduction, while taking no position on the value of individual autonomy. First, civic education turns out to encompass education for autonomy: good citizens endorse the principle of reciprocity because they actively accept the burdens of judgment in a sense that amounts to ethical autonomy. So arguments for civic education are, among other things, arguments for the civic value of individual autonomy. Second, and more important, we have just seen that the principled grounds for supporting the goal of reproducing the liberal democratic state, with its extensive package of individual rights and freedoms, rest upon an endorsement of the value of autonomy for individual lives. So arguments for distinctively liberal democratic civic education, properly understood, are also dependent on arguments for the noncivic value of individual autonomy, the way in which it makes people's lives better.

All these conclusions point to the need to reexamine the concept of individual autonomy, and it is to this task that I turn in the next part. There are a number of questions that will guide the inquiry. What is autonomy? Perhaps more importantly, as we will soon see, what isn't it? In what sense, or senses, might autonomy be considered valuable for individuals who possess and exercise it? Are any of these senses appropriate for public recognition in a multicultural, liberal democratic society? Is it possible to overcome the accusation that the value of the autonomous life is just one more sectarian position about which there is reasonable disagreement, and that to adopt it as a universal goal of public education policy would be, in the alarming words of Stephen Macedo (2000, p. 185), to declare "liberalism as holy war"?

PART II

Autonomy as a Public Value

Chapter 3

AUTONOMY, IDENTITY, AND CHOICE

MY GOAL in this chapter is to investigate and flesh out the idea of autonomy, which I also sometimes refer to as personal or ethical autonomy, in a way that lays the foundations for constructing an argument that the development of such autonomy in individuals is a legitimate, and indeed an appropriate, goal of education policy in a liberal democratic state. I do not pretend to offer a fully articulated conception of autonomy: such a task would be beyond the scope of my current project. But I do aim to make some important distinctions, to challenge the adequacy of certain conditions that have often been thought to be either necessary or sufficient for an autonomous life, and, ultimately, to offer a sketch of the nature of autonomous reflection. In chapter 1 I provided a working definition of autonomy in order to illuminate the problematic nature of political liberalism's attempt to avoid taking a position on autonomy's value. I proposed that autonomy is the combined capacity for and commitment to ongoing rational reflection on all of one's ethical commitments. But that working definition invites a whole host of questions as to whether an autonomous ethical life is truly a coherent, realistic, and attractive option for individuals. I try to address many of those questions in the course of this chapter, before proceeding in the following two chapters to argue that autonomy's value is an appropriate object of recognition not only for individual persons but also for the liberal state.

A first step in characterizing personal or ethical autonomy is to distinguish it carefully from another form of autonomy, which may be called Kantian moral autonomy. Ethical autonomy is a rationally reflective way in which a person may hold (and act according to) one particular conception of the good life rather than other conceptions, where all the options under consideration are morally permissible. Kantian moral autonomy describes a rational way in which individuals may come to and be motivated by an answer to the prior question: what maxims of action are morally permissible (and, therefore, which conceptions of the good can permissibly be pursued)? The exercise of moral autonomy defines the set of permissible options: the exercise of ethical autonomy guides the choice within that set.

As Kant makes clear (1785/1993), the morally autonomous agent is self-legislating—she thinks rationally for herself rather than being pushed around by her desires and inclinations—but there is only one right answer to the question: what maxims are morally permissible? The moral law is universal and binding on all rational beings: moral autonomy consists in freely recognizing that fact and being motivated to compliance by this recognition. There are, of course, many instances where agents face multiple permissible options, but the selection of one among these options is not a moral question, and indeed for Kant it is not a choice that can be made autonomously because reason is silent on such matters. The idea of personal or ethical autonomy is not only different from Kantian moral autonomy, it is also incompatible with Kant's strict account of the role of reason. The ethically autonomous person uses reason to guide his choice of life goals where the choice is between multiple options *all of which are morally permitted.* Hence, Raz (1986, p. 381) can say that "A moral theory which recognizes the value of autonomy inevitably upholds a pluralistic view. It admits the value of a large number of greatly differing pursuits among which individuals are free to choose."

Under the assumptions of ethical pluralism, there is no universal standard of a correct ethical choice—the right way of life—from which agents might diverge by thinking for themselves.[1] But this does not mean that one cannot make an error in one's choice among morally permissible doctrines: accepting ethical pluralism does not commit us to the radical and implausible view that *all* permissible conceptions of the good are equally valuable, only to the much weaker claim that there is no single best way of life that each person should follow. Although it makes perfect sense to claim that someone who is morally faultless has nonetheless fallen into ethical error, and we might expect often to hear private persons express this judgment about each other, it is not a judgment that the liberal state can make or evaluate without adopting a role that would be excessively intrusive and frighteningly open to abuse. But, although the state is appropriately excluded from making judgments about the substantive merits of particular morally permissible conceptions of the good, I shall argue in the next chapter that the state should require that all children be educated in a way that teaches and encourages them to make their own rational decisions about the good life, because the practice of rational ethical reflection can be expected to help them identify and lead good lives. This claim about personal autonomy's instrumental value will be the foundation

---

[1] Or, even if there is such a standard in theory, we must accept that there will always be reasonable disagreement about its content in practice.

of my paternalistic argument for adopting the cultivation of autonomy as a goal of education policy.

The conception of autonomy that I shall develop and defend has at its heart the idea of ongoing and distinctively rational reflection about one's ethical beliefs and values; this is, as Callan showed us in the previous chapter, the kind of ethical autonomy that persons develop as a result of a robust and successful liberal democratic civic education. Working with such a conception of autonomy focuses our attention on a real and important debate in multicultural liberal societies about the value of a particular type of reflective life, one that does not enjoy anywhere near universal support but that, I shall argue in the next two chapters, can nevertheless justifiably be adopted as a goal of liberal education policy. For the general purposes of political theory, as well as for my more specific purposes in this book, there is little point in defining autonomy in a way that expunges all controversial elements from the concept. My goal is not only to describe the attitude toward one's ethical beliefs and values that is encouraged by liberal democratic civic education, but also to sketch a conception of personal autonomy that is realistic and attractive as a positive goal of education policy in its own right, notwithstanding the fact that it is not and perhaps never will be universally valued in actual multicultural societies.

Raz (1986, p. 369) gives us a good starting point for our investigation: "The ruling idea behind the ideal of personal autonomy is that people should make their own lives. The autonomous person is a (part) author of his own life. The ideal of personal autonomy is the vision of people controlling, to some degree, their own destiny, fashioning it through successive decisions throughout their lives." Autonomy described this way has a broad, if not in practice universal, appeal. But the idea needs to be sharpened significantly if we are to identify the specific features to which many religious parents object. In particular, I shall argue, we must emphasize the role of reason: we need an account according to which a person is autonomous to the extent that "he can and does subject his opinions and tastes to *rational* scrutiny" (J. Feinberg, 1989, p. 32, my emphasis). What I hope to show is that we can sharpen the idea of autonomy in this way without necessarily arriving at a conception that is incoherent, undesirable, or unacceptably sectarian.

Autonomy as Ongoing Rational Reflection

Since autonomy involves reflection on one's beliefs and values, the autonomous person must both possess and exercise the capacity for second-order thought. This is a necessary condition for autonomy, but is

it also sufficient to define an attractive conception? It is worth considering why we might value the bare capacity for second-order thought.
If one possesses both first- and second-order desires, and the two sets
are more or less in harmony with one another, there is a sense in which
one may be said to identify with the life one leads. Ronald Dworkin
(2000, pp. 291–93) has argued that it is an agent's second-order endorsement or approval of her first-order tastes that allows us to ascribe
those tastes to the individual's person, rather than regarding them
merely as features of that person's circumstances. In this spirit, Gerald
Dworkin (1988, p. 15) initially proposes that autonomy is "the capacity
to raise the question of whether I will identify with or reject the reasons
for which I now act": on this account, the distinctive value of autonomy is that it enables me, by endorsing or revising my reasons for action, to achieve a kind of reflective harmony between my first- and
second-order commitments. But until something more is said about the
nature of the second-order considerations by which an agent evaluates
her first-order reasons, it is a mistake to equate identifying with one's
life, understood merely as experiencing harmony between one's first-
and second-order commitments, with the concept of living autonomously. As Riesman (1969) argues persuasively, the "inner-directed
man," whose first-order values are dictated by substantive second-
order commitments into which he has been thoroughly indoctrinated,
identifies with his choices, but he is just as heteronomous as the man
who lacks second-order preferences altogether. Second-order identification fails to capture the special quality of the autonomous life as a
kind of independence because the substance of an agent's beliefs and
values can still be dictated by others without critical examination by
the agent's own rational faculties.

   A similar problem attends Kymlicka's (1995, p. 81) attempt to assimilate the ideal of autonomy to the notion that "we lead our life from the
inside, in accordance with our beliefs about what gives value to life."
The implication of this account is that nonautonomous persons necessarily live in accordance with beliefs that are not their own but instead
belong to others. Of course, there exists the heteronomous person
whose life is simply externally directed by other people without her
ever internalizing and accepting the beliefs and values of those others—this person is the miserable slave, whose continued compliance
with the will of others is presumably guaranteed by continual coercion
or the threat thereof. But the case of heteronomy that interests us here,
in our discussion of religious education, is precisely the case of the
person who does not need to be coerced because he has internalized
the values of others and does not subject those values to rational scrutiny. As Charney (2000, pp. 43–50) points out, nonautonomous belief

and action are still typically guided by reasons that the agent accepts: even heteronomous people live their lives from the inside. Whenever immediate physical coercion is absent, from the internal perspective it will always appear that a person's actions are explained by her own reasons and beliefs (Nagel, 1986, p. 113). But therefore, if autonomy is to mean more than mere freedom from immediate external coercion, we must give up on the idea that autonomy means "leading your life from the inside" and focus instead on the way in which individuals hold the highest-order values and beliefs that regulate the first-order preferences that in turn guide their actions.

Gerald Dworkin's requirement of "procedural independence" appears at first to be an important step in the right direction, and it is certainly motivated by the appropriate concern. "Second-order reflection cannot be the whole story of autonomy. For those reflections, the choice of the kind of person one wants to become, may be influenced by other persons or circumstances in such a fashion that we do not view these evaluations as being the person's own" (1988, p. 18). By his own admission, Dworkin's account of this crucial requirement is underdeveloped, but he suggests that "roughly, the distinction is between those modes of evaluation that interfere with the rationality of higher-order reflection and those that do not" (p. 161). This emphasis on rational reflection is to be welcomed, but because Dworkin's requirement focuses exclusively on the origins of our second-order commitments and not on the actual activity of autonomous reflection, procedural independence turns out on closer examination to be neither necessary nor sufficient for autonomy.

It is not sufficient because we should not regard as autonomous the person who essentially enslaves himself by adopting the second-order commitment to obey some particular ethical authority unconditionally, *even if* that commitment is undertaken by a genuinely free choice of the person in question. If I exercise my independence from others today to commit myself irrevocably to obey you until I die, I relinquish my autonomy in the process. Autonomous persons must be the *ongoing* authors of their own lives, and this ongoing status is not guaranteed by a requirement that mistakenly focuses on the origin rather than the form of the highest-order commitments that people hold.

Dworkin explicitly rejects any such standard for evaluating the form of second-order preferences when he insists that a procedurally independent second-order commitment to obedience suffices for autonomy. "Suppose the person wants to conduct his or her life in accordance with the following: Do whatever my mother or my buddies or my leader or my priest tells me to do. Such a person counts, in my view, as autonomous" (p. 21). Dworkin maintains this view because he thinks that any scrutiny of second-order commitments beyond the requirement that they have arisen in a procedurally independent way will amount to a requirement of "substantive independence," which he argues is unacceptable because it excludes important and desirable forms of human loyalty. But, as we shall shortly see, the requirement that autonomous agents remain open-minded about the possibility that new evidence and/or arguments will warrant a change in their values or beliefs does not imperil any truly valuable human virtues.

By looking at the form of second-order commitments, we also come to see that procedural independence is not necessary for autonomy. Imagine a person who has "the procedural, second-order concern that one's choices, whatever their content, be capable of surviving a kind of deeply reflective scrutiny of and by oneself" (Hill, 1991, p. 178). This seems like a paradigmatic case of autonomy. But does it make a difference if we stipulate that this very concern was instilled by zealous liberal parents and never subsequently reviewed and endorsed by the agent? I do not think that it does. An autonomous person's first-order preferences must be procedurally independent, and this independence is precisely what we see in the case of an agent with a second-order commitment to rationally scrutinize her first-order preferences, but it is actually a mistake to extend the requirement of procedural independence to that second-order commitment. If we require for autonomy that agents rationally scrutinize not only their substantive preferences but also their higher-order commitment to rational scrutiny, we are caught in an infinite regress. But there is no good reason to be led down this dismal path: autonomous persons may choose to reflect rationally about their commitment to autonomous ethical reflection, and perhaps even about that choice, but they are not required to do so.

Ironically, Dworkin sees but misplaces the danger of an infinite regress of ever ascending higher-order preferences. Dworkin's worry is that once we start to discriminate among second-order motivations and to deny that all agents with procedurally independent second-order values and preferences are autonomous, the only way to discriminate will be to demand third-order endorsement of second-order preferences, and so on (1988, p. 19). But Dworkin here falls victim to his own stubborn refusal to evaluate the form of our commitments rather than their origins and their mere consistency with higher-order commitments. The requirement of procedurally independent second-order preferences is actually a conceptual mistake in elaborating a conception of autonomy: although we require that autonomous agents rationally endorse their first-order values and beliefs rather than passively accepting them from their environment, the same requirement does not and could not apply to the commitment to rational scrutiny itself.

The simple existence of a second- (or higher-) order commitment to ongoing rational scrutiny qualifies an agent as autonomous, no matter whence that commitment came.

In moving beyond Dworkin's account of autonomy, we embrace a positive vision of the kind of active rational reflection that defines the autonomous life. As a consequence, we should no longer heed Dworkin's advice to "guard against certain intellectualist conceptions of autonomy" according to which "the process of reflection and identification [is] a conscious, fully articulated, and explicit process" such that "it will appear that it is mainly professors of philosophy who exercise autonomy and that those who are less educated, or who are by nature or upbringing less reflective, are not, or not as fully, autonomous individuals" (p. 17). We should not be ashamed to say that autonomy is one of the many things for which education is good. Nor should we be embarrassed that conscious reflection on one's values and beliefs turns out to be a key component of the autonomous life. Neither of these things entails that it is mainly professors of philosophy who exercise autonomy, although we might expect to see these fine men and women disproportionately represented among the ranks of the autonomous. Since we are all born and raised in particular traditions, and none of us is immune to the nonrational appeal of other ways of life, you need to be thoughtful and it helps to be educated if you are to shape and actively endorse your own ethical values rather than merely acquiescing in your family's doctrine or falling for the rhetorical tricks and charms of a television evangelist.

CARICATURES OF RATIONAL AUTONOMY

Many philosophers have shied away from an ideal of autonomy that emphasizes ongoing rational reflection because of impressions that, on such a view, the autonomous life is incompatible with making real personal commitments, unacceptably demanding, or perhaps even conceptually incoherent. Brian Barry (2001, p. 357) notes wryly that autonomy, at least as it is described by some contemporary liberal theorists, sounds more like a psychological illness than a desirable approach to life. If personal autonomy is to be defended as a goal of public education policy, it will be necessary to show that these impressions are mistaken, that they flow from one or more caricatures of the nature of autonomy. As we shall see in part 3, fleshing out an idea of autonomy that is more nuance than caricature also substantially changes the implications of adopting the autonomy goal for public education policy.

So the task of showing what autonomy *is not* turns out to be at least as important as saying what it *is*.

Gerald Dworkin's central objection to including a commitment to *ongoing* rational scrutiny of one's beliefs and values as a necessary condition for personal autonomy is that this condition would render autonomy incompatible with developing the kinds of relationships and projects that require making real and lasting commitments to people and ideas. Autonomy is objectionable, on this view, because it entails that our substantive commitments can only be provisional and conditional rather than absolute. But, Dworkin suggests, a provisional commitment is not really a commitment at all, or at least human lives would be greatly impoverished if all our substantive commitments remained tentative in the sense required by the ongoing practice of critical reflection. Taking the love and commitment involved in marriage as a paradigmatic example, Dworkin worries that we will not recognize as autonomous "a wife who refuses to believe her husband has done something evil, though the evidence seems to point clearly in that direction" (1988, p. 23). Autonomy would not be an attractive ideal, according to Dworkin, if it precluded this kind of faith in one's spouse.[2]

Dworkin is right to observe that a certain type of commitment is incompatible with personal autonomy as I understand the concept, but what type of commitment is that, and should we weep for its loss? Autonomous people will not have commitments that are blind, closed off from reevaluation and possible revision regardless of the weight of considerations that would recommend a rethink to the rational and detached observer. Dworkin's wife (or at least the woman he describes in this example!) has precisely such a blind commitment to the goodness of her husband, and as such she fails to exercise autonomy in evaluating his actions. To be reasoning autonomously, she would have to be genuinely open to the possibility that he had done something evil. Of course, if their life together has given her good reason to esteem his character, she might appropriately and rationally require a considerable weight of evidence to persuade her that he had acted in a way that is apparently so out of character. And even if she forms the belief that he has indeed performed an evil act, it is a further question what she should then *do*. But an autonomous person cannot close her mind to the evidence. Is autonomy rendered an unattractive quality if it has this implication? Dworkin seems to find it obvious that the wife's blind

---

[2] It should be noted that this example concerns the nature of *moral* autonomy, not the ethical autonomy that is my focus here: it is the wife's moral judgment that is in question, not the way in which she selects one among many morally permissible conceptions of the good.

faith in her husband is a positive character trait, but this position is only plausible if we think that commitment is a matter of all-or-nothing, and therefore that the only alternative to blind commitment is no commitment. This is the specter that Dworkin conjures up when he opposes a requirement of "substantive independence." But there is no reason to accept this stark view of the nature of commitment.

As Callan (1997, pp. 56–59) and Aviram (1995) point out, the autonomous person need not and should not be constantly doubting and questioning all of her values and beliefs. The commitment to rational reflection that is central to autonomy entails the *willingness* to subject one's ethical position, as well as one's other beliefs, to critical scrutiny: it does not require that the autonomous agent engage in a daily bout of Cartesian doubt. For so long as the agent nonnegligently lacks knowledge of any significant argument or evidence that would cast doubt upon her commitments, it is entirely appropriate for her not to question them. Of course, an autonomous agent must remain open to this kind of evidence and argument—one cannot metaphorically blindfold oneself and complacently declare that nothing has come to one's attention that would justify rethinking one's deepest values—but there is no obligation to devote one's life to the search for ammunition to undermine one's commitments. As I shall argue in chapters 7 and 8, schools that aim to initiate children into the practice of autonomous reflection will need deliberately to expose their students to diverse and challenging perspectives, but autonomous adults need not continually seek out such challenges. A fully developed conception of personal autonomy would need to say more about the conditions under which autonomous agents initiate a review of their commitments, and any such conception would presumably say that one can be more or less autonomous in this as in other respects, but I do not take on these tasks here. My point is simply that autonomous persons can have real commitments, to people and to values, that are not properly described as tentative merely because they are not immune to review and possible revision in the light of new evidence and arguments.

It is not only possible but also positively desirable and in a sense necessary that autonomous agents should make ethical commitments of this revocable type. Raz (1986, p. 384) proposes that "the failure to make choices through lack of initial commitment . . . does diminish the autonomy of the agent's life," and we might go further to point out that rational choice and action are conceptually impossible without the presence of some normative commitments to provide principles of choice and action. We shall return to this issue in the next paragraph. But, of course, the conceptual need for commitments could be satisfied without the presence of lasting, settled convictions of the sort that we normally have in mind when we think about ethical commitments. Raz's response (p. 154) is to define the notion of agents with "significant autonomy" as those who can "adopt personal projects, develop relationships, and accept commitments to causes." Whether we regard the agent's demonstrated capacity to make long-term commitments as *constitutive* of personal autonomy or merely as central to the *value* of an autonomous life, we must remember that education should not seek to develop critical thinking in a way that undermines children's capacity to make the kind of commitments that autonomous persons can and should make. In particular, we shall see in chapter 8 that this concern has important implications for primary education.

Many philosophers have alleged that the concept of personal autonomy, understood as the commitment to ongoing rational reflection on one's ethical and other beliefs, is ultimately incoherent because it requires agents to make so-called "radical," i.e., criterionless, choices. This requirement is perhaps most famously asserted in the existentialist tradition of Sartre (1943/1992), and it resurfaced prominently in John Gray's recent interpretation (1996) of Isaiah Berlin. If autonomy is understood as a form of rational freedom, the presence of criteria that determine our choices seems to undermine autonomy unless those criteria were themselves freely chosen or determined by other criteria that were freely chosen, and so on. At some higher-order level, we must be capable of choosing our values and principles *ex nihilo* if the appearance of free choice is to be more than a façade. MacIntyre believes that this vision of autonomy as radical choice underpins the idea of the modern self, whose "judgments are in the end criterionless" and who must therefore be capable of abstracting entirely from all contingent features of his condition to create himself: "To be a moral agent is, on this view, precisely to be able to stand back from any and every situation in which one is involved, from any and every characteristic that one may possess, and to pass judgment on it from a purely universal and abstract point of view that is totally detached from all social particularity" (1981, pp. 31–32).

If this were the essence of autonomy, it would indeed be incoherent. As Lomasky (1987, p. 182) puts it: "it is important to avoid being taken in by an ideal of autonomy as the exercise of choice completely unconditioned by any factor external to one's faculty of practical reason [since] nothing can be made of the ideal of totally unconditioned choice." But the view that autonomy requires radical choice is a caricature: "Autonomy neither does nor could require the stepping outside of all criteria to engage in some supposedly criterionless choosing" (Dearden, 1972, p. 458). We are only led to equate autonomy with this extreme and incoherent notion if we fail to see the ways in which reason can contribute to a choice among values without entirely excluding the influence of nonrational factors. It is a sophisticated account of exactly this role of reason in autonomous reflection that preserves the conceptual space for autonomous agents to make real choices rather then simply being determined to action and belief by the things they find in their psychological makeup.

Once we abandon the notion of radical choice, we can and should admit that all persons are shaped in part by their upbringing and cultural context, and that this is no less necessary a fact for autonomous agents than for any other. Arneson and Shapiro (1996, p. 391) are right to say that "the phenomenon of choice of values by an individual that we associate with attainment of autonomy always presupposes a context in which some standards and values are held at least provisionally fixed and guide choice." There is no sense in defining autonomy in such a way that it is empirically, and indeed conceptually, impossible to attain: "a theory which required as a condition of autonomy that an individual's values not be influenced by his parents, peers, or culture would violate this condition" (G. Dworkin, 1988, p. 7). The influence is necessary because it provides the agent with a determinate starting point, a provisional identity: "a person must already possess at least a rudimentary character before he can hope to choose a new one" (J. Feinberg, 1989, p. 33). But it is important to distinguish between the absurd requirement that a person's values not be influenced by external factors and the entirely reasonable alternative that those external influences should do no more than define a starting point for autonomous reflection, and that they should themselves be subjected to rational scrutiny at an appropriate stage in the person's development.

A provisional identity is necessary not only as a conceptual precondition of ethical choice given the assumptions of pluralism, but also as a developmental stage at which children grow to understand the nature and possibility of decision and commitment in ethical matters. Importantly, the substance of the ethical starting point is less important than that there should be some well-defined "primary culture" (Ackerman, 1980), provided that an upbringing in this culture does not make it excessively difficult for the agent to think critically in the future about the values that are constitutive of the culture. As Arneson and Shapiro (1996, p. 391) and Levinson (1999, p. 57) argue, even an irrational prejudice can serve a young child as an example of a serious ethical commitment and as a place from which to commence the ethical reasoning that we hope and expect will ultimately vanquish the original prejudice. This is not an argument for raising children with prejudices, but rather an attempt to show that autonomy can develop even from the most unlikely beginnings if older children are taught to think critically about the values with which they were raised. We shall return to this question in chapter 8 when the discussion focuses on primary schooling.

The idea that one can become autonomous by rejecting the prejudices one learned as a child is sometimes implicitly transformed into the quite different requirement that one must reject one's familial or other culture of upbringing in order to achieve autonomy. After all, proponents of this particular caricature might ask, in what sense can a person be autonomous if he just believes and values all the same things he was taught to accept as a child? Those who believe that rebellion against family is a necessary condition of autonomy tend to smile knowingly when they discover the remarkable similarities between parents and children in matters of religious faith, voting behavior, or vision of a successful life. These similarities are so frequently observed that we can hardly ascribe them to coincidence—my independent rational reflection "just happens" to reach the same conclusions as my parents' even though there is no one ethical position universally prescribed by reason—but if they are not coincidences, are they not evidence of the children's lack of autonomy? It clearly will not suffice to say, with Wringe:

> Many individuals having such a[n autonomous] possibility of choice may freely and deliberately choose to continue to adhere to the beliefs, values, and ways of life current in their community of origin. This will be unsurprising when—as is of course often the case—these beliefs, values, and ways of life are indeed valuable and recognizable as such by an educated and rational person. (Wringe, 1995, p. 128)

The fact that my family's way of life can be recognized as valuable by an intelligent person does not explain why, once I have grown up and left home, I should be any more likely to adhere to that way of life than to any of the other equally valuable ways of life that find expression in my society. Children whose values and beliefs are strikingly similar to those of their parents look like prime suspects to the autonomy police.

But we should not move so quickly. The more sophisticated conception of autonomy we are sketching insists on the importance of a primary culture, and the importance of that starting point is not left behind once the process of ethical reflection begins. Remember that, according to the assumptions of ethical pluralism, the choice between reasonable ethical doctrines cannot be determined by reason alone. Some factor other than pure reason must be involved in our choice among reasonable doctrines: why should the culture of origin be any less suitable than other contingent, nonrational factors to resolve the incommensurability? It is not necessarily an affront to autonomy if "many of the most important things in our lives, rather than being consciously chosen, [are] projects we have grown up with and aspirations we discover when we first autonomously deliberate" (Waldron, 1989, p. 1112). So, personal autonomy need not mean "rescue from father and mother. Indeed, the ability to keep intact one's early associations and experience and to integrate them into adult life seems often— though not inevitably—associated with autonomy" (Coons and Sugarman, 1999, p. 73).

As Gardner (1988, p. 95) points out, the "stickiness" of our early beliefs and values is no doubt partly due to inadequate independent rational scrutiny. But Gardner is too quick to see heteronomy in this phenomenon. He is, for example, unduly troubled by the following: "Often it seems that people need what they regard as good reasons for abandoning what they believe even when they lack good reasons for believing what they do; that they believe something would appear, from their point of view, to constitute a prima facie case for continuing to believe it" (p. 96). Given that the choice among reasonable ethical doctrines or other belief systems is underdetermined before we introduce nonrational considerations, it is not irrational or incompatible with autonomy to treat one's current beliefs as the default set, to be rejected or amended only in the light of a good reason. People who suspend belief until one ethical doctrine is decisively vindicated over all others on purely rational grounds will be waiting forever! The person whose open-minded rational reflection reveals no compelling reasons either to endorse or to reject the faith in which he was raised can autonomously keep that faith, although such a person should be especially conscious of the fact that one's unchosen primary culture plays a role in shaping the outcome of one's autonomous reflection (W. Feinberg, 1995, p. 57).

All of this amounts to saying that unchosen and contingent features of an agent's history and circumstances may, and indeed must, contribute, although often in complex and unpredictable ways, to her ethical identity, and that this does not disqualify her from being considered autonomous. Some people will autonomously endorse the values with which they were raised: plenty of others will rebel against their parents' way of life without giving the matter serious rational thought. Renouncing the ethical doctrine of one's upbringing is neither necessary nor sufficient for autonomy. As Waldron (1989, p. 1119) puts it: "What matters for autonomy is not that we hold our goals independently of others, but that we currently embrace them for reasons that appeal to us using our own evaluative capacities." In most cases, as Reich (2002, p. 135) suggests, we might imagine that genuinely autonomous reflection on one's primary culture will lead neither to outright rejection nor to complete endorsement: most autonomous persons will find their primary culture to be rather like the proverbial curate's egg—good in parts.

Some readers may think that the autonomy ideal is importantly compromised by the arguments of the preceding three paragraphs. If following in one's parents' footsteps turns out to be a natural expression of autonomy, then the concept might seem to have lost much of its critical bite. But the crucial point to remember is that autonomy is indicated not by the substantive content of the agent's beliefs and values and their relation to those of others, but rather by the distinctive manner in which the agent holds these beliefs and values. A person who adheres to her parents' conception of the good can be regarded as doing so autonomously only if she has given, and continues periodically to give, serious and open-minded consideration both to the most powerful critiques of that conception and to some leading alternative value systems. As we shall see, secondary schools have an important role to play in ensuring that all persons are exposed to such challenges, encouraged to engage with them through rational deliberation and reflection, and taught the communication and reasoning skills to make such engagement fruitful.

Many of the objections to the idea that a liberal democratic state can and should uphold the value of personal autonomy stem from a flawed understanding of the concept, and especially from an excessively stark vision of the relation between autonomous reason and the kinds of attachments that help to specify the particular identity of agents. I hope to have shown that personal autonomy is not incompatible with undertaking serious commitments to persons and causes, does not require radical, criterionless choice, and does not entail that agents reject their familial culture of upbringing. At the same time, I maintain that it is the distinctive commitment to ongoing rational reflection that makes ethical autonomy both a controversial educational goal and, as I shall argue in the next chapter, an attractive ideal because of the special value that rational reflection has for us as we identify and pursue a conception of the good. My aim in the remainder of this chapter is to further explain the possibility of a conception of personal autonomy that has rational reflection at its heart but that steers clear of the caricatures I have already discussed and dismissed. The success of this venture hinges upon specifying the distinctive role of reason in autonomous reflection without losing the important insight that agents' identities are and must be shaped partly by nonrational factors.

THE NATURE OF AUTONOMOUS REFLECTION

It is sometimes maintained that the role of reason in autonomous reflection is merely to discover preexisting preferences and values and then to judge their relative strength in order to know which will prevail in cases of conflict (Telfer, 1975). Conceptions of autonomy in which the role of reason is limited in this way have been the objects of withering criticism. So, for example, Sandel (1982, p. 159) argues that if, as he believes to be the case in Rawls' work, "the faculty of self-reflection is limited to weighing the relative intensity of existing wants and desires, the deliberation it entails cannot inquire into the identity of the agent ('Who am I, really?'), only into the feelings and sentiments of the agent ('What do I really *feel* like or most *prefer*?')." Sandel is right to believe that autonomy involves more than simple discovery and weighing: agents engaged in autonomous reflection are not simply carrying out an audit of their beliefs and values, if the idea of an audit is just to record everything you find—"leave no stone unturned, but be sure to put every stone back exactly as you found it." A mere audit metaphor cannot suffice because introspection is always likely to reveal contradictory beliefs and indeterminate value weightings that the autonomous agent must actively resolve rather than passively catalogue. Autonomous reflection will typically lead persons to revise their commitments in order, at the very least, to establish internal consistency within their set of beliefs and to impose a clear rank ordering on their personal values. But internal consistency and completeness are not sufficient for the autonomous person's peace of mind because her ethical commitments do not form a closed system: autonomous reflection is typically prompted by the external challenge of some new perspective or evidence that precisely suggests the need to reevaluate one's commitments and to revise or discard those that do not withstand rational scrutiny in the light of these new considerations. Sandra finds her belief in the literal truth of the Christian Bible challenged by the evidence supporting evolutionary biology: her resulting autonomous ethical reflection will involve an inquiry into the grounds of her literalist faith and the adequacy of those grounds, followed presumably by some revision of her Christian beliefs. In this way, engaging in autonomous reflection can and often should be transformative.

But how do autonomous individuals decide which of two inconsistent beliefs to relinquish, or how to assess the new perspective that challenges their preexisting worldview? When the weight of evidence on one side is overwhelming, as seems to be the case with the scientific arguments for evolution, there is only one answer that should emerge from an adequate rational inquiry. But we must recall that although autonomous ethical reflection is a distinctively rational exercise, ethical pluralism means that there is often no unique outcome that can be determined solely by reason, unlike the case of the typical problem in mathematics or the conflict between literal Creationist views and evolutionary accounts of the origins of man. Rational principles will guide autonomous reflection and impose constraints on its outcomes, but autonomy nonetheless empowers a person to make certain types of choice about her ethical identity, about the kind of person she is and aspires to be. No one starts from a blank slate, of course, but as Callan (1994) puts it, autonomous persons are only "revocably encumbered": they possess commitments that they have not chosen, but they are also capable of casting off those commitments with which they choose not to identify. If John has been raised to seek and value traditional family life, he is revocably encumbered with a genuine desire for a wife and kids, but he can nonetheless choose to redefine his conception of the good life, to overcome and supplant the desire he finds in himself. This choice is not appropriately understood as the discovery or expression of a preexisting second-order desire, but rather as an attempt to define the type of person he is or aspires to be: a monk, perhaps, a solitary artist, or just a free-wheeling bachelor. Decisions of this sort are the essence of autonomous self-creation: they introduce new reasons to guide the agent's choice among rationally incommensurable values. "In embracing goals and commitments, in coming to care about one thing or another, one progressively gives shape to one's life, determines what would count as a successful life and what would be a failure" (Raz, 1986, p. 387). Autonomous reflection is a dynamic process through which people can define themselves in ways that go far beyond the mere acquisition of self-knowledge that is suggested by the weighing and audit metaphors.

It is crucial to see that agents can question and revise their commitments without the need for an Archimedean point from which to carry out the process. It might seem that the feasibility of doubting one's deepest ethical values requires the discredited notion of radical choice: I must somehow stand outside myself in order to think critically about my identity. But my identity is not a single, monolithic entity from which I must somehow escape altogether to review it in its entirety: rather, as Levinson (1999, pp. 32–33) observes, autonomous persons have a plurality of commitments that are each partly constitutive of their identity. The key to autonomous reflection is that one can always temporarily treat as fixed one's allegiance to a particular belief or value while questioning others. As Dearden (1972, p. 457) succinctly ex-presses the position: "All criteria may be questioned, but not all at once, if intelligibility is to be preserved." This limitation on the capacity for self-reflection entails, of course, that an individual cannot transform his whole identity in one fell swoop, but through a series of choices it is possible for an agent to adopt an entirely new ethical persona.[3]

How does autonomous reflection go beyond the discovery and weighing of preexisting values to the possibility of making choices to reject, revise, or positively endorse these values? Important elements of the answer to this question are to be found in the works of two philosophers—Charles Taylor and Alasdair MacIntyre—who are hos-tile to the ideal of autonomy as it has often been represented and, I argue, caricatured. In these two writers' reactions against views of au-tonomy that require radical choice by a self that is entirely uncon-strained by unchosen features of its identity, we actually find some of the key components of a more attractive and realistic conception of personal autonomy. Neither Taylor nor MacIntyre offers a theory of reflection and personal choice that can simply be relabeled as auton-omy, because neither theorist makes critical rationality central to their ideal, but their theories nonetheless capture some important dynamics of the process of reflection on one's ethical values and identity that must be central to a sophisticated conception of personal autonomy.

Taylor's (1985, pp. 15–44) vision of reflective agency is of an ongoing process of self-interpretation. As we have seen, competing and contra-dictory ethical values are incommensurable in the sense that abstract reason is inadequate to select one coherent set over all others. We need a thicker notion of the self than the model of the pure rational agent if ethical judgment is to be possible, because such judgment is partly a matter of introspection and there must be something there to be seen when we look inward. But although individuals cannot answer ethical questions without inquiring into their own identity, the neces-sary introspection is not an easy matter, and the answers cannot be read off from one's identity at, so to speak, an inward glance. Rather, the ethically reflective agent is involved in an ongoing "struggle of self-interpretations [where] the question at issue concerns which is the truer, more authentic, more illusion-free interpretation, and which

---

[3] There may also be psychological, as opposed to conceptual, limits on both the speed of ethical transformation and the size of each step that an individual can bear without experiencing a mental breakdown. Schools would need to be mindful of these limits, especially as they try to cultivate ethical autonomy in children who are growing up in an extremely sheltered and religiously devout home environment: a gradualist approach may best serve such children's interests in developing ethical autonomy.

on the other hand involves a distortion of the meanings things have for me" (p. 27).

However, the point is not simply that self-interpretation is difficult or that one may never be sure whether one has reached the correct answer. In an important sense, there is no correct answer, or at least there is no answer that is uniquely specified *ex ante* by the particular characteristics of an agent's identity. Ethical reflection is interpretive in the sense familiar in the arts: some interpretations will be better than others, some will be almost entirely without merit, but there is no such thing as the uniquely correct interpretation.

> Our attempts to formulate what we hold important must, like descriptions, strive to be faithful to something. But what they strive to be faithful to is not an independent object with a fixed degree and manner of evidence, but rather a largely inarticulate sense of what is of decisive importance. An articulation of this 'object' tends to make it something different from what it was before. (p. 38)

Here we can see that the gap between Taylor's vision of self-interpretation and Raz's ideal of self-creation is not as wide as might at first have been supposed. As the last quotation makes clear, Taylor believes that ethical reflection is creative, and it is crucial to Raz's ideal of autonomy that an agent's decisions are sensitive to her past, including unchosen elements of her past that continue to shape her life today.[4]

Like Taylor and Raz, MacIntyre (1981) has a theory of the self according to which agents play a role in defining their own ethical identities but are necessarily constrained by factors beyond their own control, factors without which the opportunity to choose an identity would be bewildering and ultimately incoherent. "What the agent is able to do or say intelligibly as an actor is deeply affected by the fact that we are never more (and sometimes less) than the co-authors of our own narratives" (p. 213). With his emphasis on the social roles and identities into which all individuals are born, MacIntyre is often thought to deny the possibility of personal autonomy, but the argument of this chapter is precisely that many of MacIntyre's insights, albeit tempered by a stronger and necessary role for critical reason in ethical reflection, can and should be accommodated within a sophisticated conception of autonomy. After all, social roles and identities are

---

[4] Given the incommensurable values of an ethically pluralist world, personal commitments function "to make indeterminate situations determined" (Raz, 1986, p. 388). And although many commitments are chosen by the agent, some others must be unchosen, as we have seen.

not prisons: "rebellion against my identity is always one possible mode of expressing it" (p. 221) and, although our reasoning is in some sense constrained by the traditions we inhabit, "Traditions, when vital, embody continuities of conflict . . . about the goods which constitute that tradition" (p. 222). MacIntyre's discussion (p. 219) of life as a quest whose *telos* is not fully characterized at the outset reminds us of Taylor's view that a particular self-interpretation changes or defines the very self that is being interpreted.

Taylor and MacIntyre are usually understood to reject or exclude personal autonomy as an ideal because their respective notions of self-interpretation and co-authorship are presented explicitly in opposition to a certain conception of autonomy, one that requires individuals to make choices that are radically free of all unchosen and contingent features of their circumstances. But, I have argued, an attractive and defensible conception of autonomy does not invoke this bare, rational, choosing self that MacIntyre and Taylor quite rightly find inconceivable. Instead, I propose that our conception of autonomy should draw upon the resources I have identified in Taylor and MacIntyre to provide an account of the way in which individuals can fashion their identities that is not a mystifying story of self-creation *ex nihilo*. Along these lines, Stephen Macedo (1990, p. 218) has suggested the compatibility of Taylor's approach with an ideal of situated autonomy in his characterization of Taylor's "strong evaluator."

> The strong evaluator can test, shape, and perhaps reject his dispositions and desires by reference to competing norms, ideals, and qualitative evaluations. Strong evaluation is not Kantian 'situationless' autonomy, which presupposes a transcendental subject inhabiting a realm beyond all contingency and able to act from pure reason. The ideal of autonomy is the autonomy of one informed by different standards and ideals. It stems from the ability to establish a reflective distance from our desires and deliberate on them and on ourselves more broadly.

But neither Taylor nor MacIntyre is straightforwardly an autonomy theorist: autonomous reflection is, I claim, a particular type of self-interpretation, a special way of serving as co-author of your life. The autonomous life is distinguished by the central role that reason plays in reviewing and defining the agent's ethical identity: the self "is located in the will and desires as discovered, shaped, and to an extent ordered and corrected by reflection and reason" (Aviram, 1995, p. 63; see also Lindley, 1986). MacIntyre, in particular, does not assign such centrality to critical reason, and this explains his theory's apparently conservative emphasis on tradition and inherited roles. However, I have tried to show the resources within his theory that make it possible to treat traditions and roles as grist to the mill of critical reason, even while that mill is always and inevitably situated within the very objects of its criticism. The ideas of co-authorship and self-interpretation ground autonomy in a realistic account of the self, but autonomy's emphasis on critical reasoning counteracts the illiberal overtones that we often hear in narrative accounts of the self. My goal in the next two chapters will be to demonstrate that the distinctively rational nature of autonomous reflection has certain decisive advantages over other ways of shaping one's values and beliefs, and that these advantages are sufficient to justify liberal democratic states in adopting the cultivation of children's personal autonomy as a goal of public education policy, even against the wishes of some religious parents. But to send us on our way, let us consider for a moment an account of autonomy that, although itself not fully developed, places rational reflection in pride of place and offers a positive characterization of the process of scrutinizing one's provisional commitments that are nonrational in their origins.

Conclusion

For Thomas Hill, Jr., ethical autonomy entails an ongoing commitment to the practice of "rational deep deliberation" about one's values and goals. Rational deep deliberation means, in particular, taking a certain attitude towards the nonrational and unchosen motivations that exist within us all. "One's inclinations are not viewed as forces which fix one's ends without one's cooperation. Rather, one actively reviews and examines one's inclinations as background facts about which one has a decision *to make*, presupposing that one can discount and act contrary to any given inclination even if one continues to *feel* it after full reflection" (1991, p. 183).

In part, my decision about a particular inclination is made on the basis of its relation both to my other inclinations and to the evidence available to me. But, of course, under the assumptions of ethical pluralism, many inclinations with great significance for the conduct of my life are neither uniquely selected nor ruled out by these tests of consistency. Yet the rational nature of ethical reflection is not exhausted once my inclinations are shaped to be internally consistent and supported by the external evidence (although this would be a remarkable achievement in its own right). "Searching for reasons is not simply trying to discover one's inclinations, just as weighing reasons is not simply trying to introspect the relative strength of one's inclinations" (Hill,

1991, p. 183). Deep rational deliberation is an attempt to construct a vision of one's life that both discovers and defines the self, in the spirit of MacIntyre and Taylor: by inquiring critically and interpretively into the extent to which particular inclinations are consonant with and expressive of my aspirations and identity, I play a part in shaping those aspirations and that identity.

Chapter 4

THE VALUE OF AUTONOMY IN
A PLURALIST WORLD

IN THE LAST CHAPTER, I sketched a conception of ethical autonomy that I believe is moderate, realistic, and attractive without being vacuous. But, needless to say, it is still a controversial ideal. Significant numbers of religious parents, among others, would be likely to object to the proposal to adopt the cultivation of autonomy as a goal of public education policy: I shall address directly a number of these likely objections in the next chapter. But first I want to consider the positive arguments that can be made for the noncivic value of ethical autonomy and to ask whether any of these arguments are of a type suitable for use in the political sphere of a liberal multicultural society.[1] I believe that ethical autonomy's *instrumental* value to individuals seeking to find and lead a good life can be demonstrated in ways that satisfy the conditions on acceptable public justification in a pluralist society; mandatory education for autonomy of the sort I propose would therefore be justified liberal paternalism, because it would reliably serve the interests of all children without illegitimately appealing to particular conceptions of the good. But, before developing and defending this position, it will be instructive to begin by surveying the form of arguments for the *intrinsic* value of leading an autonomous life and understanding why such arguments are unsuitable to ground public policy in a pluralist state.

JOHN STUART MILL, JOSEPH RAZ, AND THE INTRINSIC VALUE OF AUTONOMY

In the third chapter of his *On Liberty* (1859/1989), John Stuart Mill makes a series of arguments for the value of "individuality," a way of

[1] Recall that by specifying the "noncivic" value, I mean to exclude from consideration arguments (such as Callan's, discussed in chapter 2) that ethically autonomous persons are better citizens. I concluded in chapters 1 and 2 that there are good civic reasons to support an education that will cultivate children's autonomy; the question now is whether there are claims about the noncivic value of autonomy that the state can legitimately employ to block parental objections to such an education.

life that features a robust commitment to a kind of independent rational reflection that has much in common with the idea at the core of our conception of ethical autonomy. Mill's arguments for individuality are an excellent example of an attempt to show the *intrinsic* value of independently shaping one's own life by taking a critical-rational approach to the beliefs and values of one's society and/or those in which one was raised. But Mill is not defending ethical autonomy as I understand that concept, so, to avoid any confusion, it is worth taking a moment to show how Millian individuality differs from ethical autonomy. The key point is that Mill is not indifferent between the choices that persons might make when they exercise what I would call ethical autonomy. For Mill, individuality goes hand in hand with originality in the war against debilitating custom. "Millian individuality entails the overall superiority of lives that exhibit eccentricity, dissent, and innovation over others ... a more expansive doctrine than liberalisms which take their bearings from a general idea of autonomy that is neutral on the choice between individualistic and more conventional ways of life" (Callan, 1997, pp. 18–19). As Callan notes, one can argue for the intrinsic value of ethical autonomy without taking this quite independent position on the value of originality: indeed, as discussed in the last chapter, reflectively endorsing one's culture of upbringing may be a natural expression of autonomy for many persons. Nonetheless, Mill's claims about the value of individuality offer a model for arguments intended to show the *intrinsic* value of ethical autonomy.

The essence of Mill's position is that a life of individuality is, by its very nature, a dignified and flourishing life for a human.[2] He intends to offer us an inspiring vision: through individuality, "human beings become a noble and beautiful object of contemplation" (Mill, 1859/1989, p. 63).[3] Mill was all too aware that his vision was not widely shared in his day; indeed, much of chapter 3 of *On Liberty* reads as a lament for the stagnant conformism that Mill believed was stifling individual happiness and social progress in England in the mid-nineteenth century. But when Mill writes (p. 57) that "individual spontaneity is hardly recognized by the common modes of thinking, as having any intrinsic worth, or deserving any regard on its own account," he does not, as many contemporary liberals would, treat this as a case of reasonable and irreconcilable disagreement between the many

---

[2] Although Mill goes on to show that one man's individuality is typically a good for others (1859/1989, pp. 64–67) and, more generally, a catalyst for social progress (pp. 70–74), these claims of value are only secondary to Mill's main contention that individuality is partly constitutive of a good human life.

[3] Mill (1859/1989, p. 58) attributes this view of man's highest ends to Wilhelm Von Humboldt.

who favor more traditional, unreflective ways of life and the few who believe that individuals should actively and creatively fashion their own lives. Instead, he sets himself the challenge of proving the common modes of thinking wrong by demonstrating the intrinsic value of individuality.

Political principles that rest on claims of autonomy's intrinsic value (and that therefore implicitly appeal to some argument that is closely analogous to Mill's for the value of individuality) are uncommon today, but they are not unknown. Take, for example, Raz's clear statement of the position:

> The true moral theory for our societies recognizes that there is special value in people freely developing their own understanding of the meaning of life and the ways one can flourish, and also in people living in accord with their own freely developed conception of the good. This means that those whose lives are not guided by such freely chosen conceptions of the good are diminished and that those who are so guided are better off for being so guided, *even if their particular conceptions of the good are mistaken.* (1994, p. 64, my emphasis)

These last words make clear what is entailed by saying that autonomy has intrinsic value: autonomous reflection adds value to a human life even if its function, over the course of that life, is to lead the person into error that she would have avoided if she had not thought for herself. The value of autonomy does not consist solely, or perhaps even primarily, in its being a reliable means to an independently defined good life: rather, "we regard the fact that a life was autonomous as adding value to it" (p. 105). Autonomy for Raz, much like individuality for Mill, is partly constitutive of the good life.

Those who believe in the intrinsic value of autonomy often do so because, in the words of a critic of such positions, they "understand human dignity to consist largely in autonomy" (Tamir, 1995, p. 10).[4] How might this claim be defended? Again, it will be instructive to consider the form of Mill's argument for individuality. Mill claims, in strikingly Aristotelian fashion, that individuality is necessary for a dignified and flourishing human life because only the life of individuality develops and exercises the distinctively human faculties. "To conform to custom, merely as custom, does not educate or develop in him any

---

[4] Although this phrase sounds eminently Kantian, the case for ascribing intrinsic value to *ethical* autonomy is at most only quasi-Kantian since, as we saw in chapter 3, the idea of ethical autonomy is both different from and strictly incompatible with Kant's notion of moral autonomy.

of the qualities which are the distinctive endowment of a human being. The human faculties of perception, judgment, discriminative feeling, mental activity, and even moral preference, are exercised only in making a choice" (1859/1989, p. 59). Interestingly, Kant offers a similarly teleological argument for governing oneself by reason early in the *Groundwork* (1785/1993, p. 8), before he goes on to develop the famous characterization of rationality as freedom. The idea, in these arguments of both Mill and Kant, is that the purpose and higher modes of life of a human consist in cultivating and exercising those capacities that distinguish humans from other species. Since "he who lets the world, or his own portion of it, choose his plan of life for him, has no need of any other faculty than the ape-like one of imitation" (Mill, 1859/1989, p. 59), he is failing to make appropriate use of the distinctive gifts given to him by nature. Evidently, a similar argument could be advanced on behalf of the conception of ethical autonomy that I developed in the previous chapter.

Mill was, as I have said, acutely aware that his view of the value of individuality was not widely shared in his society, and it will be instructive to review the way in which he responded to his opponents as a segue to a consideration of the contrasting way in which most contemporary liberals propose to respond to those who deny the value of autonomy. Mill identifies the Calvinists as his paradigmatic opponents and refers to their celebration of obedience to authority when he remarks, acidly, that "many persons, no doubt, sincerely think that human beings thus cramped and dwarfed, are as their Maker designed them to be" (p. 62). Mill's response to his notional Calvinist interlocutor is both shocking and, I somewhat mischievously propose, invigorating to those of us who have been comprehensively schooled in the doctrine of ethical pluralism, political liberalism, or "the diversity state" (Galston, 1995, p. 524). Mill takes it upon himself to tell the Calvinists what their doctrine really is, or at least what it should be. "If it be any part of religion to believe that man was made by a good Being, it is more consistent with that faith to believe that this Being gave all human faculties that they might be cultivated and unfolded, not rooted out and consumed" (p. 62). Since Mill makes his own political pitch for liberty in terms of a comprehensive vision of the human good, he has no reason to hold back from engaging critically with the comprehensive doctrines of others, whether Calvinists or those, like Susan Mendus (1995, p. 42), who advance secular reasons for the value of virtues like humility and obedience. Characteristically, Mill needs no second invitation to join the fray, telling Calvinists and others of like mind that the state needs "a conception of humanity as having its nature bestowed upon it for other purposes than merely to be abnegated" (p. 63).

Contemporary Liberal Responses to Mill:
The Neutrality Condition

Mill's defense of the intrinsic value of individuality could easily be
recast as an argument for the value of ethical autonomy, and it might
be an appealing argument at many levels, but it would not be appropriate as the grounds for making public policy in a liberal pluralist
state. Political liberals, led by John Rawls in his later work, have argued conclusively that a liberal polity must not be based on or endorse
any conception of the ultimate purposes of human lives and human
nature. Whether one believes in pluralism as a metaphysical fact or
merely as the inevitable and permanent inability of human reason to
settle the major questions of ethics, the state cannot justify its actions
by invoking a particular conception of the good life about which there
will always be reasonable disagreement. Claims about the intrinsic
value of ethical autonomy, of the sort that must underlie Raz's position
discussed above, are contestable conceptions of the good life just as
much as religiously based claims about the duty of self-abnegation.
Therein lies the truth of Evan Charney's charge (2000, p. 36) that so-
called autonomy liberals are being inconsistent by refusing "to extend
value pluralism to include the manner in which persons come to have
those ends and forms of life." As Arneson and Shapiro (1996, p. 399)
put it, autonomy conceived as valuable for its own sake "would have
to be judged a sectarian goal, not suitable as a consensual basis for
public policy," although I shall argue later in this chapter that it is a
mistake to regard actual consensus as the hallmark of political legitimacy. Similarly, I agree with Galston's view (1989, p. 100) that the liberal state cannot make claims about the intrinsic superiority of the examined life without "throwing its weight behind a conception of the
human good unrelated to the fundamental needs of its sociopolitical
institutions and at odds with the deep beliefs of many of its loyal citizens," but I will nonetheless maintain that the liberal state can mandate education for autonomy on the grounds of its instrumental value
to persons concerned to find and live the best life for themselves.

So Rawls was right to follow the logic of respect for reasonable pluralism and renounce all reliance on claims about the intrinsic value of
the ethically autonomous life. Justice as fairness, in its later formulation, explicitly "does not seek to cultivate the distinctive virtues and
values of the liberalisms of autonomy and individuality" (1993/1996,
p. 200) but rather "leaves the weight of ethical autonomy to be decided
by citizens severally in light of their comprehensive doctrines" (p. 78).
If these statements are understood only to mean that political liberal-

ism remains agnostic on the *intrinsic* value of an autonomous life, then they should be accepted, but, as I discussed in chapter 2, even political liberals need to invoke the value of autonomy in some form if they are to justify their unwavering insistence on the familiar package of liberal rights and freedoms. Perhaps this difficulty explains why Macedo seems to tie himself in knots, frantically attempting to convince us that he is not endorsing the value of autonomy while making statements such as: "Critical thinking about one's own convictions is an important part of moral education" (2000, p. 124). Liberals must attach a special value to individual autonomy, but in so doing they must not fail to respect the reasonable views of those who attach no *intrinsic* value to an autonomous life. If we are to judge the success of any attempt to walk this fine line, we shall need a clearer formulation of the constraint imposed by respect for reasonable pluralism.

If ethical autonomy is to be pursued by a liberal state, it cannot be because autonomy is valued *as* a conception of the good or part thereof. To do so would be to overstep the bounds of liberal political legitimacy. As Ackerman (1980, p. 10) puts it, "nobody has the right to vindicate political authority by asserting a privileged insight into the moral universe which is denied the rest of us." If autonomy is to be defended as something that we all can and should value, it must not be presented as part of a contestable vision of the good life for an individual. What are the alternatives? I shall devote much of the rest of this chapter to developing the claim that ethical autonomy has important instrumental value to individuals seeking to identify and lead a good life for themselves, and I shall argue that this claim is one that liberal states can legitimately make. But first I want to consider an alternative way in which some liberals have tried to justify the adoption of autonomy as a political value, namely, by tying autonomy to the notion of moral responsibility. I shall suggest that this strategy, although not entirely without merit, is insufficient, and that my own account of autonomy's instrumental value is still needed to justify the liberal project of defending and promoting the exercise of ethical autonomy.

AUTONOMY AND MORAL RESPONSIBILITY

It can be argued that our conception of individual moral responsibility relies for its justification upon the assumption that individuals enjoy ethical autonomy. This would not be to claim that only ethically autonomous people can be held responsible for committing immoral acts: as I explained at the start of chapter 3, ethical autonomy refers only to the way in which a person comes to accept and live by one morally permitted conception of the good rather than another, and it is quite another question whether, why, and how people accept moral constraints on their actions. The conception of moral responsibility I have in mind is not responsibility for immoral actions but rather an individual's responsibility to bear the consequences of his or her conception of the good. The beliefs and values I hold that define what would be a successful life for me entail certain costs: if I measure the success of my life by the number of original van Goghs that I am able to collect, then I shall either have to work exceptionally hard at a very high-paying career or, more likely, resign myself to a life that is minimally successful by my own standards. One might ask, as Ronald Dworkin (2000) and others have, why I should be solely responsible for the wretched implications of this expensive taste when it could be viewed as a handicap for which society ought to provide some compensation.

Dworkin's own position is that individuals are responsible, in the sense of being ineligible for compensation, for their expensive tastes if and only if they identify with those tastes. But it turns out that the fact of identifying with a taste is significant in large part because Dworkin (p. 291) thinks that tastes with which the agent identifies "are interwoven with judgments of endorsement and approval," and that these judgments have been made against a background of information about the costs of satisfying those tastes in the agent's society. Dworkin is wrong to claim that identifying with a taste, or indeed a conception of the good, entails the presence of "judgments of endorsement and approval": one can have a neutral or negative attitude toward one's tastes without feeling *alienated* from them. But he is right to believe that these kinds of judgments, or at least the capacity to make them independently and rationally, are important for our conception of individual responsibility. And, of course, only an ethically autonomous agent is capable of making judgments about her conception of the good in this way. I suggest that we are justified in holding a person responsible for her values because, or to the extent that, we are justified in assuming that she possesses the capacity, and has the ongoing opportunity in full knowledge of her social circumstances, rationally to revise or endorse those values.

My claim is not that, as a practical or even a theoretical matter, we ought to assess a person's level of ethical autonomy before deciding whether to compensate him for having an expensive conception of the good. There would be myriad problems with such a policy, not least being the problem of perverse incentives: we would not want to encourage people to retard the development of their own and their children's autonomy in order to qualify for compensation. Except in cases where people suffer from addictions or cravings that can be clinically diagnosed, the liberal state should not generally be in the business of compensating people for the costs or inconveniences of their conception of the good. But if I am right that a vision of the ethically autonomous person underpins our claim to be justified in holding people responsible for their conceptions of the good, then it seems that the educational policy of the liberal state should quite properly be to encourage the development of ethical autonomy.

The significance of autonomy for individual responsibility is defended by Aviram (1995) and by Joel Feinberg (1989, p. 42), who argues that *"de facto* autonomy, it would seem, is a conceptually presupposed condition of most judgments of responsibility," although I suspect that Feinberg has in mind more expansive notions of autonomy and responsibility than I discuss here. Taylor (1985, p. 42) argues that the capacity for self-interpretive reflection grounds our notion of "responsibility for self" because it is "an essential feature of the person": I would argue that it is only when such reflection takes on the flavor of independent, critical rationality that it explains our willingness to hold a person—rather than his parents, his peers, or his whole society—responsible for the implications of his ethical orientation. To reiterate, I do not think that this argument from individual responsibility is sufficient to justify liberal states in adopting the development of ethical autonomy as a goal of education policy, in part because I accept Dearden's (1975, p. 10) observation that "relating ascriptions of responsibility to personal autonomy is . . . only one possible basis for such ascription," but I think Dearden is right when he goes on to say that this basis is "deeply embedded" in our thinking about responsibility. It is tempting to argue, following Rorty (1989, 1991), that it suffices for justification to show that ethical autonomy underlies *our* conception of individual responsibility, in *our* liberal societies, but I do not pursue this thought here, in part because I recognize the tensions between such a view and the emphasis I shall place on universally valid rational justifications for public policy as the means whereby liberal states should respect the plurality of ethical doctrines in society.

If the argument from moral responsibility is indeed insufficient to justify adopting autonomy as a public value, we must continue the search for an argument that does not illegitimately appeal to autonomy's supposed intrinsic value. In rejecting arguments from intrinsic value, we have resolved that any normatively acceptable public justification that invokes the value of autonomy must ultimately be grounded in the value of an end that is conceptually separable from the cultivation of ethical autonomy, even if such cultivation is in practice the best means to that end. What this suggests, of course, is that the liberal state might be permitted to recognize ethical autonomy as having instrumental noncivic value to individuals. But the discussion so far establishes only the theoretical possibility of an account of autonomy's instrumental value that does not implicitly rely upon an account of its intrinsic worth: it remains to show that such an account exists. We must also ask why the phenomenon of reasonable disagreement does not rule out political recognition of the instrumental value of autonomy in just the same way as it rules out recognizing the claims of intrinsic value offered by Mill and Raz. How can one justify invoking the instrumental value of autonomy in making a political decision that will be binding on persons who deny that autonomy has this instrumental value? It is to these difficult tasks that I now turn.

Arguments for the Instrumental Value of Autonomy

The instrumental value of ethical autonomy to a person lies in its being a means to that person's living a successful life but not necessarily a part of that success (J. Feinberg, 1980, pp. 143–44). The essential idea is that rational reflection about one's beliefs and values is an effective way for one to find and live a life that is good for oneself. As Brighouse (1998, p. 729) sets out the idea, "children will be significantly more able to live well if they are able rationally to compare different ways of life" because "the basic methods of rational evaluation are identifiably somewhat reliable aids to uncovering how to live well." To some readers, these claims will seem unproblematic, but they are not uncontroversial. In particular, we need to understand and substantiate such claims in the light of the particular conception of autonomous reflection sketched in the preceding chapter. Given that there is no single truth in ethics, no conception of the good that is best, some work must be done to explain how and in what sense rational reflection promises to pay dividends. The choice between ethical doctrines is, we have seen, underdetermined by reason, so what sense can be made of the notion that autonomous reflection will help persons to find and live good lives? The various mechanisms by which the practice of ethical autonomy can be instrumentally valuable in a pluralist world have not been adequately discussed in the literature: in the next few pages, I shall present the case for autonomy's instrumental value by making a number of these mechanisms explicit.

A useful starting point is Callan's (1997, p. 66) observation that "the attempt to formulate one's best judgment about how to live must proceed in light of due reflection on the conflicting judgments of reasonable others, who may understand something important we ourselves have yet failed to grasp." One way to put this is that we should be

humble enough that, when surrounded by sensible people who disagree with us, we do not simply assume that we are right and they are
wrong. To say that the choice of an ethical doctrine is not determined
by reason alone is not to say that reason does not have an important
part to play in guiding the choice. Even if we feel confident in the basic
contours of our conception of the good, we should remain open to the
possibility that it can be refined and improved by critical attention to
details, especially on issues where other people have had more experience or have deliberated more than we have. My views on the value
of mountain-climbing or parenthood are likely to be informed and improved by reflecting on the perspectives of mountain-climbers or parents, even though these are not areas in which I should simply defer
to the experts ("You *will* enjoy climbing Ben Nevis!"). Callan reminds
us that autonomous reflection is not simply the exercise of an individual mind in isolation, but rather an integral part of what should be an
ongoing dialogue with others—a dialogue that is, explicitly or implicitly, about the nature of the good life.

In chapter 7 of his *Theory of Justice*, Rawls (1971/1999) introduces the
idea of "deliberative rationality" to define a normative standard for a
good life. The basic proposition is that the best life for a particular,
situated individual is the life that he or she would have chosen as the
outcome of a process of rational deliberation under hypothetical ideal-
ized knowledge conditions. This is not to say that autonomous reflection is, in practice, sufficient to find the best life for oneself: we lack a
great deal of the knowledge required to gauge and compare the implications of the different life choices we might make. But there is some
reason to think that, if the standard for the best life is defined as the
outcome of hypothetical rational deliberation, the most promising way
to approach knowledge of that best life in the real world will be via an
actual, ongoing commitment to rational reflection. "With great luck
and good fortune some men might by nature just happen to hit upon
the way of living that they would adopt with deliberative rationality.
For the most part, though, we are not so blessed, and without taking
thought and seeing ourselves as one person with a life over time, we
shall almost certainly regret our course of action" (p. 372). And, Rawls
goes on to note, even if the unreflective man never actually experiences
regret about his course of life, we may still quite reasonably ask
whether his life truly went as well as it would have done if he had
paused to scrutinize his ethical values and beliefs.

Religious parents might respond that their children are in fact
blessed to know the best ethical doctrine for themselves without the
need for reflection because they have been the beneficiaries of a good
upbringing. But public education policy would be reckless in the ex-

treme to assume that parents reliably perform this service for their children so well that the latter will never have need to think for themselves. The parents' beliefs and values may be misguided in some way, and/or they may be distorted in transition to the younger generation. The world may have changed in ways that make the parents' ethical doctrine inappropriate or incomplete for their children. But, even more fundamentally, the parents' ethics may simply not suit the particular child: "the child's traits and evaluative dispositions might be significantly different" from the parents' (Arneson and Shapiro, 1996, p. 402). As we have seen, part of the explanation as to why reason alone does not select a unique ethical doctrine for all people is that the best doctrine for me must fit my distinctive identity and aspirations, as well as the physical and mental endowments I received from nature.

Mill (1859/1989, p. 67) neatly articulates this important ground for ascribing instrumental value to autonomy: "If a person possesses any tolerable amount of common sense and experience, his own mode of laying out his existence is the best, not because it is the best in itself, but because it is his own mode. Human beings are not like sheep; and even sheep are not indistinguishably alike." When Galston (2002, pp. 59–60) proposes that "the diversity of human types is part of what exists prior to cultural self-determination," he intends to lend weight to claims for minimal government interference in the lives of families. But unless one believes, against all the evidence, that children always turn out to be of the same type as their parents, then the natural fact of diversity supports each child's interest in exercising autonomy in an effort to discover and define the best way of life for herself, a way of life that is likely to draw upon features of the ethical doctrine in which she was raised but also to diverge from that doctrine in certain respects. In short, children are often different from their parents, they live in a different world from that of their parents, and no parents are infallible ethical guides. As people seek to find and live the best lives of which they are capable, they are well served by thinking for themselves. We even find this view expressed, of all places, in Rawls' *Political Liberalism*, a work that is devoted in no small part to arguing against the idea that liberals should endorse the value of autonomy. We have already seen, in chapter 2, how Rawls' attribution to all citizens of an interest in securing the political conditions to exercise their second moral power—the capacity for a conception of the good—amounts to a tacit endorsement of the value of autonomy. And as Rawls (1993/1996, p. 313) develops this idea, he explains that the value to individuals is instrumental, though he continues to shy away from using the word "autonomy." "There is no guarantee that all aspects of our present way of life are most rational for us and not in need of at least minor if not major revision. For these reasons the adequate and full exercise of the capacity for a conception of the good is a means to a person's good."

Skeptics about the argument so far made to support the instrumental value of ethical autonomy might protest that little has been said that counts in favor of a distinctively *rational* reflection: would it not be sufficient for agents periodically to ask themselves whether they still identify with the beliefs and values they hold, whether or not these have rational grounds? In the last chapter, I insisted that the rational nature of reflection is a hallmark of the autonomous life, so it needs to be shown that reason plays a key role in the form of ethical reflection that is most likely to lead agents to the good life. At the same time, we can explore the different ways in which autonomous reflection may prompt agents to revise their conception of the good despite the fact that there is no single ethical truth toward which reason should be leading us. As I shall soon discuss, there will always be those who deny that rational reflection is a valuable means for individuals seeking to find and live good lives, but the mere fact of dissent from this contention is not sufficient to disqualify it from adoption as a principle guiding public education policy in a liberal democratic state. For the moment, I concentrate on fleshing out the argument for ascribing instrumental value to ethical autonomy; later in this chapter I address the problem of public justification in the face of dissent.

One important way in which rational reflection is likely to improve the quality of one's conception of the good is by exposing false beliefs. Mill (1859/1989, p. 21) famously reminds us that, as fallible humans, we should permit and remain open to the expression of dissenting views even when we are confident that we know the truth; much the same argument can be made for encouraging individuals to practice ongoing rational reflection on their beliefs and values rather than trusting in the infallibility of their parents, their priests, or their own previous judgments. As Arneson and Shapiro (1996, p. 399) put it, "people do not merely wish to live a valuable and worthy life according to their current beliefs about what constitutes such a life. They want to lead a life that truly is valuable and worthy." Recall that pluralism, whether understood as a metaphysical fact about ethical value or merely a claim about the limits of human reason, does not entail the impossibility or incoherence of judging an ethical belief to be false. The idea that there are *many* rational conceptions of the good should not be confused with the false notion that *all* conceptions of the good make rational sense. Large numbers of conceptions rest on false beliefs: people who hold these conceptions are to some degree either ignorant or irrational. Even if no evidence or rational standard exists by which a given belief can be conclusively disproved, it is likely that the weight of evidence and considerations supporting that belief can be appraised, and it can be rational to be swayed by the greater weight of reasons even if some doubt remains. Indeed, we typically regard as irrational those people who refuse to be swayed by the ever-mounting evidence against their belief on the grounds that some ideal and probably unattainable standard of proof has yet to be met.

It might be objected that there are certain types of fundamental ethical orientation that simply cannot be shown to be false. An example might be Mike's belief that he should devote his life to serving God. As I shall soon argue, these types of belief and value can still provide the fodder for demanding tests of rational consistency among one's ethical commitments, but they may also be connected in complex ways to those of our beliefs that are empirically verifiable, such that the discovery of false beliefs of the latter type might prompt changes in our fundamental ethical orientations. Mike might well revise his commitment to a life in God's service if it were shown that his priest and mentor is a fraud, although such a discovery would not in any way show Mike's belief about the purpose of his life to be false. At the very least, we would expect Mike to think again about what it means to devote one's life to serving God. This example may be extreme, but it is natural to assume that most people's conceptions of the good rest in some part on beliefs and assumptions of a type that could, in principle, be shown to be false. Rational reflection on one's own epistemological commitments is proven to be a good, albeit of course imperfect, method for uncovering false beliefs. The process must be ongoing to take account of our developing knowledge, but it can be periodic rather than incessant. As Kymlicka summarizes the position:

> Since we can wrong about the worth or value of what we are currently doing, and since no one wants to lead a life based on false beliefs about its worth, it is of fundamental importance that we be able rationally to assess our conceptions of the good in the light of new information and experiences, and to revise them if they are not worthy of our continued allegiance. (1995, p. 81)

Often, rational reflection will bring to light inconsistent beliefs and values within our conception of the good without being able to determine that some particular false beliefs are the cause of the inconsistency. Indeed, this is probably the most common way in which the exercise of ethical autonomy might prompt an agent to revise his conception of the good. Reason plays an important role in exposing these kinds of conflicts even if it does not also dictate a resolution of the conflict. As we saw in the last chapter, Sandel (1982, pp. 158–63) argues that the Rawlsian agent is capable of only an impoverished form of autonomous reflection because his rational faculties can do no more than weigh and order preexisting desires and preferences. My first response to Sandel was to propose a conception of autonomy in which reason has a much greater role in defining the identity of the agent, albeit in ways that are inevitably conditioned by cultural context. But my second response, which I develop here, is that the weighing and ordering of preexisting ethical beliefs and values constitutes a far more sophisticated form of ethical reflection than might first be thought. For persons who wish to live a successful and worthwhile life, it is no small concern to discover that one's own set of principles and values contains internal contradictions, and the quest to reestablish consistency expresses a natural desire to live a life of ethical integrity and coherent purpose.

I suggest that the use of reason to identify contradictions within one's conception of the good is the single most important, and probably the most common, form of autonomous ethical reflection. Just as no person wants to lead a life premised on false beliefs, no one aspires to a life whose meaning and coherence is compromised by contradictory goals and commitments. Sandel thinks that finding out "what I really want" is not a serious ethical achievement because it simply involves weighing desires and declaring the victory of the weightiest. But I suspect that Sandel underestimates both the difficulty of this task and the nature of the objects to be weighed. Autonomous reflection is not a matter of agonizing over the proverbial choice between chocolate and vanilla ice cream. The ethically autonomous person is committed to scrutinizing her deepest life purposes and values with a view to imposing an order on her life rather than merely drifting in the direction on which she was started by her parents. Given that we all find ourselves with multiple competing life priorities and only a finite supply of time and resources with which to pursue them, the task of establishing meaning and direction in one's life by making difficult choices among one's values is scarcely a trivial one. And it is no easy charge to identify and resolve the kind of inconsistencies internal to one's conception of the good that threaten to undermine the value of one's life, whether or not one is aware of their existence.

The use of autonomous reflection in the quest for consistency in an ethical life can be analogized to Rawls' (1971/1999, pp. 18–19) method of "reflective equilibrium" for reasoning about justice. Equilibrium requires that each principle or commitment is consistent not only with other principles of the same level of generality, but also with our considered judgments about cases that are more or less concrete and particular. So, my general philosophy of parenting must be in harmony

with my considered judgments about the best way to respond to particular cases in which my child misbehaves, my belief in the literal truth
and absolute authority of the Bible must be in harmony with my considered judgments about the validity of scientific theories of evolution,
and so on. Disequilibrium is especially likely to arise in cases where
abstract ethical principles are applied to concrete cases in very different
spheres of one's life: consider, for example, the inconsistent ways in
which many of us sporadically invoke or rely upon the ethical principle
of acting "in accordance with nature." The method of reflective equilibrium does not dictate the proper resolution of the tensions it exposes,
in ethics any more than in a conception of justice, but it does highlight
the need to revise or refine some of one's commitments. Individual
lives go better to the extent that they realize a coherent set of goals and
value weightings, and autonomous reflection is the best way to verify
and establish the coherence of those goals and weightings.

So far, I have argued that the exercise of ethical autonomy helps persons to find and lead better lives by detecting false or inadequately
supported beliefs and by identifying the presence of inconsistent values or applications of principles within one's conception of the good.
In both of these respects, the instrumental value of autonomous reflection lies in its rational nature. One might add that the capacity rationally to scrutinize one's ethical commitments is an important safeguard against exploitation and manipulation by others (Dearden, 1975,
p. 14). People who are unable or unwilling to question the rational
grounds for a certain belief, or the rational connection between a value
they endorse and a suggested course of action that is asserted to further that value, are peculiarly vulnerable to exploitation by persuasive
others. People who are accustomed to trusting nonrational forms of
ethical authority may be fortunate enough to be raised in an environment where those authorities are both competent and benign in their
intentions, but one cannot be guaranteed a life of such good fortune.
Blind faith in the advice of priests serves one well only until one meets
a corrupt priest; unswerving obedience to the ethical injunctions of
one's parents may not be such a good idea when one's parents are no
longer of sound mind. In short, in a world where people constantly try
to influence one another's ethical beliefs, and not always with the best
of qualifications or intentions, one is well served by developing the
capacity and inclination to subject all advice to rational scrutiny.

In addition to these general arguments about the instrumental value
of autonomy to individuals seeking to define and live the good life,
it has been argued, most notably by Raz (1986), that the capacity for
autonomous reflection and rational deliberation is a prerequisite for
successful functioning in the social conditions of modern liberal de-

mocracies. In part, Raz's argument appeals to the rapid pace of social change in the modern world and the corresponding need for persons to develop the independent capacities to navigate in an environment radically unlike their parents': autonomy is "an ideal particularly suited to the conditions of the industrial age and its aftermath with their fast changing technologies and free movement of labor" (p. 369). Raz offers no examples, but one might consider the ethical dilemmas raised by advanced communications technology or the development of genetic science: the ethical wisdom inherited from one's parents may not extend to questions about Internet dating or embryo screening. As Gutmann (1999, p. 57) puts it: "the inadequacy of habitual behavior is acute in modern societies where people confront new problems for which old habits supply insufficient guidance." But Raz also argues that the problem of modernity for nonautonomous people is not merely rapid change in general, but the particular direction of that change as we witness the continued weakening and/or liberalization of traditional social structures, such as the family and hierarchical religious institutions, that supported people leading less autonomous lives.[5] "Since we live in a society whose social forms are to a considerable extent based on individual choice, and since our options are limited by what is available in our society, we can prosper in it only if we can be successfully autonomous" (1986, p. 394).

THE INSTRUMENTAL VALUE OF AUTONOMY AND THE NEUTRALITY PRINCIPLE

I hope to have shown in the last few pages that there is an impressive case to be made for the *instrumental* value of ethical autonomy. But, readers might well be thinking, didn't John Stuart Mill suggest how one might make an impressive case for the *intrinsic* value of autonomy? If political liberalism has taught us anything, it is that we must think twice before assuming that our own reasons for living in a certain fashion are adequate to justify imposing that same way of life on others. When Stephen Gilles (1996, p. 976) protests that for liberal politics "to appeal to the capacity for critical deliberation is to make a controversial judgment about the extent to which we should rely on reason to govern our lives," this objection might appear to count equally against

[5] There is a risk of circularity here. Liberals must beware of arguing that autonomy is valuable because we can no longer rely on parents and priests for comprehensive ethical guidance while simultaneously invoking the value of autonomy to justify public policies that diminish the power of those same parents and priests.

appeals to the instrumental or intrinsic value of ethical autonomy. In similar fashion, Macedo (2000, p. 166) insists that the liberal state cannot endorse autonomy as the path to truth any more legitimately than it can endorse the intrinsic superiority and dignity of the autonomous life. Of course, Macedo is operating with what I regard as a caricature of autonomy: his opposition to mandating education for autonomy is expressed, for example, in the claim that "schools should not aim to strip away all of the beliefs and allegiances that parents might seek to inculcate in their children" (p. 238). But this aside, we must still ask how arguments for the instrumental value of autonomy can be any more admissible into liberal democratic politics than are Mill's heroic efforts to characterize individuality as a necessary and intrinsic part of the good life for man.

The arguments for the intrinsic and instrumental values of ethical autonomy are both controversial, but the key to establishing the latter as admissible to liberal democratic politics is to draw a distinction between the types of controversy involved in each case. Brighouse (1998) makes this move in an important article where he argues that one can assert the instrumental value of ethical autonomy without thereby failing to respect the reasonable conceptions of the good held by people who deny that autonomous reflection is the best path to a good life. According to Brighouse (p. 738), the instrumental argument for autonomy "invokes not a moral claim but a true epistemological claim: that rational evaluation is more reliable than other methods for discovering the good. This is controversial, but the controversy concerns epistemology, not morality." Why is the distinction important? By insisting that all children learn to operate as autonomous ethical agents, the liberal state would not be taking a stand on the worth of the parents' conception of the good but would instead declare a position on the question of how children can best determine for themselves whether that conception of the good is better for them than the various others they will encounter in their lives. Education policy in a pluralist liberal state should not mandate instruction in any particular ethical doctrine, but it can and should equip children with the best means to identify their good, and liberal states are not obliged to stay silent on the contested question of what means are best for that purpose. "Neutrality does not prohibit sincere appeal to controversial empirical premises; it prohibits only appeal to controversial moral claims" (p. 738).

If Brighouse is right, then we need not be alarmed by Gilles' observation that, by mandating education for autonomy, the liberal state would be making "a controversial judgment about the extent to which we should rely on reason to govern our lives." The liberal state rightly insists upon the superiority of rational methods for assessing evidence and arguments, even against the objections of some parents and other citizens. When a child is severely ill and doctors recommend traditional biomedical remedies but parents maintain that prayer alone is the best means to the child's good of regaining health, liberal states can and should insist upon the (not uncontroversial) judgment that the treatment should be determined by using rational standards to assess the empirical evidence that supports each position. It might be argued that the question of the best means to finding and living the good life is quite different from purely empirical questions about the best means to physical health, but we have already seen that ethical values are often bound up with the truth or falsehood of empirically verifiable conjectures, and such verification is best performed by rational methods. Furthermore, liberal states can and should use rational analysis and deliberative procedures as the best means to assess rival policies on the coherence of their principles and the consistency of their goals with existing policy commitments. And states rightly expect judges and jurors to use rational standards to evaluate arguments offered in court. In similar fashion, I suggest, liberal states are entitled to judge that these same methods of rational reflection and deliberation are the best means whereby individuals can assess the coherence of their particular ethical doctrines.

Returning to issues of education policy, we might usefully compare mandatory education for autonomy with mandatory instruction in what used to be called "the three Rs": reading, writing, and arithmetic. Most, if not quite all, liberals accept that the state can impose these latter basic curricular requirements despite the objections of cultural or religious groups who say, for example, that it is contrary to their way of life for women to learn such skills. By comparing autonomy with the three Rs, I do *not* mean to suggest that autonomous reflection should be taught merely as a skill and not also promoted as a valuable activity. When schools teach children how to read, write, and perform mathematical calculations, they should not claim to be agnostic about the wisdom of using these skills throughout one's life. Schools in a liberal state rightly *promote* reading, writing, and quantitative reasoning as valuable ways of learning about and interacting with the world. There is nothing illiberal about the idea that schools should encourage children to continue using these skills throughout their lives. Similarly, I suggest, there is nothing illiberal about the idea that schools should urge their students to adopt the method of autonomous reflection as a lifelong approach to ethical issues.[6]

If the state can override objections to teaching the three Rs, why can it not similarly override objections to teaching autonomy? One re-

---

[6] I return to this issue in chapter 5 in my discussion of the view that schools should enable but not promote autonomy.

sponse might be that illiteracy and innumeracy are severe barriers to effective civic participation. But, as we saw in chapter 2, Eamonn Callan has shown that good citizens of the liberal polity will also need to practice autonomy. There are civic reasons to mandate all these educational goals, but what can the liberal state say in answer to the objection that children are being corrupted by being taught to read and write, multiply and divide, and to think critically about their values and beliefs? I argue that the liberal state can and should refute these claims, as opposed to merely asserting, implausibly in my view, that they may be true but that they are necessarily outweighed by civic imperatives. *Yoder* was decided in favor of the Amish parents in large part because the Court decided that civic educational goals carry less weight in the case of a community that eschews engagement in politics and the larger American civil society.

Liberal states should confront directly the issue of children's individual interests in finding and leading good lives. Literate persons are empowered and free to read and write about any substantive ethical view; numerate persons have the skills to make their own judgments about a host of complex ethical issues in the world; autonomous persons are equipped to identify and pursue a good life for themselves, whatever that life may involve. The liberal state's endorsement of autonomy is akin to its endorsement of literacy and numeracy: in each case, there is a sufficient justification that is neutral in the sense that it appeals only to instrumental value and imposes no substantive constraints on the ethical positions one may accept as a result of reflection, reading, writing, or quantitative reasoning. It is one thing to say that liberal states cannot make ethical judgments: it would be quite another to say that they cannot make judgments about the best methods for individuals to use in making their own ethical judgments.

Of course, the preceding argument relies upon the premise that judgments about the best means to finding the good life for oneself are not themselves ethical judgments. To put the same point another way, we must accept that epistemological principles are in some sense separable from beliefs about the good life, and that only the latter are properly considered part of an individual's conception of the good, upon which the liberal state can make no judgment. Barry (2001, p. 123) relies upon this distinction to argue as follows that "autonomy-promoting liberalism [is] a bona fide form of liberalism."

> Autonomous people can have any substantive beliefs they like. What we mean by saying that people are autonomous is simply that whatever beliefs they do have will have been subject to reflection: their beliefs will not merely be those that were drummed into them by their parents, community and schools.

If we do not make this distinction between the substantive content of a conception of the good, on the one hand, and the manner in which that conception is held by a person, on the other, we are led to odd conclusions.

Consider the case of religious parents who claim that their conception of the good includes not only a set of beliefs and values but also the idea that those beliefs and values must be held in a way that is beyond rational reflection: these parents were themselves indoctrinated into this faith, and now they claim the right to indoctrinate their own children. Many liberals believe both that religious parents should have the opportunity to raise their children in the faith and that children should eventually be given the chance to reflect rationally on whether their parents' faith is right for them. In the case above, if we accept the parents' description of the status of their opposition to autonomy, these two liberal commitments are actually inconsistent: a school that successfully cultivates autonomy would necessarily destroy the parents' opportunity to raise their children in the faith, even though the children may exercise their autonomy to endorse all the substantive religious commitments with which they were raised. The mistake is to admit such an expansive characterization of the conception of the good in which parents may legitimately raise their children. Liberals should respect the right of parents to raise their children in their conception of the good *qua* substantive ethical beliefs and values, but not in the sense that such an upbringing might by definition have to constitute ethical indoctrination. We shall return to this question in the next chapter when we consider the objections of Stolzenberg (1993) and others made on behalf of adherents to religious traditions that emphasize innocence and faith in the absence of exposure to alternative ethical systems.

Some readers will probably still be troubled at the prospect of the liberal state's making and acting upon a judgment, namely, that rational reflection is the best means to finding the good, that many, especially religious, citizens will reject. How can a liberal state justify to dissenting parents the requirement that their children be educated for ethical autonomy? It might seem that a requirement of this sort fails to show appropriate respect for the sincere judgments of the parents, even if, as I argue above, it does not violate the principle of neutrality by failing to respect their conception of the good. One possible response is to point out that it is not parents, but rather their children, who are required to receive the education: on this argument, it would be unacceptably paternalistic of the liberal state to impose the ideal of ethical autonomy on adult parents, but there is no such objection to directing paternalism at children. Indeed, paternalism is and must be the essence of all educational requirements that aim to advance the private good of children. But liberals are normally content to leave these kinds of paternalistic judgments to parents, on the grounds that parents are generally both better placed and better motivated than the state to act in the best interests of their own children. So I think we still need an explanation of how the liberal state can be justified in overruling the judgments of those parents who maintain that an education for ethical autonomy would not serve the interests of their children.

What we need, in the words of Gaus (1996, p. 3), is "a normative theory of justification—a theory that allows [us] to claim that some set of principles is publicly justified, even given the fact that they are contested by some." The key to such a theory is the concept of "open justification": a person is openly justified in holding a particular belief if and only if that belief could survive perfect rational reflection in the light of full information, and similarly a principle is openly justifiable to a person who currently rejects it if that person would be committed to endorsing the principle with full rationality and perfect knowledge (pp. 31–32). Under the terms of open justification, the fact that some parents reject the principle that ethical autonomy has instrumental value does not settle the question of whether that principle is in fact justifiable to them. If they reject the principle because they lack knowledge, we do not fail to respect them by refusing to respect their ignorance. And the matter is still not settled if they (would) continue to reject the principle in the light of all relevant information. Gaus' theory of public justification contains normative standards of reasoning and inference, and these standards work in two ways. First, if citizens would assent to a given law only because of a failure in their rationality, this assent is insufficient to justify the law: liberal states must not exploit the irrationality of their citizens. Second, and more important for our purposes, if citizens dissent from a law only because of a failure in their rationality, this dissent is insufficient to show that the law is illegitimate: liberal states need not be paralyzed by the irrationality of their citizens. As Gaus persuasively argues, liberal politics would be a hopeless project if public justification, and hence legitimacy, relied upon actual universal assent, even among a well-informed populace. "People can withhold their assent because of obstinacy, selfishness, laziness, perversity, or confusion" (p. 131). In light of the arguments made earlier for the instrumental value of ethical autonomy, surely it is irrational to deny that rational reflection is an important means to finding and living the good life for oneself.[7]

---

[7] As I shall argue in the next chapter, adopting autonomy as a public value would not mean sending recalcitrant adults to autonomy boot camps for their own good—the liberal state should respect the preferences of adult citizens who opt to live nonautonomously, just as it respects their right to live according to a conception of the good that

One might protest that Gaus' concept of open justification begs the question because it simply invokes once again the same disputed standard of rationality. It comes as no surprise that a theory of public justification containing normative standards of rationality and inference will license an educational policy that seeks to teach people to live by those exact same standards. Citizens and parents who deny that rational reflection is an important means to determining the nature of the good life may well equally deny that rationality is always a good standard by which to assess proposed public policies, especially those that seek to prepare people to find and live good lives. Parents who object to the requirement that their children be educated for ethical autonomy are asking the liberal state to respect their preference for nonrational methods, so they are unlikely to be impressed by the response that they themselves are rationally committed to acknowledging the instrumental value of ethical autonomy. At root, the argument rests on the question of whether the liberal state, in regulating the forms in which children's education will be delivered to achieve paternalistic objectives, can insist upon the normative standard of rationality or whether it is obliged to accommodate and respect the opposing views of parents who reject this standard.

Needless to say, this is a formidable question and one that I cannot hope to resolve in a fully satisfactory fashion here, or indeed in my lifetime. But I think that Jean Hampton made an impressive case, in *The Authority of Reason* (1998), for insisting on the normative force of propositions that take the form of imperatives of rationality. My awareness of the fact that a given course of action is prescribed by reason may not actually motivate me to perform the action, but that does not mean that such an imperative of rationality merely provides me with information that I am free to ignore. To say that I should perform the action if I am rational is not like saying that I should perform it if I like vanilla ice cream (Hampton, 1998, pp. 127–42). Imperatives of rationality have "directive authority over us" (p. 49), and this authority cannot be escaped by denying that one is rational. The "instrumental norm: act so as to perform the most effective means to a desired end" (p. 144) carries objective authority and, I would add, the question of which means is actually most effective is not simply a subjective judgment. Recognition of the objective authority of reason is implicit in our everyday moral practice: "our normal reaction to irrational

---

is irrational—but it would mean requiring that all schools aim to cultivate autonomy in children for their own good, even against the objections of parents. It is one thing to paternalistically coerce adults, quite another to overrule their judgment about the formal education that best serves their children's interests.

people presupposes that they have defied the authority of the instrumental norm" (p. 151), and we are perfectly entitled to criticize them
for this defiance.

How is legitimate public policy in a liberal state limited by the need
to respect pluralism and, more generally, the existence of disagreement
among citizens? Gaus and Hampton propose similar answers to this
question by emphasizing the need to look beyond the phenomenon
of actual agreement and disagreement and to inquire into the rational
adequacy of citizens' views. The premise that underlies both theories
is the idea that the liberal state truly respects its citizens not by heeding
their prejudices and legislating their misconceptions, but rather by defending and advancing their rational interests. Of course, the mantra
of respecting people's rational interests rather than their declared opinions could be, and often has been, a cloak for tyranny, but all good
ideas are subject to abuse, intentional or otherwise. Liberal states must
guard against abuses of the "open justification" concept. In particular,
it is not a legitimate political claim that a single ethical doctrine ultimately defines the rational interests of all people; as we saw in the last
chapter, human reason is inadequate to select one such doctrine as best
for all persons. So the approach I recommend respects the plurality of
rational and reasonable conceptions of the good that command support in free societies while acknowledging the distinctive value of rational ethical reflection to individuals as they seek to identify and pursue the good life for themselves.

It might be objected that, notwithstanding the various arguments so
far presented to support the instrumental value of ethical autonomy,
not all persons can be expected to live better lives if they rationally
reflect on their goals and values than if they simply defer to an external
authority. Some people may be so bad at rational reflection, even after
receiving an education for ethical autonomy, that the risk of their going
astray outweighs the various reasons for believing that individuals
need to think for themselves. Certain mentally handicapped people
might fall clearly into this category, but skeptics about the instrumental
value of autonomy could propose that it is really only the gifted few
who can expect to profit from exercising ethical autonomy rather than
following the wisdom of the ethically sagacious. We must beware of
putting too much faith in ordinary people.

One problem with this line of argument is that it is not at all obvious
that the people who emerge as the ethical leaders will necessarily be
the most qualified for the role, the sages rather than the "ordinary people." And there are additional problems with relying on others in ethical matters: as we have discussed, heteronomy leaves one open to exploitation, and the ethical principles prescribed by even the best

authority figure may not suit the identity and needs of each disciple. It is true that a full account of the instrumental value of autonomy would need to identify, at least roughly, the degree of cognitive impairment beyond which autonomous reflection could not be expected to pay dividends. I cannot engage that task here, but I believe that the arguments of this chapter suffice to confirm Mill's view (1859/1989, p. 67) that actively fashioning one's own life is a better bet not only for "persons of decided mental superiority" but also for the person who "possesses any tolerable amount of common sense and experience." As Arneson and Shapiro note, to deny the instrumental value of ethical autonomy "one must deny that an individual of normal potential competence is likely to benefit from such exercise of critical reasoning skills. One must hold that the epistemic strategy of uncritical acceptance of the values that the individual was taught is a superior strategy for maximizing the goodness of the life the individual will have" (1996, p. 403). With the exception of a small class of severely cognitively impaired persons, I therefore believe that all children should receive an education that will prepare them for an autonomous ethical life.

CONCLUSION

I hope to have shown that, although appeals to the intrinsic value of ethical autonomy are out of place in liberal politics, a strong case can be made for the instrumental value of autonomy without violating the liberal principle of neutrality by asserting the superiority or inferiority of any particular conception of the good life. Exercising a developed capacity for ethical autonomy is the best way for individuals to detect false or inadequately supported beliefs, root out and resolve inconsistencies in their ethical doctrine, adjust their goals to suit their particular character and aspirations, guard against exploitation and manipulation by others, and prosper in a modern society whose social and economic institutions require and encourage the exercise of individual choice. Liberal states can justify invoking the value of ethical autonomy even against the opposition of religious parents and others if they can show that the objections are ultimately irrational or grounded in ignorance: coercive policy backed by the authority of reason need not fail to respect the plurality of conceptions of the good found in modern societies. Liberal states can and should take a stand on the special value of rational reflection and deliberation as a means to good decision making, in ethics and elsewhere. Mandatory education for autonomy may also strengthen the foundations of our conception of individual responsibility for one's conception of the good.

In developing my positive argument for the instrumental value of autonomy and trying to demonstrate the suitability of that argument for liberal politics, I am aware that I have given short shrift to the objections that might be raised, by religious parents and others, to a policy requiring specifically that all children be educated for ethical autonomy. In the next chapter, I focus on a number of these objections and try, through my responses, both to defend and to further develop my claim that liberal states can and should require education for ethical autonomy on the grounds that it serves the best interests of children. In so doing, I have no illusions that I shall satisfy or convert all my critics, but I hope to lay out clearly my reasons for believing that mandatory education for autonomy serves the interests of children without violating any parental rights or contradicting any other core liberal commitments.

Chapter 5

AUTONOMY AS A GOAL OF EDUCATION POLICY:
OBJECTIONS AND RESPONSES

IN THE PRECEDING CHAPTER, I hope to have shown that the instrumental value of ethical autonomy can be demonstrated by arguments that do not violate the appropriate conditions on public justification in liberal democratic politics. My purpose in doing so is to defend the claim that liberal states can and should adopt the cultivation of ethical autonomy as a goal of public education policy, overriding the objections of parents where necessary. But we are not yet in a position to make such a claim: even if the value of personal autonomy can be publicly justified, there might be other reasons to oppose the requirement that all children be educated for autonomy. Of course, there are a potentially infinite number of reasons that might be advanced against such a policy, and I cannot hope to list all these arguments, much less respond to them. But in this chapter, taking the conclusions of the previous chapter as given, I set out what I take to be the principal remaining objections to mandatory education for autonomy: roughly in decreasing order of importance, I consider objections grounded in parental rights, fairness to traditional cultures, possible conflicts with civic educational goals, the suffering of children, and autonomy itself. In each case, I develop the objection before explaining why I do not regard it as invalidating the claim that liberal states can and should require that all children be educated for personal autonomy.

PARENTAL RIGHTS AND INTERESTS

The argument in chapter 4 focused almost exclusively on the question of whether all children have an interest in developing personal autonomy. But this hardly settles the larger question about educational policy unless we believe that the interests of children are the only factors we need to consider to determine such policy. Some people do believe this: Shelley Burtt (1996, p. 414) proposes that "authority over children ought to be distributed according to the ability and willingness of the relevant parties to meet children's needs" and certainly not according to the "biological accident" (p. 424) of parentage. In fact, Burtt goes on to argue that children's needs, including their interest in developing the capacity for autonomous reflection, are best met by granting parents broad discretion to direct their children's formal education: her arguments to this effect will be considered in chapter 8. But the crucial premise of Burtt's argument is that parental rights can only be justified by showing that they serve children's best interests. Critics of this premise insist that parents have legitimate claims to direct their children's upbringing that are not grounded in assumptions about the distribution of authority that best serves children's interests. If these claims are indeed legitimate, they may be sufficient to block the inference from children's interest in autonomy to the state's right, and perhaps even duty, to educate all children for autonomy against the wishes of parents.

Charles Fried is often cited as a modern theorist who gives a strong account of parents' rights over their children: he argues that "the right to form one's child's values [is an extension of] the basic right not to be interfered with in doing these things for oneself" and goes on to claim, in a phrase that has many liberals frothing at the mouth, that "the child is regarded as an extension of the self" (Fried, 1978, p. 152). In defense of this position, Fried offers essentially two arguments. First, he claims that parental rights over their children are necessary to respect the sexuality of parents: to deny parental rights "implies that the parents' reproductive functions are only adventitiously their own" (p. 153). This first argument is disturbing to liberals to the extent that it resembles an ownership claim, and it also cannot account for the rights of adoptive parents. Second, Fried (p. 155) makes a claim about the essential meaning of the enterprise of raising children: "Parenthood is the closest many of us come to overcoming the fact of mortality . . . a kind of physical continuity . . . which is also bound up with spiritual and moral continuity through our influence on our children." This argument again threatens to neglect the independent moral identity of children, who are not merely vessels through which parents may extend their lives.

The critique of Fried I sketch in the last paragraph is a commonplace of the last two decades' liberal writings about education. Most liberal theorists have taken it for granted that Fried's conception of parental rights is hostile to children's autonomy and have therefore found it important to wage war on his arguments. But I would like to suggest that Fried's theory is not actually in any necessary tension with the idea that all children should develop as autonomous persons, at least according to the conception of autonomy I outlined in chapter 3. Ethical autonomy does not require radical choice, unconditioned by upbringing, and is therefore not incompatible with a parental prerogative to shape the child's earliest ethical beliefs provided that the child subsequently develops and utilizes the capacity to reflectively evaluate these beliefs. Fried does not allow parents' rights to override the interests of the child, which could include, as I argue they do, an interest in personal autonomy. He merely asserts that, since the child's ethical starting point must be given, not chosen, we should acknowledge the right of parents to give that gift. In the crucial passage that removes the impression that Fried supports parental rights that could clash with and override a child's interest in developing as an autonomous person, he writes that a child's "independent status is sufficiently recognized by *obliging* the parents to care for and educate the child *in the child's best interests*. The child's most intimate values and determinants, however, must come from somewhere. The child cannot choose them— rather, they choose the child" (p. 154, my emphasis).

If one is looking for a theory of parental rights according to which the state is never justified in overriding parental judgments about the best educational interests of the child, one must look beyond Fried. But one can find such a theory in the libertarian writings of Chandran Kukathas. Kukathas' (1992a) primary concern is to defend the sovereignty of minority cultural groups within a multicultural, liberal state. According to his theory, a voluntary association of religious parents could legitimately deny their children an education for autonomy, although it is unclear whether the same right should be accorded to a single religious parent who does not belong to any larger association.[1] However, the key point is that Kukathas would allow certain religious parents to direct the education of their children without being constrained by any independent specification of the best interests of those children. For Kukathas, this conclusion is dictated by the need to respect freedom of association, the right of individuals to live together on whatever terms they wish. If freedom of association is the foundational freedom, then "the right to be free to leave [the community] . . . has to be the individual's fundamental right; it is also his only fundamental right, all other rights being either derivative of this right, or rights granted by the community" (pp. 116–17). But, as Barry (2001, p. 239) has noted, the right of exit presumably does not belong to children, and certainly cannot be exercised by young children, so children in Kukathas' theory enjoy no rights whatsoever against the community

[1] Kukathas' work raises a host of complex questions about the definition and boundaries of the cultural groups about which he writes. For my purposes, however, it suffices to observe that some traditional religious communities, for example, the Old Order Amish, are meant to fall within the scope of Kukathas' theory.

with which their parents voluntarily associate, at least where their education is concerned. Since children have no rights against their parents' community, the liberal state has no grounds for legitimate intervention: "The wider society has no right to require particular standards or systems of education within such cultural groups" (Kukathas, 1992a, p. 117) and therefore, if Amish or Gypsy parents were to decide, in accordance with their religious and/or cultural beliefs, not to provide *any* formal education for their children, this decision would have to be respected (p. 126).

Whereas Fried's theory turned out, on closer examination, to grant parental rights only on condition that they be exercised in the best interests of children, Kukathas proposes to license (communities of like-minded) parents to design their children's education (or lack thereof) entirely without regard for the independently specified best interests of those children. If Fried's position actually concedes too little to parents, as I shall shortly argue, Kukathas' position surely concedes too much by conceding virtually everything. Why do I say "virtually"? It may seem that Kukathas' theoretical framework leaves children entirely without rights of any sort: Barry (2001, p. 239) evidently reads the theory that way when he accuses Kukathas of proposing that "the state should stand by and let parents mutilate their children with impunity." But I do not think that Kukathas means to say this: children are presumably at least minimally protected by his principle that freedom of association is limited by "norms forbidding slavery and physical coercion" and "prohibitions on cruel, inhuman, and degrading treatment" (Kukathas, 1992a, p. 128). Nonetheless, there is something deeply unpersuasive about Kukathas' stark distinction between the moral status of adults and children: adult individuals can protect themselves by exercising an almost unqualified freedom of association, but their children, who will one day enjoy that same freedom as adults but at present lack the all-important right of exit, are to be protected only against slavery, torture, and other forms of what might uncontroversially be deemed cruelty. It is reasonable to maintain that children and adults enjoy somewhat different moral rights, and it is necessary to establish legally a conventional age above which persons assume the rights of adults, but the mere fact that young people are unlucky enough to be unable to exercise a right of exit if they find themselves in an oppressive community is inadequate to justify the claim that children's rights should be as few and limited as Kukathas proposes.

A decent and coherent political and moral theory must give more than minimal normative weight to the identity of children as persons distinct from their parents, even if it then goes on to argue that parents are justified, for their own sake as well as for their children's, in treating their children in ways that they could not legitimately treat other people, including other children. Without full recognition of the moral importance of the separate identity and interests of children, "the parental freedom to control the education of children can itself be a form of tyranny—especially if such control extends to a view of the child as the parents' property" (Macedo, 2000, p. 101). Not only must the separate interests of children be fully recognized in theory, they must also be properly protected in practice: if children have an interest in developing into ethically autonomous persons, this interest must be defended by a trustee if it is not advanced by the parents. "Children are not legally capable of defending their own future interests against present infringement by their parents, so that task must be performed for them, usually by the state in its role of *parens patriae*" (J. Feinberg, 1980, p. 128). All too often when education policy is discussed, the distinction between children and their parents is blurred in a way that threatens to neglect entirely the independent interests of the former where they diverge from the preferences of the latter. For example, Michael McConnell (1991a, p. 150), writing in defense of school vouchers, argues that "with educational choice, each school could teach from a coherent moral-cultural perspective—one that is *chosen* by its student body." Let us not forget that, in many if not most families, especially when the children are young, these kinds of choices are made by parents.

John Stuart Mill's position on the need to recognize and protect children's independent interests, as opposed to those of their parents, looks oddly inconsistent to the contemporary reader. Mill's staunch advocacy of the value of individuality might suggest that liberal states should regulate education to prevent parents from indoctrinating their children. And it seems that Mill is setting up for this conclusion when he writes: "It is in the case of children, that misapplied notions of liberty are a real obstacle to the fulfillment by the State of its duties. One would almost think that a man's children were supposed to be literally, and not metaphorically, a part of himself, so jealous is opinion of the smallest interference of law with his absolute and exclusive control over them" (1859/1989, p. 105). Yet Mill uses this observation only to rail against parents who fail to provide their children with any formal schooling at all: in his haste to warn of the dangers of state-controlled education, he ignores the risk that parents, through their choice of school, might equally constrain the child's development of individuality. To avoid the dangers of a state-imposed orthodoxy of opinion, Mill argues for a scheme of educational diversity with minimal public regulation designed only to ensure that children learn to read and write and that they acquire an adequate level of general knowledge. In particular, Mill insists that "all attempts by the state to bias the conclusions of its citizens on disputed subjects, are evil" (p. 107). Presumably, Mill does not mean this statement to entail that the state cannot endorse the value of individuality and critical thinking, although he certainly realized that this was a "disputed subject": Mill's political argument in *On Liberty* is precisely that states should uphold the familiar liberal freedoms in the name of individuality, notwithstanding the controversial nature of that appeal. Mill's vigorous distrust of government interference in education surely ought to be balanced against the dangers that unchecked parental authority can pose,[2] so I think it is in the spirit of his celebration of individuality to say that the state can and should regulate education to ensure that children's interest in developing as ethically autonomous persons is not ignored when it runs contrary to their parents' beliefs.[3]

In rejecting the view of Kukathas, I hope to have established that, if parents have rights over their children that are not grounded solely in the best interests of those children, such rights do not trump, but must rather be balanced against, the children's independent rights and interests. As Burtt (1996, p. 421) argues, it is unacceptable to recognize that children have independent interests but nonetheless to insist that parental preferences are always sovereign in cases of conflict: such a position "ends up privileging the rights, desires, and life plans of one class of individuals in our society (parents) over others (their children) without offering sufficient justification for this favoritism." But one might go further and ask whether and why parents have any rights to treat their children in ways that are not in the children's best interests. Since Fried's view turned out to impose on parents the general obligation to serve the best interests of the child, and Kukathas' view of parental rights has been rejected, we have yet to find an acceptable theory of parental rights according to which parents' interests can ever legitimately prevail in cases of conflict with the interests of their children. In what follows, I sketch such a theory before explaining why it does not challenge the principle that the state can legitimately require that all children be educated for ethical autonomy.

[2] As Gutmann (1999, p. 44) notes, professional educators have the potential to be a third force that limits the authority of both parents and democratic majorities: certainly, in a recognizably *liberal* democracy, government actions are not automatically legitimate merely by virtue of their being the outcome of democratic decisions. But, in practice, as I argued in chapter 1, the survival and flourishing of a liberal democratic regime must ultimately rely on the virtues of its citizens rather than on the checks that can be provided by institutions, since these institutions can always be sidelined or undone by democratic politics.

[3] In the next chapter, I consider in more detail Mill's concern that government management and/or regulation of education, especially where control is local, creates schools that propagate majority ethical opinion rather than cultivating children's autonomy.

"Parents Are People Too"

Adult citizens of liberal states are free to live as they see fit, subject to certain limits that apply to all. As David Bridges (1984, p. 57) explains the familiar idea:

> The liberal assumption is that an individual should enjoy such freedoms at least up the point at which they start to impinge on other people's freedom. At this point, which may of course arrive fairly quickly within the close confines of the family, a judgment has to be made as to the course of action that will most fully and fairly allow competing parties their freedom of action.

How should we resolve these conflicts within the family? If parents' rights to direct their children's upbringing are grounded exclusively in the best interests of those children, then we can only ever resolve conflicts in favor of allowing parental freedoms if it can be shown that the diminution of the child's freedom is a valid form of paternalism, that is, limiting the child's freedom genuinely serves his or her interests. But it is not obvious why this should be the only adequate justification for requiring children to sacrifice some of their freedom for the sake of their parents' freedom. As Bridges (p. 57) puts it, "parents are people too and have, on the face of it at least, *no less* right than their children to lead the kind of life they choose." It is in the nature of parenting and family life that many activities must be pursued by all or none: if the parents go to church, the young children will have to go too; if the children stay home, so must the parents. Many theorists propose that these kinds of daily decisions about family activities need not be made exclusively with regard to the interests of the children.

Galston (2002, p. 94) argues persuasively that parents have a legitimate, albeit not trumping, "expressive interest in raising their children in a manner consistent with their understanding of what gives meaning and value to life," *even if* this upbringing is not in the best interests of the children. This parental interest should, I propose, be understood as an extension of the usual adult freedoms into the particular and distinctive circumstances of family life: if we did not acknowledge the legitimacy of such an interest, parents would be unable to live and express their deepest convictions in their role as parents if doing so would impose even the slightest burden on their children. It might appear tempting to respond that, by bringing children into the world and undertaking to raise them, parents have voluntarily introduced into their own lives a sphere in which it is illegitimate for them to express their convictions at the expense of defenseless others. As I shall shortly argue, this is a profoundly unappealing view of the life one assumes by becoming a parent: it overemphasizes the significance of the child's lack of choice in being born by placing the extraordinary burdens of family life exclusively on the parents. But it also misses the key point that we want parents to approach their family life not as a sphere in which they must routinely suppress their ethical values but rather as an opportunity to express those values, albeit in ways that are balanced by a concern for the interests and freedoms of children. As Callan (1997, p. 142) puts it, "the role of parent is typically undertaken as one of the central, meaning-giving tasks of our lives" and it would be cruel to suggest that parents should regard themselves merely as custodians of the child's independently defined interests.

But if Devins (1992, p. 837) is right to claim that there is a legitimate parental interest in "living one's life through one's children, [which] ought to be called the parent's right to exercise his religion through the child, and to extend through the child ideas, language, and customs which the parent believes to be important," whence does the legitimacy derive? We do not generally grant people the right to coerce others so as to live vicariously through them, so in what morally relevant ways is the relationship between parent and child special? First of all, since parenting is a major commitment and an activity of tremendous social importance, it is vital that it should be a satisfying role for persons to play. The point is not so much that we must be careful not to deter potential parents, though I think this is a concern, but rather that we simply do not want to make parenting any more burdensome or difficult than it has to be. Requiring that all decisions made by parents that will impact their children be justified exclusively in terms of the interests of the children makes parenting seem like martyrdom, and we do not expect, or perhaps even desire, that all parents should be so infused with the spirit of self-sacrifice. As Bridges (1984, p. 59) observes: "The potential for joy in parenthood . . . does seem to depend on parents being able in general to raise their children as they see proper, perhaps to extend through them what they see as good in life, and on their being able to establish a particularly intimate network of relationship and influence." Of course, we hope and expect that parents will often be able to find joy in their lives in exactly this way without any cost to the child but, as and when conflicts occur, I do not think we should stipulate in advance that it is always the parents' joy that must be sacrificed.

Callan (1997, pp. 145–46) offers an interesting hypothetical case to illustrate the claim that parents must sometimes be allowed to make choices that do not best serve their child's interests. He imagines that "the parents of a musically talented and interested child" choose to take the child to Disneyland rather than to buy a piano. Perhaps the decision is "unfortunate, even stupid," Callan suggests, and *ex hypothesis* it does not serve the child's best interests, but is it illegitimate? Callan seems sure that the Disneyland choice is "within [the parents'] rights," although I think that much of the appeal of that judgment lies in our understandable reluctance to grant anyone the power to intervene in parental decisions of this sort: Callan concedes that the legitimacy of the parents' choice is a separate question from the desirability and feasibility of establishing a body to prevent parents from making the various kinds of illegitimate purchases they might be considering. But I do not think we have to work too hard to amend the case into one in which the parents' decision is clearly legitimate despite its going against the child's best interests.

Imagine that the most suitable music lessons for the child in Callan's example happen on Sunday mornings, many miles from the family's church. The child shows no interest in attending church, and the parents have given up all realistic hope that she will develop a meaningful faith. But nonetheless, the parents insist that the whole family will go to church: they are not willing to miss church themselves, they could not find or afford any other way to get their child to the music lessons, and anyway, they are determined that their daughter will share the church-going experience with her parents. Assuming for the moment that this decision cannot reasonably be thought to serve the child's best interests, it still seems to me eminently legitimate. The parents are not morally required to sacrifice their own interests and their vision of Sunday morning family life for the sake of their child, although we might consider it admirable if they did. Parents are people too, and they should not be reduced to "a state of bondage" (p. 146) by their commitment to raising a child.

> If the moral burden of rearing children is not to engulf entire lives without residue, the burden must be curtailed by the recognition that parents have lives beyond the service they give their children, and that some discretion in how they balance that service against responsibilities that flow from other projects and roles, as well as the claims of self-interest, rightfully belongs within their sphere of personal sovereignty.

While it is true that children did not ask to be born and could not choose their parents, it is not unreasonable to expect them to accept some give and take in the resolution of the many conflicts that arise between their own interests and those of their parents. As Bridges (1984, p. 60) notes, this claim is supported by a casual observation of the number and extent of the extraordinary demands that children make upon, and that we expect to be satisfied by, their parents: "We allow and expect that children will make demands on their parents—their love, their patience, their pockets, their understanding—that would be unthinkable in almost any other relationship." The principle of reciprocity suggests a corresponding "parental entitlement to a level of interference in *their* children's lives which could not be justified in their relations with any other people, including other children." Although parents brought their children into existence and thereby acquired a considerable set of responsibilities to attend to their needs and interests, the legitimate role of the parent is not limited to service. "A better model is more nearly reciprocal: parents and children serve, and are served by, one another in complex ways" (Galston, 2002, p. 103).

The stage is now set to consider whether parental rights include the right to except one's child, presumably on conscientious grounds, from a policy that furthers the child's best interests by mandating formal education designed to promote autonomy. I have argued above that parents do have a legitimate interest in directing and conditioning the upbringing of their children according to their own preferences and values, even when the parentally preferred upbringing would not serve the children's best interests. But merely to say that parents are people too, with their own legitimate interests at stake, is obviously not to say that parental interests always trump those of children: we must assess the two competing interests, and strike a balance between them, across the full range of cases that occur in family life. The question is therefore not whether it is sometimes justifiable for parents to act against their children's best interests, but whether we should recognize as legitimate such parental discretion in the particular case of parents wishing not to send their children to formal educational institutions that seek to cultivate ethical autonomy in students. Where does this case fall as the state tries to balance its responsibilities to secure the best interests of the child against its obligation to respect the legitimate freedom of parents to shape the life of their family?

States should, and liberal states typically do, recognize that parents should have very considerable and, in a sense, extraordinary freedom to raise their children as they see fit. Outside the sphere of formal education, parents should be left free within very broad limits to exercise power over their children: coercing them to attend church, indoctrinating them with bedtime stories from the Koran, etc. We grant parents these freedoms in part because it is good for children to be grounded in the culture and values of their family (as will be discussed in chapter 8) and in part, as Callan (1997, pp. 145–46) notes, because we rightly fear to authorize agents of the state to intrude in domestic life except in the clearest and most egregious cases of child abuse. But this does not tell the whole story: we respect the broad discretion of parents in directing their children's extracurricular lives in part also because we recognize the great significance of family life to parents and the legitimacy of their pursuing their own independent interests through their children. During the overwhelming majority of hours in a year, when children are not required to be receiving formal instruction, conflict between parents' and children's interests should, in principle, be resolved by a balancing procedure that does not systematically favor either side. But, in practice, the liberal state must permit parents to strike the balance as they see fit in all but the rarest and most extreme cases, given the dangers associated with granting to state agencies the power of routine intervention in family life.

But, given the substantial discretion that parents must be granted at home, liberal states should take a different approach to their regulation of the periods of formal schooling that children are required to receive, in one form or another. Parents cannot be forced to advance the cause of their child's autonomy at home,[4] but they should not be permitted to frustrate the satisfaction of such an important interest in every sphere of the child's life. Our conception of parents' rights is not Kukathas': the independent interests of parents and children must be balanced, so public education policy counterbalances sweeping parental prerogatives at home by carving out a portion of children's lives in which their own interests will be paramount. The institutions of required formal education, whether they be public or private schools, are precisely the venues in which the liberal state can and should insist upon the cultivation of ethical autonomy in the best interests of the child. Parents who complain that their rights are being trampled when they are required to send their children to schools that promote autonomy must be reminded both that they do not own their children and that there are great swathes of their family life in which they are largely free from state interference to direct the ethical and religious upbringing of their children.

As Gutmann (1999, p. 29) argues, there is no "right of parents to insulate their children from exposure to ways of life or thinking that conflict with their own," even though parents rightly enjoy a great deal of influence over the environment in which their children are raised. The independent rights and interests of parents are an important element of a liberal theory of child-rearing, as we have seen, but they do not justify parents in withdrawing their children from publicly regulated schools

---

[4] Home schools are a special case: my argument certainly entails the need for considerable public regulation of the practice of home schooling, difficult as this would inevitably be.

that serve the best interests of children by developing in them the capacity and inclination for autonomous reflection. Notice, however, that an analogous argument would not have worked in chapter 2 to justify giving absolute priority to civic concerns in the sphere of formal education while giving parents a relatively free rein elsewhere. Because the reproduction of the liberal democratic state is a good that depends upon the level of civic skills and virtues among the citizenry as a whole, whereas the development of a person's autonomy is a private good for that individual, the educational balance between parental authority and civic concerns should be struck over the domain of all children, whereas the balance between parental authority and children's independent interests must be struck separately and fairly for each child.

The Death Knell for Traditional Ways of Life?

A second important objection to mandatory education for autonomy was touched upon in the previous chapter: such a policy, if successful, will necessarily extinguish certain traditional and religious ways of life that are partly defined by elements of character that are incompatible with personal autonomy. Notice that the argument here is not merely that children who are educated to think critically about their culture of upbringing will be more likely to renounce it later in life, but rather that the very fact of receiving an education for autonomy displaces an individual from certain cultures. In both an important U.S. Supreme Court case, *Wisconsin v. Yoder* (1972), and an influential series of judicial proceedings culminating in a U.S. Sixth Circuit Federal Appeals Court case, *Mozert v. Hawkins* (1987), parents claimed the right to withdraw their children, wholly or partially, from public schools on the grounds that these schools were corrupting their children by exposing them to ideas and practices not found in their familial culture. The *Mozert* case is especially interesting for our purposes because the plaintiffs argued at length that the development and practice of critical thinking about social and ethical issues are expressly forbidden by their fundamentalist Christian beliefs. If the plaintiffs' children were exposed to unbiblical ideas and ways of life without continually being told by their teacher that such deviations from fundamentalist Christian norms are wrong, this would implicitly encourage the children to think independently and open-mindedly about the merits of alternative perspectives rather than simply deferring to biblical authority. But, by encouraging this kind of independent critical judgment, schools would be teaching children a value or practice that is directly at odds with the parents' system of values.

One way to respond to the parents in the *Mozert* case, and also in *Yoder*, has already been discussed at length in the first two chapters of this work: rather than engaging directly with the parents' claim that an education that encourages critical judgment and open-mindedness to other ways of life is at odds with their private values, one might instead focus on the fact that such an education is necessary if children are in the future to play their part as good citizens of the liberal democratic state. Specifically with reference to the *Mozert* controversy, Gutmann and Thompson (1996, pp. 63–69) offer precisely this response to the objections of religious parents, arguing that the request for an exemption from measures necessary for a good civic education fails the test of reciprocity: all citizens should abide by those conditions that are necessary for continued fair social cooperation, but the parents in *Mozert* propose illegitimately to violate reciprocity by free-riding on others' compliance with these conditions. The problem with this response, as I argued in chapter 2, lies in its unwarranted assumption that the civic purposes of education trump the claims of parents who want to avoid a significant burden on their ability to raise their children in accordance with their cultural values or religious beliefs. As Galston (1999b, p. 45) puts it, "there is . . . an important public interest in educating good citizens. But there are other morally significant interests with which the formation of citizens sometimes comes into conflict and to which the claims of citizenship must sometimes give way." A few free-riders do not doom the liberal democratic enterprise. So although the civic case against granting the *Mozert* parents' request carries important weight, it does not settle the question. We still need to decide how to weigh the *noncivic* value to children of an education for autonomy against the parents' claims that such an education would prevent them from raising their children according to their religious beliefs.

The plaintiffs' arguments in *Mozert*, as documented by Bates (1994) and analyzed by Stolzenberg (1993), turned standard liberal assumptions on their head. The fundamentalist parents objected to "the cultivation of individual reason, objective judgment and rational critical thought . . . as a form of indoctrination," in direct opposition to the conventional view that "the state eschews indoctrination by encouraging its citizens freely and critically to choose among competing beliefs" (Stolzenberg, 1993, p. 611). To educate children for personal autonomy is to indoctrinate them into pluralism, to teach that "the significance of the Bible is a matter of opinion" and therefore that fundamentalism is "just one among many belief systems from which an individual might choose" (Stolzenberg, 1993, p. 627). From the fundamentalist perspective, this trivializes religious belief (Carter, 1987, 1993). Worse still, once children have been programmed to think critically about their values and about religious authority, they are already estranged from their parents' way of life, no matter what decisions they ultimately make about social and ethical issues.

> Even if the children adhere to their parents' beliefs, they do so knowing that those beliefs are matters of opinion [which] transforms the meaning of remaining (or in the case of the children, becoming) attached to them. It is one thing for beliefs to be transmitted from one generation to another. It is another to hold beliefs, knowing that those beliefs are transmitted, that they vary, and that their truth is contested. (Stolzenberg, 1993, p. 633)

The mode of epistemic commitment that Stolzenberg describes—in which a daughter endorses her parents' beliefs only after independently and open-mindedly assessing the merits of alternatives, and while recognizing the reasonableness of ethical disagreement (and perhaps also the role of contingent cultural context in shaping her ethical doctrine[5])—is precisely the hallmark of ethical autonomy as I characterized it in chapter 3, and it is manifestly at odds with certain religiously grounded traditional ways of life.

Stolzenberg regards this case as exemplifying a paradox of liberal neutrality: liberals want both to promote autonomy and not "to judge or to undermine diverse ways of life" (p. 660), but *Mozert* brings these two goals into direct conflict. How should liberals respond? For Kukathas (1992a, p. 122), our duty to respect different cultures must extend to respecting different cultural judgments about the value of autonomy, or lack thereof: "Culture is not simply a matter of colorful dances and rituals, nor is it even a framework or context for individual choice." We cannot seriously claim to be respecting the fundamentalist parents and their way of life while overriding their sincere objection to having "different visions of ultimate truth . . . laid out before their young children as equally valid alternatives. The word *heresy* is rooted in *haeresis*, meaning 'choice'" (Bates, 1994, p. 309). If fundamentalist parents are required to send their children to schools where they will be educated for autonomy, they are "being forced to act in ways that they believe will lead to divine retribution" (Stolzenberg, 1993, p. 630).

In responding to Stolzenberg, Bates, and Kukathas, it is important to remember the specific grounds of our concern that children should

---

[5] I have in mind the person, discussed in chapter 3, who feels that she lacks conclusively good reasons to accept the ethical doctrine in which she was raised, but who also lacks good reason to accept any other substantive ethical values or beliefs; I suggest that such a person might continue to live by her parents' doctrine and be regarded as autono-

be educated for autonomy. Kukathas (1992b, p. 678) observes that children educated in and by cultures that reject autonomy are likely to grow up "so completely committed to their respective faiths, and ignorant of alternatives, that the idea of changing faiths or questioning their own fundamental beliefs is beyond contemplation," and he goes on to argue that "it is not clear that this is objectionable if one's concern is the freedom of the individual to live as he or she prefers." Of course, if this were our only concern, we would have no reason to value autonomy: indeed, an extremely thorough and effective indoctrination into the dominant local culture would be a very good way to ensure that a child will be able to live the rest of his or her life "as he or she prefers." But the key to recognizing the instrumental value of autonomy is to see that living as one prefers is not necessarily the same as living the best life for oneself. Inability to think critically about one's ethical doctrine and ignorance of one's alternatives are both serious impediments to finding and living a life whose values are coherent, supported by evidence and true beliefs about the world, and expressed in terms that both suit the agent's deepest aspirations and provide comprehensive ethical guidance as social conditions change. None of this involves the notion that Kukathas (1992a, p. 124) considers and rightly rejects as the basis for liberal politics: "that human flourishing requires that the individual be capable of autonomy or have the capacity to choose his or her way of life on the basis of critical reflection on a range of options." Appeals to the intrinsic value of autonomy as a constituent of the human good admittedly provide inadequate justification for imposing educational goals on children and their parents, but liberal states can and should insist upon the instrumental value of personal autonomy to individuals seeking to find and live the best life for themselves.

How, then, is the liberal state to justify a policy that sounds the death knell for certain traditional, especially religious, ways of life? One first point to make clear is that ways of life themselves have no survival rights: at base, we care about people, not cultures, which we value only insofar as they enhance the lives of individual people. Kukathas (1992a, pp. 116–17) accepts this too. Do the fundamentalist parents? I think they do, although of course they insist that theirs is the *only* culture within which it is valuable for a person to live. But even if some citizens assert that cultures themselves make moral claims upon us, regardless of their significance for people, I think this claim must be rejected at the foundational level of liberal political morality. As a sec-

---

mous on condition that she also continues to engage in rational ethical reflection and recognizes the contingency and provisional nature of her present ethical commitments.

ond point in preparation for the liberal response, it should be noted that there is no contradiction involved in a policy whose promotion of a person's autonomy removes a particular way of life from the set of options available to that person. As Raz (1986, p. 410) makes clear, autonomy depends upon the availability of a diverse range of valuable options, but it does not and could not require that all valuable options be available, still less that all options whatsoever be sustained. Of course, one might protest that it is particularly valuable for children to have the option of sharing their parents' way of life, and, as we shall see in chapter 8, I think this is true, but it is not in the interests of a child to secure this one option at the expense of her being exposed to, and taught rationally to assess the merits of, *all* other options.

The main response to this important objection from traditional cultures, apart from restating the argument for the instrumental value of autonomy, is to insist that although the "innocence" or "unreflective faith" that characterizes certain ways of life cannot by definition be chosen by an autonomous agent, the substantive beliefs and values that make up that way of life are still available to those who have been educated for autonomy. In particular, we are not entitled to assume with Dewey (discussed in Macedo, 2000, pp. 139–45) that adequate critical reflection necessarily spells the end of religious faith. Religious beliefs can be held autonomously although, as Callan (1988) notes, this requires a very different type of faith from what many people currently have: autonomously held religious beliefs must take the form of "sophisticated belief," which combines "a vigorous faith with an intelligent humility about the possibility of its reasoned vindication" (Callan, 1997, p. 38).

As discussed in the previous chapter, and in Barry (2001, p. 123), liberals can legitimately draw a distinction between the substantive beliefs and values that constitute a conception of the good, on the one hand, and the attitudes toward autonomy that are partially constitutive of certain ways of life, on the other: the state is bound to respect the former, but not the latter. Liberal concerns about paternalism are sufficient to rule out policies that coerce adults into developing and practicing autonomy, but these concerns do not debar the state from pursuing the best interests of children by teaching them autonomy against parental objections: the upbringing of children is necessarily a paternalistic endeavor, and parents do not have exclusive authority to determine the form of that upbringing. The liberal state rightly insists that all children receive a formal education that meets certain standards, even against the objections of parents who claim that these standards are contrary to their way of life. The argument of chapters 4 and 5 has been that the cultivation of ethical autonomy should be one of these nonnegotiable standards: within the sphere of mandatory formal education, children should be taught to think for themselves about their ethical commitments not only because of the civic importance of autonomy, but also to equip those children with a demonstrably effective method to find and lead a good life for themselves.

Needless to say, this argument will not fully satisfy those who believe that the primary concern of liberalism is to safeguard the liberty of adult citizens by accommodating and respecting cultural diversity: for liberals of this stripe, and indeed for many nonliberals, the distinction between "substantive" beliefs and values and "attitudes" toward autonomy will appear arbitrary and bogus, reminiscent of Kukathas' concern that culture not be reduced to "colorful dances and rituals." The rhetorical appeal of this slogan is unquestioned, but it does of course grossly misrepresent the nature and extent of the respect I advocate for cultural pluralism. The liberal state should not take sides in the reasonable disagreement about substantive ethical values in a pluralist society where citizens affirm many diverse conceptions of the good, but the state should assert the value to all individuals of being able to think rationally for themselves about which of these conceptions to affirm. This is *not* equivalent to treating culture as no more than "colorful dances and rituals." But it does resolve the supposed "paradox of liberal tolerance," a paradox that Stolzenberg (1993, p. 667) insists "will haunt us" because we can do no more than look it "in the face." Recall that the paradox supposedly arises when the twin liberal goals of respecting diversity and promoting autonomy conflict with each other. The resolution lies in declaring, in the spirit of Kymlicka (1989), that liberals do not value cultural diversity and cultures for their own sake, but rather for their significance in enabling individuals to find and live good lives, respectively. Adults who have committed their lives to a particular ethical path should not be coerced into reflecting on alternative paths, but children deserve the opportunity to find their best path in life. On this view, it would be perverse of the liberal state to attempt to justify, in the name of respecting culture, any restriction on the development of children's capacities to make good lives for themselves.

OTHER OBJECTIONS AND RESPONSES

Having devoted considerable time to stating and responding to two objections—one from respect for parental rights, the other from fairness to traditional cultures—to adopting the development of ethical autonomy as a goal of public education policy, I complete this chapter by dealing more tersely with three further objections. The first objection is that education for ethical autonomy may be in tension with civic education. If schools develop in future citizens both the capacity and the inclination for critical thinking, it must be expected that the beneficiaries of this schooling will sometimes apply their critical thinking skills not only to their ethical doctrines but also to the principles and norms of the liberal democratic polity in which they live. And, as Galston (1989, p. 91) observes, rational reflection and deliberation may be insufficient to generate and sustain a robust allegiance to principles of liberal justice, so the worry is that the liberal state might undermine its own foundations in popular support by educating citizens for autonomy. "Very few individuals will come to embrace the core commitments of liberal society through a process of rational inquiry. If children are to be brought to accept these commitments as valid and binding, it can only be through a pedagogy that is far more rhetorical than rational." But Galston's observation does not imply that education for autonomy is at odds with civic educational goals, unless one insists upon a view of the role of reason in autonomy that I have already rejected as a caricature. If children were given a blank slate and encouraged to think rationally about the best form of political society, it is presumably true that very few would reason their way to the exact form of liberal democracy in which they live. But autonomous decisions need not, indeed cannot, be made without being conditioned by cultural context, and so there is no need for teachers to eschew entirely the kind of rhetorical pedagogy that Galston advocates. The future autonomy of a young child is not threatened by her being brought up to believe that liberal democratic principles are fair and just, so long as she subsequently develops the necessary capacities for rational reflection to think critically about this belief. If liberal democratic principles are indeed worthy of our allegiance, it is likely that many people who are raised in the liberal democratic political tradition will not discern sufficient grounds to renounce those principles once they are able to critically scrutinize them.

But, of course, one should not deny that free, critical thinking may lead people to conclusions we wish they had not reached. Galston may exaggerate the risk, but the risk does exist. However, as Brighouse (1998, p. 720) argues, it is a risk that liberal democracies must be willing to take for the sake of their own legitimacy. Popular support for the principles of the liberal democratic state only confers legitimacy on government if that support can reasonably be regarded as free and considered, as opposed to having been manufactured by government propaganda. So "civic education is permissible only if it includes elements that direct the critical scrutiny of children to the very values they are taught." Both Macedo (2000, p. 279) and Gutmann (1999, p. 15) endorse this idea that liberal democratic civic education, unlike other forms of civic education, must involve developing the capacity of future citizens to think critically not only *within* the political sphere but also *about* the nature and rules of the political sphere. Otherwise, "an originating point of the consent of the governed [is] controlled by the government," which illiberally "becomes a kind of political perpetual-motion machine, legitimizing its long-term policies through the world view and public opinion it creates" (Arons, 1983, pp. 207, 203). Liberal democracies must make room for autonomous dissenters from their own principles.

Furthermore, as discussed in chapter 2, Callan argues persuasively that ethical autonomy is conceptually inseparable from an active recognition of the burdens of judgment: since civic education in a liberal democracy must aim to develop in citizens this grasp of the burdens of judgment, it must necessarily encourage ethical autonomy. Callan himself notes that widespread autonomy is both a blessing and a curse for liberal democratic states, although his reasons are slightly different from Galston's. "Even if a wide-ranging ethical autonomy is intrinsic to political virtue, its free development may often pull against the civic responsibility those same virtues entail. Autonomous reflection does not necessarily lead everyone to a way of life in which civic engagement has an impressively prominent place" (Callan, 1997, p. 11). Whether autonomous reflection prompts certain citizens to deny the authority of liberal democratic principles or merely to shirk their civic duties (and here one is tempted to think of those economists and game theorists who don't vote because they have figured out that it is not rational to do so), there is no doubt that a kind of tension exists between civic education and education for autonomy. But it is a tension that liberal democratic states must accept on pain of illegitimacy. The stability of liberal democratic regimes cannot be guaranteed precisely because the continued consent of autonomous individuals can never be taken for granted: true supporters of liberal democracy are obliged to engage in a ceaseless process of persuasion that must not cross the fine line to become an exercise in brainwashing. The fact that education for autonomy might undermine support for the liberal state is not a reason to oppose education for autonomy, but it does alert us to the dangers of complacently assuming that the future health of our political order can ever be assured.

The next objection I want briefly to consider centers on the misery that children may suffer if they are torn between a deeply religious familial culture, with parents who oppose ethical autonomy and believe, for example, that the authority of the Bible should be accepted without reflection, and a school that seeks to instill in children a commitment to critical scrutiny of their values and beliefs. Mandatory education for autonomy is intended especially to benefit children from these kinds of traditional or fundamentalist homes, and yet ironically they are precisely the children who will suffer most from the dissonance between home and school environments. Perhaps the instrumental value of ethical autonomy is outweighed in certain cases by the damage that would be done to the child by establishing such a rift between the educational goals of home and school. Whether the child identifies with the values of one sphere of her life more than the other or, as seems more probable, she is buffeted around in confusion between these two starkly different places, she is likely to experience great discomfort, no little misery, and perhaps lasting psychological damage. Can all this be justified in the name of cultivating ethical autonomy for its instrumental value?

I think this objection rests, in part, on a flawed but common assumption about the best way to design schools so as to cultivate ethical autonomy in the children of religious fundamentalists. As I shall argue in chapter 8, pronounced dissonance between home and school values is unlikely to help develop autonomy in young children, and so this approach should not be prescribed by a liberal state whose education policy is informed by the autonomy goal. But it is true, I shall argue, that the development of autonomy in older children of many religious parents will be best served by placing those children in schools that represent a definite break from the familial culture. Such children can indeed be expected to experience some problems oscillating between the two worlds of home and school, although the phenomenon of teenagers warring with their parents is hardly limited to cases of families in which the parents have been constrained by the state in their choice of secondary school. A degree of suffering as children develop their own identities and conflict with parental expectations is not surprising, and it may reasonably be regarded as a necessary evil in the case of children from families that oppose the development of ethical autonomy. Children have a long life to lead after they leave home, and it would require an unacceptably short-term perspective to believe that they are better off without ethical autonomy just because its development would exacerbate the tensions of their teenage life.

One might try to sharpen the objection by specifying the most likely cause of suffering among older children who are required to attend a school where the official enthusiasm for autonomous reflection contrasts starkly with the familial culture. These children will suffer, the objection might run, because they are forced to think and act in ways that are offensive to *their own* values. Although they are still children, the teenage progeny of devoutly religious parents may well have strongly held beliefs and commitments that the liberal state should respect as constitutive of their identity and life plan. Just as the state may not force adult fundamentalists to attend an autonomy boot camp, it should not forcibly expose teenagers to alternative ethical doctrines and compel them to reflect critically about their own. But we should beware this line of argument: we should not cut childhood short just because parents have succeeded in instilling in their fifteen-year-old child a deep commitment to the parents' preferred ethical doctrine. As Brighouse (1998, p. 738) argues, "we should not regard children's conceptions as their own, because they are unequipped to make them genuinely their own." Of course, people can identify with their conceptions nonautonomously, as was discussed in chapter 3, but there is still every reason to assume that teenage children have not yet reached the level of intellectual, social, and emotional maturity to be regarded as having their own, settled ethical convictions. So, although we should not delight in children's feelings of pain and confusion when they confront an alien school environment, nor should we feel duty-bound to spare them any such experience that offends their fledgling values.

The final objection I address posits that the liberal state should stop short of actively *promoting* autonomy but should instead ensure that all persons receive an education that *enables* them to live an autonomous life, should they so choose (Brighouse, 1998, p. 733). Enabling means teaching children *how* to engage in autonomous reflection, something that is admittedly best learned through practice, much like the art of painting. But one can still teach someone how to paint without promoting painting as an activity. "I'm making you do this to expand your skills and future options," the teacher can periodically explain, "but when you leave school there's no reason to continue painting unless you happen to like it." Those who support enabling but oppose promoting autonomy might like to see autonomous reflection taught like painting, as a skill that one might rationally decide not to use in one's future life.

I suspect that this objection to promoting autonomy is grounded in the sense that there is something strange, perhaps even contradictory, about "the compulsory inculcation of autonomy" (Barry, 2001, p. 120). Perhaps the idea of schools forcing children to think for themselves has the superficial flavor of a paradox, but there is certainly nothing paradoxical about forcing parents to send their children to schools whose curriculum and institutional culture will positively encourage autonomy rather than merely enabling it. In the next chapter, I consider more fully the view that schools, as institutions of social control, are inherently ill suited to encourage free thinking, and I argue that this view rests on a failure to distinguish between conditions suitable for the *cultivation* of autonomy and those that facilitate the *exercise* of autonomy. If it is true, as I have argued, that people stand to benefit by developing ethical autonomy as children and that the liberal state can legitimately adopt this principle as part of its education policy, then it will be an important task for education researchers to identify the forms of schooling that best promote autonomy: I certainly cannot take on that task in full, but I offer some reflections in the remaining chapters of this work.

For some theorists, including White (1982) and Aviram (1995), the idea that the liberal state should merely enable, not promote, personal autonomy seems to mean that the liberal state cannot urge children to endorse the intrinsic value of an autonomous life. Aviram may have this in mind when she objects to the idea that the liberal state might insist upon autonomy as a "life ideal." To the extent that this phrase alludes to the intrinsic value of autonomy, Aviram is absolutely right: as I discussed in chapter 4, the liberal state has no business promoting the autonomous life as a vision of human flourishing. But it is less clear what to make of Aviram's (p. 70) insistence that autonomy "is only a springboard from which the student may jump to the life ideal of his/her choice and even forsake autonomy, if the chosen life ideal contradicts it." If this means that the liberal state cannot promote the instrumental value of maintaining a commitment to think critically about ethical questions throughout one's life, then I think Aviram is wrong. The value of reflecting rationally on one's ethical doctrine is not exhausted by a one-time autonomous decision at age eighteen. But if Aviram means only to say that adults who have been educated for autonomy are always at liberty to renounce autonomy without fear of being coerced by the liberal state, then she is right. The liberal state's endorsement of autonomy does not undermine its opposition to paternalism of adults: autonomy can and should be publicly valued and encouraged in children through schools, but adults must not be discriminated against if they choose not to exercise autonomy in their own lives.

It is worth taking a moment to explain and justify this proposed difference between the liberal state's treatment of children and its conduct toward adults. The liberal state legitimately judges that parents who deny the instrumental value of personal autonomy are wrong and consequently demands that their child receive a formal education that will serve her best interests by cultivating autonomy. Why, then, is the state not also entitled to send the recalcitrant parents to autonomy boot camp on the basis of a similar judgment about their own best interests? The answer lies in the liberal state's strong opposition to paternalistic coercion of adults.

There are two fundamental ethical values at stake—the freedom to live as one prefers, and the value of living a good life—and a conflict arises between these two values when the goodness of the life one prefers is compromised by the fact that one's conception of the good contains false beliefs or inconsistent values or does not fit one's character and aspirations. The liberal state wants to see its citizens live good lives and asserts the value of autonomous reflection as a method for improving the goodness of the life one prefers. As I shall discuss in the conclusion, such a state should therefore adopt policies that encourage the development and exercise of autonomy among its adult citizens. But the liberal state's primary commitment to adults is to safeguard their freedom to live as they prefer (within the bounds of moral permissibility) and in accordance with their settled ethical convictions, whatever these may be and whether or not they are held autonomously. In other words, in its treatment of adults who prefer not to live autonomously, the liberal state prioritizes the freedom to live as one prefers over coercive measures that would increase one's chances of finding and leading a better life.

Children, by contrast, are regarded neither as having settled ethical convictions[6] nor as being sufficiently mature agents to have their life preferences respected when doing so would stymie their development of autonomy and thereby diminish their chances of finding and leading a better life. There is much debate over the exact age at which childhood should legally end for the purposes of education policy, and I will not enter that debate here, except to assert that the decision should be guided principally by our knowledge of the emotional and cognitive development of adolescents, rather than by cultural or economic considerations.[7] But, leaving aside this difficult line-drawing issue, there should be no serious disagreement with the proposition that there exists a category of "young" children for whom paternalism is appropriate. "The question is not whether six year-olds will be independent in the manner of adults. That was decided by nature. What nature has left to society is the design of the paternalism most likely to advance the interest of the individual child" (Coons and Sugarman, 1999, p. 47).

I have argued in this chapter that paternalistic reasoning justifies dividing authority over children between parents, who should have

---

[6] In Rawlsian language, we would say that children lack a developed capacity for a conception of the good.

[7] For an example of the kind of argument that belongs in this debate, see Coleman (2002), who uses evidence from developmental psychology to argue that we should draw the line significantly below the age of eighteen.

broad discretion to direct children's upbringing outside of institutions of formal education, and the state, which should insure that all children receive a formal education that cultivates their personal autonomy. It may also help to recall that both the state and parents have legitimate nonpaternalistic interests in children's upbringing: the state properly pursues civic educational goals through its education policy, and parents are entitled to express their own values through child-rearing. A comprehensive liberal account of the treatment of children would have to balance the paternalistic and nonpaternalistic claims of both the state and parents to determine the justified division of authority in all of the various spheres and phases of children's lives.

Conclusion

In chapter 4, I argued that a liberal state can legitimately endorse the instrumental value of ethical autonomy in spite of the objections of religious parents and others. In this chapter, I have tried to show that the liberal state can and should act on that judgment by mandating education for personal autonomy. In particular, I argued that such an education policy is not objectionable either as a violation of parents' rights to direct their children's upbringing or as a failure to show appropriate respect for traditional ways of life that are incompatible with autonomy. Parents do have rights, and cultures do have value for their members, but neither of these claims can be extended to argue that children can legitimately be denied a formal education that equips them to try to find and live the best life for themselves. Autonomous individuals may be more likely to dissent from liberal democratic principles, but this is a risk that liberal democracies must take: nonautonomous citizens' political participation will not be informed by the requisite virtue of reasonableness, and their consent will not confer legitimacy upon the regime. Children from some traditional families may suffer as they are torn between the attitudes at home and school, but that suffering can reasonably be seen as a necessary and short-term evil. Because children are not regarded as having settled ethical identities and convictions, the state may legitimately require that they be exposed to ideas and arguments that offend their embryonic values: childhood is the phase of a person's life during which the liberal state can and should act paternalistically to teach both the capacity and the inclination for autonomous ethical reflection.

PART III

Religious Schools and Education for Autonomy

Chapter 6

SECULAR PUBLIC SCHOOLS: CRITIQUES

AND RESPONSES

THE ARGUMENT of the previous part might seem to suggest that religious schools should not be supported, or perhaps even permitted, by the state unless they can be demonstrated to be effective instruments of education for autonomy. But we must be careful not to move too quickly. Before we can assess the implications of the autonomy goal for public policy toward religious schools, and certainly before we can mount any kind of autonomy-based argument against religious schooling, we need to ask whether the alternative, namely, secular schooling, can reasonably be expected to advance children's development of autonomy. Of course, as I discussed in chapter 2, some religious parents object to secular public schools precisely because they believe that such schools have the effect of promoting ethical autonomy. But perhaps this belief, on further examination and especially when seen in the light of the more nuanced conception of autonomy I developed in chapter 3, will turn out to be false.

It might be a mistake to characterize the ethical dimension of secular education as mere even-handed exposure to and critical engagement with a diverse range of doctrines. More fundamentally, it might be a mistake to think that these kinds of encounters with ethical diversity during one's formative years are likely to develop one's autonomy. Even if certain forms of religious education do little to advance the autonomy goal, it may be that secular education is typically no better. We must also consider the charge that any attempt by public authorities to regulate and control schools poses a threat to children's autonomy, ironically even if the intervention's stated purpose is precisely to promote education for autonomy. And, most radically, it may be that we are misguided in thinking that the school as an institutional form is capable of encouraging genuinely independent critical-thinking skills and inclinations in children. If some or all of these concerns turn out to be well-founded, then there would be no clear public policy implications of any finding that certain types of religious school fail to cultivate children's ethical autonomy.

So, in this chapter I defend secular schools, and especially those controlled by the state, from a diverse range of critiques, all of which aim
to show that such schools are unsuitable to play a positive role in education for autonomy. I shall not deny that many existing secular public
schools in contemporary liberal democracies fail to advance children's
autonomy, but that empirical fact tells us little about what suitably re-
formed and restructured secular public schools could achieve, especially if teachers and other educational professionals were encouraged
to adopt the cultivation of autonomy as a primary goal for their efforts
and liberated from the relentless pressure to improve children's performance on a whole battery of dubious tests. My defense of the viability
of effective education for autonomy in secular public schools will set
the stage for the final pair of chapters, where I ask whether and under
what conditions religious primary and secondary schools can live up
to the standards of education for autonomy that can realistically be
achieved in secular public schools.

In what follows, I shall explore a sequence of increasingly radical
critiques of the idea that secular public schools are suited to advance
children's ethical autonomy in a way that might plausibly mark them
as superior to certain types of religious school. In responding to these
critiques, I shall not suggest that any of them is obviously and exclusively misguided. Rather, I shall argue that such critical perspectives
are important reminders that a liberal democratic state must always
be vigilant lest the schools it authorizes and supports become sites of
indoctrination or otherwise fail to cultivate children's autonomy. It is
beyond the scope of this work to propose a detailed model of a liberal,
secular school, complete with its curriculum, pedagogical methods,
structures of administration and government, mechanisms of teacher
accountability and incentives, disciplinary code, etc.[1] I hope to show
through my responses that the dangers to autonomy associated with
secular education, public control, and the institutional form of schools
are not necessarily so grave that we should abandon the idea that education for autonomy can effectively be pursued through secular public
schools and therefore that religious schools have a benchmark to meet
or exceed. My responses may appear hopelessly optimistic to some
readers: I shall often say that a particular danger is real, but that an
enlightened liberal democracy, genuinely committed to the value of
autonomy and vividly aware of precisely that danger, can realistically
hope to avoid it. Liberal education, just like liberal democracy more

---

[1] I shall, however, advance some thoughts that bear on these matters in the next two
chapters when I propose the respective hallmarks of primary and secondary *religious*
schools that should be considered compatible with the goal of education for autonomy.

generally, is a demanding ideal to realize, and it probably does take a certain degree of optimism to believe that the difficulties can be overcome. In what follows, I can do little more than allude to the grounds for that optimism, but I hope, despite these disclaimers, that my responses will appear substantive and perhaps even persuasive.

WHAT'S WRONG WITH SECULAR EDUCATION?

According to certain defenders of religious education, it is a mistake to think that the secular character of common schools makes them more suitable than religious schools for cultivating ethical autonomy in students. Perhaps the most commonly encountered form of this argument in America is the charge that secular schools are really preaching the "religion" of "secular humanism," an effort at socialization (or even indoctrination) into a substantive ethical doctrine that is therefore vulnerable to all the same autonomy-based criticisms that might be leveled at religious schools. The plaintiffs in the *Mozert* case, discussed in chapter 5, made a version of this argument, among many others. And Brian Crittenden (1988, p. 149) is clearly sympathetic to the view:

> Public schools uphold (in fact if not by intention) various forms of a secular ideal of human life. Depending on the group of teachers and other conditions, the ideal as it affects knowledge is likely to be a form of scientific rationality or romantic relativism or some combination; and in relation to values of life more broadly, it may well be strongly tinged by possessive individualism or egalitarianism (or, perhaps, some curious mixture of the two).

Some educational professionals and policy-makers, along with some regular citizens, doubtless believe in the tenets of "secular humanism" and may see it as desirable and proper that secular schools should promote this ethical doctrine. Such people are, according to this critique, essentially no different from religious believers who want to see their faith taught in schools: neither group could plausibly invoke the value of autonomy selectively to indict the other group's preferred schools.

But those who are opposed to the idea that schools should teach children to be good secular humanists may nonetheless support secular schools because they believe that these schools do not, or at least *need not*, have the effect of promoting secular humanism. Secular schools, properly conceived, do not preach an atheistic religion: rather, they equip and encourage children to make their own reflective ethical choices among options that include traditional religious doctrines. In responding to this defense of secular schooling, critics frequently make one or both of two claims about the impossibility of ethical neutrality in education, in an effort to show that we can choose our normative biases but never eliminate them. First, and most obviously, critics point out that ethical neutrality is impossible if it means giving equal time and consideration to the study of all ethical doctrines, or even just to all those with significant numbers of adherents in the society (or the world?). As McConnell (1991a, p. 143) quite rightly observes, any serious attempt to give equal time in this manner would rapidly lead to curricular incoherence and overload: therefore, any school's curriculum will always exhibit a certain bias in favor of particular substantive ethical doctrines and against others. But McConnell (p. 142) also makes, in a curious tension with the first claim, a more sophisticated and contentious second claim, namely, that a school's policy of remaining "neutral" on questions of religious truth has the inevitable and undesirable effect of encouraging students to believe in a form of ethical relativism. This is not a substantive ethical doctrine but rather a meta-ethical view that turns out to be at odds with the value of ethical autonomy itself.

Ethical relativism here refers to the idea that there is and can be no truth in ethics that is universal; if there are right answers, even better answers, to be found, these normative judgments will properly apply only within particular traditions or communities. Relativism therefore implies that there is little progress to be made in ethics through dialogue between these traditions or communities: since Helene and James inhabit different groups, they rightly recognize different standards of justification and/or sources of evidence in ethics, so there is no scope for Helene rationally to persuade James of the superiority of her own doctrine. An ethical relativist might argue that schools should remain "neutral" on ethical questions because there are never any universal, rational grounds for preferring one ethical doctrine to another;[2] critics turn this claim around to suggest that a secular school's neutrality is, or at least appears to be, underpinned by a meta-ethical commitment to ethical relativism.

A radical version of ethical relativism, and one that especially concerns many critics of secular schools, might appropriately be labeled ethical subjectivism, according to which the unit within which particular ethical judgments rightly apply is limited to the individual person whose judgments they are. Some version of ethical relativism, perhaps subjectivism, apparently underlies the so-called Values Clarification

---

[2] This is not, of course, the only way one might apply ethical relativism to education policy: one might argue instead for separate schools for separate communities, each of which would then be free to teach its ethical doctrine to its own children.

strategy for teaching personal ethics, which has found favor in the American public schools at various times in recent history (Dent, 1988, p. 869). According to advocates of "Values Clarification," students' ethical development is properly pursued merely by encouraging children to reflect on and choose (or otherwise identify) their own values, without imposing any particular standard to guide this process.[3] Critics charge that the even-handedness and "neutrality" of all secular schools favor and promote ethical subjectivism or relativism, whether or not this is the intention of those who run the schools.

The ideal of ethical autonomy, as I sketched it in chapters 3 and 4, does share some ground with the principle of ethical relativism: there is no single best way to live that can be shown to apply to all persons, and the best ethical doctrine for an agent is partly a matter for choice or self-definition by that agent. If that were all that McConnell's charge amounted to, then secular schools should not be afraid to endorse ethical relativism. But McConnell means to make a more worrying claim, namely, that secular schools' bracketing of religious questions and truth-claims encourages children to believe that nothing can be gained by arguing rationally about ethics because ethics is ultimately just a matter of nonrational individual preference or taste (Callan, 1997, p. 207). If secular schools do indeed prompt children to give up on rational reflection and deliberation about ethical issues, then such schools are hardly promoting the ideal of autonomy that I have proposed. Ethical relativism in its fullest sense is the parent of a conception of autonomy that is altogether less valuable than the one I have tried to describe. Barry (2001, p. 224) characterizes this debased notion of autonomy in typically scathing terms: "On an all-too-common conception of autonomy, what it calls for is encouraging children to express the way they feel about a thing, whether or not these feelings have any adequate grounding in reality."

So, we have now reviewed three different arguments for the conclusion that secular education has no special claim to be autonomy-promoting. First, secular education is really inculcation into a substantive ethical doctrine, popularly known as secular humanism. Second, education for autonomy would require neutrality in the form of equal treatment of and equal time for all ethical positions, but this is impossible. Third, secular schooling encourages a kind of easy ethical relativ-

---

[3] Notice that I am not discussing "Values Clarification" as a technique of moral education, to help children form their views about the moral status of murder and rape—see my distinction between moral and ethical autonomy at the beginning of chapter 3. I therefore do not consider here the important question of whether children's moral development is better served by the authoritative teaching of accepted moral values or by stimulating autonomous moral reflection.

ism rather than the serious rational reflection and deliberation that are the hallmarks of the autonomous person. The first two of these concerns, I hope to show, are misguided, but the third deserves our attention: fears that even-handed exposure to ethical diversity with the accompanying civic lessons in toleration will actually discourage sustained ethical deliberation must be acknowledged and combated as we design schools, train teachers, and make educational policy.

The idea that secular schools (and other supposedly religion-free institutions of the liberal state) actually preach the so-called religion of secular humanism emerged from the Christian fundamentalist movement in America, which itself arose in the nineteenth and twentieth centuries in opposition to the practice of critical Bible scholarship.[4] As has often been pointed out, it is unclear what "secular humanism" really amounts to, and the decision to label it a "religion" was apparently a legal strategy designed to open the possibility of challenging the system of exclusively secular public schools as a violation of the U.S. Constitution's First Amendment prohibition on established religion. If secular humanism means only a commitment to the value of critical-rational inquiry in all domains of human knowledge, including religion and ethics, then it is another name for autonomy, and the critics' charge just reduces to pointing out that some religious people sincerely deny the value of autonomy. I have already responded to this charge in chapter 4. But if secular humanism means something more than autonomy, and in particular if it is alleged that a secular education necessarily espouses substantive ethical commitments of a sort that are fundamentally at odds with religious belief, then I think the allegation is unfounded.

Secular schools need not aim to eliminate or even to discourage religious belief: they are called secular because of the absence of a religious purpose, not because of any opposition to religion. As we have seen, certain types of religious faith—those that are incompatible with or necessarily exploded by adequate critical-rational thought and those that rely on the absence of exposure to alternative ethical doctrines—cannot be held by a truly autonomous person. But, as Callan (1988; 1997, p. 38) has argued, religious faith is not incompatible with ethical autonomy, although the faith of an autonomous person is a more self-conscious and intellectually sophisticated matter than what might be called the "faith of innocence." Certain religious beliefs ought not to survive the development of ethical autonomy because they are manifestly contra-

[4] For a brief, interesting history, see Stolzenberg (1993, pp. 614–28).

dicted by the empirical evidence.[5] Other beliefs should be discarded when autonomous reflection reveals to the agent that they are isolated from and inconsistent with many of her most settled convictions. But ethical autonomy does not rule out religious faith in general, even though ethically autonomous persons will often have decisive reasons to reject particular religious beliefs that some nonautonomous persons accept as a matter of faith. Typically, many articles of a person's faith are perfectly capable of surviving genuine and thorough autonomous reflection: there is no decisive evidence against them, and they are not at odds with the person's existing structure of beliefs and values. Admittedly, autonomous reflection might result in certain persons' discarding particular religious beliefs that were nonetheless *capable* of surviving such reflection, but other persons may well adopt those very same religious beliefs through the exercise of ethical autonomy: this is only to be expected given the burdens of judgment (Rawls, 1993/1996, pp. 54–58). As I discussed in chapter 3, autonomous reflection is a form of choice and self-definition, albeit guided both by the standards of reason and by one's unchosen cultural background. The development of autonomy will hopefully be revelatory and/or liberating for many persons, and it is likely to lead persons to make some revisions to the beliefs and values with which they were raised, but it is not incompatible with maintaining or acquiring religious faith.

We should not be disturbed by the second concern about secular schools as sites of education for autonomy, namely, the claim that only an educational regime of equal time and consideration for all ethical doctrines would establish conditions of true ethical neutrality: no such demanding conditions are necessary to cultivate autonomy. As Raz (1986, p. 410) has pointed out, autonomy does not require that all valuable options be equally available for choice. As we shall see in the next chapter, all that we should require of secondary schools is that children be exposed to a significant diversity of ethical doctrines, extending well beyond the particular religious or other ethical commitments of their parents, and that the exposure be managed in an institution that teaches and encourages open-minded, critical-rational engagement with this diversity. A secondary school whose curriculum included critical examination of Christian, Hindu, and secular ethics could not be faulted on autonomy grounds for failing to cover Buddhism or Islam. This is not to deny that there will often be controversy about the composition of the curriculum and student body in secular schools:

---

[5] The belief that the Earth was created only a few thousand years ago is one good example.

although the development of autonomy does not and could not require exposure to all reasonable doctrines, it is possible that children are more likely to see the merits of a particular way of life if they are exposed to it at school, whether through a class in the comparative study of religion or through peer interaction with children of a certain faith. The key point for my purposes, however, is that education for autonomy does not require complete neutrality and equality of exposure: political battles will be fought over the organization of secular schools, and there may be important principles other than autonomy at stake in these battles, but none of this calls into doubt the principle that secular schools can effectively promote children's autonomy without meeting the chimerical requirement of giving equal time to the study of every ethical and religious doctrine.

Lastly, I want to address what I consider to be the most serious concern about the suitability of secular schools to cultivate children's autonomy. Critics charge that the failure of a school to espouse a substantive ethical doctrine, and methods like "Values Clarification" that often accompany this studied neutrality on questions of the good life, might give children the impression that ethics is simply the domain of subjective caprice and therefore that serious rational reflection would be a waste of time. In a sense, this concern is the inverse of the charge that secular schools inevitably preach, or at least favor, particular substantive conceptions of the good: according to this last line of criticism, the problem with secular schools is precisely that they take no concrete position on ethical questions and thereby set a bad example to their students. Children will be exposed to and encouraged to discuss a diverse range of ethical views, but the secular school can never come down on one side of the debate, and this may lead children to believe in some version of ethical relativism or subjectivism. Callan (1997, p. 196) voices this concern about effective education for autonomy (which is also for him, in light of his argument that good liberal democratic citizens must be ethically autonomous, a concern about civic and moral education). "Dialogue that merely gives expression to divergent moral views might encourage among children or adolescents a sense of the futility of deliberation about the good and the right or engender a feckless skepticism or relativism in the face of apparently intractable differences."

Since in ethics, unlike in mathematics, there is no answer that can be conclusively shown by a process of rational deliberation to be correct for all persons, children's expectations must be carefully managed if they are not to be disappointed by the outcome of the exchange and examination of ethical views that secular schools are concerned to facilitate. As Callan (p. 214) notes, sometimes "dialogue may take us nowhere because there is no more balanced and sober truth to be had."

But ethical dialogue does not have to be unsatisfying simply because it will not lead us all to agree on a universally best way of life. As I argued in chapter 4, ethical autonomy has real instrumental value for persons seeking to live a good life, and children should be helped to see that value for themselves even when debate does not converge on a single right answer. The secular school does promote meaningful standards for evaluating ethical positions—internal consistency among one's beliefs and values at various levels of abstraction, claims supported by reasons and evidence rather than assertions and shows of power—although those standards do not select a unique winner. So, as Reich (2002, p. 184) argues, proper liberal education does not promote "nonjudgmental relativism," but it does try to shape ethical deliberation by encouraging "a slowness to judge or an interpretive generosity that precludes knee-jerk assessment of other cultures, cultural practices, or cultural products from one's own point of view."

We all know that debates about ethics can quickly descend into intolerant name-calling and disrespect for other religions and cultures. But just as bad, or arguably even worse, these debates may deteriorate into the wholly uncritical exchange of views in which participants do not dare to ask each other for justification, perhaps because they are ignorant of what form justification might take or skeptical that it is a meaningful possibility in ethics. This is the important truth in McConnell's (1991, p. 143) discussion of ethical relativism and Dent's (1988, p. 869) concerns about "Values Clarification": the lessons to be learned by those who support education for autonomy are that it is a demanding aspiration and that there are certain pits into which secular schools are especially liable to fall. We must redouble our efforts to find effective pedagogical and curricular strategies for cultivating students' ethical autonomy through classroom exposure to and deliberation about diverse ethical doctrines.[6] Secular schools will never fully live up to our ideals in this respect, but that is no reason to give up on those ideals or on the realistic belief that such schools can be effective in educating children for autonomy.

PUBLIC CONTROL OF SCHOOLS

Next, I want to consider the claim that public control of educational institutions is itself inimical to the autonomy goal, a claim that is most famously made by John Stuart Mill in *On Liberty*.

---

[6] Many of the strategies I propose in the next two chapters are readily applicable to secular schools.

That the whole or any large part of the education of the people
should be in State hands, I go as far as anyone in deprecating. . . .
A general State education is a mere contrivance for moulding people to be exactly like one another: and as the mould in which it
casts them is that which pleases the predominant power in the
government, whether this be a monarch, a priesthood, an aristoc-
racy, or the majority of the existing generation, in proportion as it
is efficient and successful, it establishes a despotism over the
mind. (1859/1989, p. 106)

More recently, Stephen Arons (1983) has made this same critique of the
American public schools, which he argues socialize children into a set
of orthodox beliefs and values. It is worth noting that, although Mill
and Arons both focus much of their energy on direct public management of schools, their objections also extend to anything more than
minimal public regulation of the operation of private schools. When
Arons (1983, pp. 189–90) proposes a "complete separation of school
and state" so that government will cease to be a "deadening agent of
repression" in education, he is opposing almost all forms of government intervention in the decisions that parents make about their children's education. And, as we have seen, Mill (p. 107) believed that the
state's role as an overseer of private educational arrangements was
merely to ensure that the most basic and uncontroversial skills and
knowledge were being taught in an effective fashion. Minimally regulated private religious schools may not enhance children's capacity for
ethically autonomous reasoning, but, on this view, schools that are run
or extensively regulated by the state simply have the effect of promoting a nonreligious doctrinal orthodoxy that is no friendlier to the
autonomy goal.

As Mill notes, the particular orthodoxy that public control of education promotes depends on the form of government: in a democratic
state, the fear is that schools that are managed or extensively regulated
by the government simply transmit majority opinion to students. Of
course, to the extent that the spirit of liberalism infuses a particular
society, its schools will not intentionally and consciously seek to indoctrinate children in the tenets of majority opinion,[7] but the effects of

---

[7] As I discussed in the first part of this work, schools in the liberal democratic state
can and should teach the moral values that underlie liberal democracy, but even this
instruction must not descend into indoctrination: since the legitimacy of a liberal democratic regime relies on the free consent of the citizenry, the liberal state must not manu-
facture unreflective and nonrational civic commitments. And, as Dennis Thompson
pointed out to me, the state must be wary of teaching one particular political conception
of liberal democracy to the exclusion of other reasonable conceptions.

public control are, according to many critics, insidious. Coons and Sugarman (1999, pp. 42–43) make this point in their description of contemporary American public schools: "by and large the schools shun explicit treatment of controversial moral or political views. Implicitly, however, they endorse majoritarian social and political norms." In a diverse pluralist society, ethical norms that command majority support in the state as a whole may be few in number and rather general in nature: the notion that material affluence is an important measure of personal success might be an example of such a norm in many contemporary liberal democratic states. But, especially in countries like America where control of schools is highly decentralized, the more pressing concern is that local majorities with a deeper and more extensive set of shared ethical values will (perhaps unconsciously) shape schools in such a way that they promote a relatively narrow conception of the good life. One might think, for example, of homogeneously Christian regions of the American South and the influence of their local dominant ethical norms on the character of their public schools.

On this account, public control of schools is no kind of safeguard of children's autonomy interests: the choice is simply between allowing parents to socialize their children into their particular ethical worldview and mandating the forced assimilation of all children to a public orthodoxy (McConnell, 1991a, pp. 136–37). If this were the rather bleak choice, one might reasonably think that liberals should prefer the former option, albeit perhaps balanced by the civic concerns discussed in part 1 of this work. According to Mill (1859/1989, p. 73), all forms of education actually tend to promote conformity and assimilation "because education brings people under common influences, and gives them access to the general stock of facts and sentiments." This is not, of course, an argument against compulsory education, but it is a warning to liberals to beware the homogenizing effects of schools and not to aggravate the problem by placing the primary authority over schools in the hands of democratic majorities. Ironically, even if public control is justified precisely by the goal of ensuring that schools promote children's autonomy, the political reality may be that such state intervention is counterproductive.

What are we to make of Mill's and Arons' claim that democratic control of schools is a kind of tyranny of the (local) majority that serves to transmit to the next generation the orthodox beliefs and values of the present generation, in violation of the principle that children should be learning to think critically and for themselves? Undoubtedly, there is a real and omnipresent risk that supposedly liberal democratic educational authorities will sacrifice the liberal value of ethical autonomy to an insufficiently constrained democratic majoritarianism; this is especially likely to happen at the level of the local school board, whose members and constituents often have a shared commitment to a much broader and deeper set of substantive ethical values than could command majority support at the level of national education policymaking. When majority opinion becomes the ethical orthodoxy in publicly controlled schools, it is common to assume that the only people who are really harmed are the children and parents of families whose ethical doctrines are minority views. But, interestingly, if education aims at satisfying all children's interest in developing autonomy, it is arguably the case that more harm is done to the majority than to the minority.

As I shall argue in opposing certain types of religious secondary schools in the next chapter, all children lose out on an education for autonomy when their secondary school teaches a particular ethical doctrine to the exclusion of the critical thinking skills and exposure to diversity needed to prepare them for choice among doctrines. But children whose parents subscribe to a minority view at least hear a different story at home, and it is possible that the conflict between the ethics of home and school may prompt some serious attempts at ethical reflection in these children. By contrast, children whose parents belong to the ethical majority are most in need of a genuinely detached school to stimulate their autonomy. Therefore, the fact that Arons focuses on the complaints of minority religious groups reminds us that his argument against public control of schools is not in the name of children's autonomy, but rather in defense of parents' rights to raise their children in the faith.[8] In fact, the orthodoxy that many devout religious parents identify and vehemently oppose in the public schools is precisely a belief in the value of ethical autonomy: as I have argued, even in a liberal pluralist society, there are some values, both civic and noncivic, that we should aspire to instill in all children.

The preceding analysis makes clear that the autonomy liberal's response to the dangers of an ethical orthodoxy propagated by public schools cannot be to relinquish public control of education and leave the matter to individual families. Exclusive parental control of education is at least as great a threat to children's autonomy as is public control, and we do not want simply to replace one evil with another. Of course, if education is unavoidably going to be mere indoctrination, then there is no autonomy-based argument for insisting that the state rather than the parents get to choose the content of that indoctrination. But I do not think we are obliged to accept this bleak conclusion. The views of Mill, Arons, and others serve as forceful and necessary reminders to liberal democratic citizens that public secondary schools

---

[8] I responded to arguments based in supposed parental rights in chapter 5.

can all too easily fall off from their mission of cultivating autonomy. This falling off may be the result of deliberate subversion or of an equally worrying but less easily detected unconscious bias on the parts of teachers, administrators, and school board officials. Realistically, schools will probably always transmit some ethical values without giving students sufficient opportunity and encouragement to engage in critical reflection. But although the theoretical ideal may be unattainable, some schools will approximate it far more closely than others, and so the best response to Mill and others is not despair but vigilance. Those like Levinson (1999, p. 89) who sincerely believe in the autonomy goal must remain vividly aware of the worry that even secular public schools are liable to "teach a culturally situated informal curriculum that will reflect and reinforce the norms of the dominant culture in society." One practical measure to help ensure that public schools do not simply transmit the ethical commitments of the majority is Gutmann's (1999, p. 44) proposal that a significant share of educational authority be vested in independent educational professionals, who can serve as a third force against both parents and democratic majorities.[9] However, the long-term stability and success of a policy of education for autonomy depends upon maintaining in citizens both an active support for the goal and a heightened awareness of the continual tendency for public schools to serve simply as conduits for transmitting majority values and beliefs to children.

AUTHORITY AND AUTONOMY

Finally, I want to consider a truly radical claim, Ivan Illich's contention that compulsory school attendance, regardless of who controls the schools and whether they can teach religious doctrine, is at odds with the liberal goal of encouraging autonomy in children. The problem, according to Illich, lies with the basic features of the institutional form we call "school." Education in schools is "teacher-centered" in that it "requires an authoritarian presence to define for the participants the starting point for their discussion" (Illich, 1971, p. 20): there is a stark incompatibility between the educational goal of autonomy and "the fundamental approach common to all schools—the idea that one per-

[9] Gutmann casts educational professionals specifically as custodians of children's independent interest in developing autonomy, but more would need to be said, especially about mechanisms of training and accountability, to substantiate the claim that educational professionals can reliably be expected to play this role, rather than to pursue a different conception of children's good or some sectional interest unrelated to children's needs altogether.

son's judgment should determine what and when another person must learn" (p. 42). In short, "compulsory learning cannot be a liberal enterprise" (p. 65). While both the state and parents are capable of subverting or, in a limited form, supporting a child's development of autonomy, no authority in the child's life can effectively mandate an educational path to autonomy because all such stipulations will crush the child's embryonic autonomy. If Illich is right, the development of children's autonomy is frustrated not only by religious schools but also by secular schools, so the state cannot invoke the autonomy goal to justify any preference for the latter over the former.

Much of Illich's critique of schools focuses on the role of the teacher. In a powerful evocation of the personal and formal authority that teachers possess in relation to their young charges, Illich (pp. 30–31) declares that teachers simultaneously play the roles of "custodian," "moralist," and "therapist" in the lives of their students. As Crittenden (1988, pp. 148–49) notes, it is widely accepted in contemporary liberal democratic societies that schools have a broad educational role to educate "the whole person," albeit in a way that tries to respect the reasonable pluralism of ethical doctrines that may be represented by the families of the children in a single classroom, especially a public school classroom. Crittenden wonders, and one might be tempted to ask of Illich, whether it would be possible for schools to circumscribe their goals more narrowly and for teachers' authority therefore to be confined to matters of technical expertise and basic discipline. But, I suggest, even to ask this question is to see the impossibility of reforming schools so that they will not engage sensitive matters of ethical concern. A school is a community of real people who spend significant portions of their lives in that institution: whether or not "ethics" appears on the formal curriculum, it cannot be imagined that schools could operate without routinely engaging ethical questions and shaping the ethical lives of their students. The question is rather whether the impact of schools on children's ethical development is necessarily at odds with the autonomy goal.

For Illich, the fact that the school experience inevitably has a large ethical dimension entails the necessity of disestablishing education, and not just in the sense that Arons proposes when he talks of "separating school and state." For Illich (p. 11), society must be "deschooled": it is no more acceptable that governments require children's attendance for ten years at an accredited school than it would be for governments to make church attendance mandatory. Mandatory church attendance would scarcely be made more legitimate by the fact that individuals were free to choose their own church from an approved list of options, many of which would not be run by the state. Mandatory school attendance laws require that children assemble daily as a captive audience for institutionalized indoctrination: "Children are protected by neither the First nor the Fifth Amendment when they stand before that secular priest, the teacher" (p. 31). In education, as in religion, Illich (p. 11) insists that "there shall be no ritual obligatory for all." If we endorse Illich's stark assessment that the school's role in ethical education will always amount to ethical indoctrination, we can have no grounds for invoking the educational goal of autonomy selectively to oppose only religious schools. Rather, we must either abandon compulsory schooling altogether or resign ourselves to the thought that public education policy cannot meaningfully take the cultivation of children's autonomy as a goal, in which case any autonomy-based case against religious schools would collapse.

Is Illich right to claim that schools are inherently unsuited to deliver education for autonomy? We must proceed carefully. He is certainly right to observe that inequalities of status and power, such as we typically see between teachers and children in schools,[10] generally exist in a clear tension with the autonomy of those in the subordinate position. But the crucial point is that children in schools are not yet autonomous, and so the exercise of paternalistic authority over them in the name of their own *future* autonomy is not obviously contradictory or incoherent. Undoubtedly, the authority of the teacher can be abused and there is a standing danger, as Levinson (1999, p. 88) acknowledges, that hierarchical "structures that are intrinsic to the process of formal education may at the same time be deleterious to children's development of autonomy." But Illich's (1971, p. 31) assertion that "the claim that a liberal society can be founded on the modern school is paradoxical" is too strong: there is a compelling argument to be made that education for autonomy can and probably must rely on a degree of paternalistic authority and even coercion that could not justifiably be directed at most adults. As Joel Feinberg (1980, p. 127) puts it, "Respect for the child's future autonomy, as an adult, often requires preventing his free choice now," and there is every reason to think that this requirement includes mandatory school attendance (see also Levinson, 1999, pp. 38–41). Certainly, the structures of authority in schools are not necessarily hostile to the goal of cultivating children's autonomy.

It is worth noting that this supposed tension between education for autonomy and failure to heed the present desires of children is to be

[10] Of course, in certain troubled public schools, the authoritative status of the teacher is very much in doubt; I owe this important observation to Dennis Thompson. Nonetheless, we must ask whether the conventional *ideal* of the classroom teacher as an effective authority figure is at odds with the autonomy goal.

found in arguments with conclusions less radical than Illich's. Coons and Sugarman (1999, pp. 85–86) accept that the young child is not qualified to make decisions about his own education, but those same authors insist that a teenager should be allowed broad latitude to choose his secondary school in order "to advance his own autonomy." If the development of autonomy is our goal and one school environment is more suitable than another as an institutional means to that goal, it seems to me profoundly mistaken to leave the choice to children.[11] There is every reason to suspect that a child of fourteen will have at most a hazy view of the potential value to his life of developing the capacity for rationally autonomous reflection. And, even if the teenage child truly seeks to "advance his own autonomy" by his educational choices, he is unlikely to be a good judge of the best means to that goal. Therefore, if one is serious about treating the development of autonomy as a goal of education, one cannot simply devolve educational choices to children, let alone to their parents as do most advocates of "school choice."[12]

Coons and Sugarman seem to share Illich's belief that there is a kind of conceptual incoherence in the idea that one can advance an older child's autonomy while refusing to respect her express preferences. I suspect that this belief derives from an inadequate conception of autonomy, according to which one qualifies as autonomous merely by making choices without being constrained by others. As Dearden (1975, pp. 11–14) argues, freedom is a necessary condition for the *exercise* of autonomy, but it is neither a necessary nor sufficient condition for the *development* of autonomy, which requires learning both a set of intellectual capabilities and a certain self-discipline that cannot be expected to arise spontaneously in children who are granted the freedom to chart their own educational course. "Nurturing the capacity for and exercise of autonomy must come before we respect it" (Reich, 2002, p. 108). Of course, the tension between allowing children to exercise their developing autonomy, on the one hand, and constraining them paternalistically for the sake of further cultivating that autonomy, on the other, becomes more acute as children approach

[11] My argument here has no implications for the question of whether children (or parents) should be allowed to choose between schools all of which are fully compatible with education for autonomy.

[12] Coons and Sugarman (1999, p. 63) write that "we have preferred to call it family choice instead of parent choice because of our conviction that the child's role in the process of selection will be very important in most families." But, whatever may be the case in "most families," parents who oppose their child's development of ethical autonomy are presumably the least likely to take the child's independent preferences into account, especially if he wants to choose a school "to advance his own autonomy."

the age of majority and/or the end of their required formal education, beyond which the liberal state is committed to respecting their choices (p. 95). But, I suggest, until that line is crossed, paternalism remains the right policy: the state should insist that all children attend a secondary school that serves their interest by continuing to cultivate their ethical autonomy. Teenagers might be allowed to choose among autonomy-promoting schools, and teachers within such schools might judge that the best way to encourage a teenager's autonomy is increasingly to respect her choices as she approaches the end of her school days, but teenagers should not be permitted to opt out of education for autonomy.

CONCLUSION

I cannot embark here on any attempt to answer the complex practical questions of how secular public schools should best be run to pursue the autonomy goal: there is a need to address everything from the level of classroom teaching through curriculum design to systemwide issues of public policy and administration. Levinson (1999) offers a sketch of the autonomy-promoting detached school, but her philosopher's blueprint leaves many practical issues unresolved. In the next two chapters, I offer some thoughts on autonomy-friendly curricula and pedagogical methods; although my remarks are geared toward religious schools, they also have important implications for secular schools. For example, children at secular schools might appropriately be addressed by practitioners of various faiths as part of a course in religious studies that encourages fair-minded rational deliberation about the merits of different ethical doctrines.

Doubtless we have a long way to go in identifying effective methods of education for autonomy, but I do not think we need be as pessimistic as Gutmann (1999, p. 60) about the current state of knowledge: "Although is it possible that there is a way that schools can teach autonomy, nobody has come even close to finding it." Presumably there is no single best way. Some of our questions may be settled by empirical research, while many others will doubtless remain fiercely controversial for generations to come. But, I propose, neither these controversies nor the inevitability that any actual system will fall far short of our best models should lead us to abandon our conclusion that secular public schools offer a realistic hope of effective education for autonomy that sets the standard for acceptable religious schools. The various critiques of secular and publicly controlled schools as instruments of education for autonomy are not fatal: rather, we can and should use the misgivings of opponents—about the inherently authoritarian nature of schools, the dynamics of public control, and the message sent by ethical neutrality—to help us identify and guard against the most common errors into which secular public schools tend to fall.

The purpose of this chapter was to show that, contrary to the views of certain prominent critics, secular schools under public control are not necessarily at odds with the educational goal of promoting children's autonomy. Of course, any particular secular public school might (and many existing schools do) operate in a way that is incompatible with this goal, but my responses to the critics are merely intended to vindicate the claim that there is nothing about secular education, schools as institutions, or public control of education that contradicts the autonomy goal. It is not my purpose to provide a model of the ideal autonomy-promoting secular school, but rather to defend the proposition that secular public schools can realistically serve as instruments of education for autonomy. In the next two chapters, I ask whether and under what conditions the same can be said of religious secondary and primary schools. I shall argue that the autonomy goal does not rule out religious schools—indeed it may favor certain types of religious primary school—but that it does impose limits on acceptable pedagogy, and, at the secondary level, that it makes certain demands on the school's curriculum and its openness to those beyond the community of faith.

Chapter 7

RELIGIOUS SECONDARY SCHOOLS AS

THREAT TO AUTONOMY?

IN THE PREVIOUS CHAPTER, I defended the view that secular schools, suitably managed or regulated by the state, can be effective instruments for cultivating children's autonomy. If this is so, we must next ask whether a liberal state that aims to ensure that all of its citizens develop as autonomous persons can consistently fund, or even permit the operation of, various religious schools as alternatives to these secular, autonomy-enhancing institutions. If, as I shall argue, nonschool institutions and experiences cannot be relied upon to develop children's autonomy, liberal education policy must take seriously the possibility that certain types of religious school might pose an unacceptable threat to children's future autonomy. In this chapter, my focus is on secondary schools: I contend that radical opponents of religious education go too far by calling for a virtual prohibition on religious schools, but that their arguments do justify a much more extensive scheme of public regulation than is found in most liberal democracies. Toward the end of the chapter, I indicate the scale and nature of the proposed regulations by sketching the hallmarks of what should be considered a permissible religious secondary school. In the next chapter, I propose that religious primary schools should also be subject to significant regulation, but that the demands made of primary schools should be different and less extensive because the particular developmental needs of preadolescent children from religious families are such that a distinctively religious primary education can play a positive role in laying the foundations for future autonomy.

THE DEVELOPMENT OF AUTONOMY CANNOT
BE TAKEN FOR GRANTED

As we shall see in the next chapter, by the age of eleven or twelve (when secondary schooling begins), most children have the cognitive capacity for the kind of formal thought and hypothetico-deductive reasoning involved in autonomous reflection. But, of course, this bare cognitive capacity is not autonomy itself but merely the *potential* for autonomy: children must develop and practice the skills and commitments of the autonomous person if they are to realize this potential. Does the liberal state need to use its control of formal schooling to help ensure that each child's potential autonomy becomes actual? Some defenders of religious secondary schools concede that such schools do little or nothing to advance children's autonomy but nonetheless maintain the compatibility of religious schooling with the autonomy goal: the key claim here is that the ethical autonomy of children who attend religious secondary schools will tend to develop through their interactions with the wider society outside of and after school. In essence, this amounts to saying that children can be expected to develop autonomy *despite* receiving a religious secondary education.

Liberals who oppose religious secondary schools on autonomy grounds stand accused of overestimating the importance of school in a child's overall educational and developmental experience. In the social conditions of a contemporary liberal democratic state where a plurality of religious and nonreligious ethical doctrines vie for support against the background of predominantly secular popular and political cultures, it is frequently argued that children of religious parents are hardly likely to lack exposure to alternative belief systems and skeptical perspectives on their faith, even if they attend a religious secondary school. Coons and Sugarman (1999, pp. 85–86) may be right to say that "the average child of twelve should be ready to cope with and profit from the challenge of increasing ideological and cultural dissonance," but what implications does this fact have for policy toward religious schools? Theorists such as Galston (1989, 2002) and Gilles (1996), who oppose the adoption of autonomy as a goal of public education policy, agree with those like Burtt (1996) and Crittenden (1988), who support the autonomy goal, that the deck is already stacked against unexamined religious faith and in favor of autonomy. There is no need for the liberal democratic state to pursue the autonomy goal through its policy on schools because the background culture of modern pluralist societies already has the measure of the task. Children typically only attend secondary school for five days a week, forty weeks a year, and, perhaps most crucially, seven or eight years of their life. Outside of school and after the period of compulsory education, the children of religious parents will be exposed to, perhaps inundated by, the messages of alternative ethical doctrines.

Galston (2002, p. 106) proposes that "In a contemporary liberal democratic society, it is impossible for small groups to seal themselves off from ways of life very different from their own." Burtt (1996, p. 426) puts the same point more colorfully: "When it comes to providing the next generation of American citizens with a sense of the different ways in which one can be a good human being, it seems to me that the message of the dominant secular culture is not in danger of being drowned out by the strictures of marginal sectarians. (Even Waco's Branch Davidians watched television.)" On this view, the reality of life in a contemporary pluralist society absolves the liberal democratic state of any obligation to use its education policy to guarantee that children of religious parents will be exposed at school to sufficient ethical diversity to enable them to develop as autonomous persons. I suspect that Galston and Burtt are too hasty in dismissing the possibility that determined parents might succeed in significantly isolating their children from unwanted ethical and cultural ideas, but I do not want to focus the debate on this empirical question. It is far more important to show that the mere fact of exposure to alternative perspectives, however much parents fear that this may lure their children away from the faith, does not suffice to develop children's autonomy.

Several theorists find great significance for the autonomy debate in the fact that children whose home and school lives are thoroughly religious nonetheless not only are routinely *exposed* to ethical alternatives but also frequently *defect* from their parents' faith to endorse one of those alternatives. In this vein, Crittenden (1988, p. 153) notes that "there are many examples of young people who, notwithstanding a full programme of schooling that broadly reinforces their family's values, adopt beliefs and ideals different from those of their parents." Likewise, Gilles (1996, p. 977) is keen to reassure autonomy liberals that "numberless children, after an initial education in religious or ideological orthodoxy, have renounced their parents' faith later in life." But this kind of reassurance misses the mark. As I argued in chapter 3, autonomy does not require and may not even be strongly correlated with people's rejecting the ethical doctrine in which they were raised. As Brighouse (1998, pp. 742–43) quite rightly points out, the frequency of defections "may indicate how easy it is to exit a faith, but tells us nothing about the process by which people decide to exit or remain; and it is the character of the process, rather than the numbers involved, that interests liberals."

Once we attend to the process by which people choose among ethical options, we shall no longer be so sure that mere exposure to alternatives satisfies children's interest in developing autonomy.

> Social diversity is certainly not a *sufficient* condition for individual autonomy, since an individual may well be confronted by diversity but have no way to respond to it in an autonomous fashion. As well as living in a diverse society, an individual must possess

the *personal* capacities for critical thought, toleration, values pluralism, and so forth if she is to be able to exercise autonomy. (Levinson, 1999, p. 72)

Whilst we may be entitled to assume that all children in contemporary
liberal democratic societies will be exposed to multiple ethical options,
there is no reason to be confident that they will face those options with
any kind of capacity to make discerning, reflective judgments and
choices. The kind of intelligent understanding of ethical diversity that
distinguishes the autonomous agent is not simply "picked up in the
public world of contemporary pluralistic societies. What is picked up
there is a seductive sense of the many glittering variations that a life of
heedless consumption and trendy group-think can now take" (Callan,
1997, p. 134). Callan's rhetorical flourish may overstate the point, but it
helps us to see what empty consolation the autonomy liberal will find
in Galston's (1989, p. 101) observation that parental attempts to insulate
their children from knowledge of other ways of life are not only likely
to fail, as we have seen, but may well actually prove counterproductive:
"as every parent knows, possibilities that are known but forbidden take
on an allure out of all proportion to their intrinsic merits."

Autonomy liberals are not determined that children should renounce their parents' way of life and certainly do not want children to
value alternatives "out of all proportion to their intrinsic merits." Galston may be trying to reassure us that a religious upbringing is not an
inescapable prison, but in fact he merely focuses our attention on the
need for children to learn the reasoning capacities that will enable
them to make an autonomous decision whether or not to "escape." As
Brighouse (1998, pp. 742–43) observes, "the mainstream culture . . .
does not always exert its appeal through rationality-respecting mechanisms," and therefore children need to be equipped to deal with this
nonrational allure. Casual exposure to ethical diversity is insufficient
to develop autonomy: "to cultivate the capacity for critical reflection,
students need sustained *intellectual* engagement with diverse values
and beliefs" (Reich, 2002, p. 162, my emphasis).

Those who believe that certain religious secondary schools are serious threats to children's autonomy need not and should not deny that
formal schooling is only one of many important factors in a child's
education and development. But it is important to recognize "the
unique institutional role the school is able to play in fostering the development of autonomy" (Levinson, 1999, p. 61). As we shall see in the
next chapter, primary schools play only a preparatory role in education
for autonomy, since children under the age of eleven have distinctive
developmental needs and have not yet developed the cognitive capaci-

ties necessary for autonomous thought. But secondary schools, I shall argue, can and should be dedicated to rational inquiry and reflection on the rival merits of diverse approaches and answers to ethical (and other) questions. Only during the period of compulsory education can the state ensure that its citizens are exposed to ethical diversity in a controlled environment that is explicitly oriented to, among other things, the informed, critical, and respectful exchange of ideas about the good life. Once children become adults, they have the option to discontinue formal education and/or to cloister themselves away in communities of like-minded persons; liberal democratic states must respect these choices of adults. But, through its requirement that children attend secondary schools and its policy as to which secondary schools will be permitted and funded, the state must seize the one opportunity it will have to set all children on the path to ethical autonomy.[1] The question that remains is: what does this mean in practice for policy toward religious schools?

Of course, as some readers will no doubt already be thinking, this is in principle an empirical question: how far do the religious character and content of a school experience and the typical child's encounters with ethical diversity outside and after school affect his or her development of personal autonomy? Once the nature of autonomy is properly understood, the vital role of schools can perhaps be accepted without empirical evidence: as a rational-cognitive ideal, ethical autonomy is not something that children can reliably be expected to pick up outside of formal educational institutions. But it might still appear that the question of the suitability and effectiveness of different types of schooling to cultivate autonomy is a matter for empirical research rather than theoretical conjecture. The undoubtedly complex causal relationships between a school's curricula (both formal and informal), pedagogical methods, structures of authority, and the composition of its body of students and teachers, on the one hand, and the ways in which children come to hold their ethical beliefs and values, on the other, are certainly not issues I can hope to resolve decisively in two chapters of theoretical analysis. As McLaughlin (1985, pp. 119–20) puts it: "since any attempt to specify the kind of upbringing likely to produce 'open-mindedness' involves variable empirical considerations, no philosophical argument alone can determine the character of that upbringing."

---

[1] My argument so far and the regulations I shall shortly propose for religious schools both suggest the need to regulate the practice of home schooling much more rigorously than is common in most countries today. Parents should not be permitted to exempt their children from an education for autonomy, whether by entrusting instruction to a stay-at-home parent or by sending them to a minimally regulated private religious school.

But I believe, as indeed does McLaughlin, that there is valuable work to be done here without venturing "into the field." And this is probably just as well, since the prospects for successful empirical work look bleak. As Reich (2002, p. 161) puts it, the creation of a test to measure the development of ethical autonomy "may be desirable, but it seems highly unlikely. The empirical measurement of autonomy, especially in children, seems to me an exceptionally difficult and probably quixotic quest." So, we must instead proceed by asking: "What structural aspects of the educational environment might promote or retard autonomy? What features of schooling are essential to fostering autonomy?" In the rest of this work, I try to answer these questions as they touch upon religious schools. In the next chapter, I show that careful attention to the more nuanced conception of autonomy I sketched in chapter 3, conjoined with some insights from widely accepted theories of child development and some uncontroversial observations about the social conditions that prevail in most contemporary liberal democracies, can lead us to tentative but important conclusions about the positive role certain kinds of religious primary schools might play in preparing some children for future autonomy. In this chapter, I propose that adequate secondary education for autonomy requires schools that both expose children to a diverse range of ethical doctrines and manifest a commitment to the critical-rational scrutiny of those doctrines, a requirement that certain types of religious school do not satisfy. As we shall see, this conclusion does not permit the liberal state to prohibit all religious secondary schools, or even to rule out public funding in all cases, but it does mean that the state can and should regulate secondary schooling so as to prohibit the kind of narrow education in the faith that significant numbers of parents and local communities desire for their children.

The Autonomy Case against Religious Schools

Those who believe that all religious schools are obstacles to the development of children's autonomy typically argue that the inculcation of faith is directly at odds with the encouragement of autonomous, critical scrutiny of one's own beliefs and values. In his earlier work, Eamonn Callan (1985) characterizes religious education as a form of indoctrination because it seeks to instill beliefs and values in a student using methods that are both nonrational and designed to decrease the likelihood that the student will, at some stage in the future, engage in serious critical evaluation of those ethical commitments. Religious instruction need not lead to the formation of *unshakeable* beliefs for it to qualify as indoctrination: according to Callan's (1985, p. 115) less restrictive definition, "the necessary effect of indoctrination on the mind of the learner is a belief which is maintained without due regard for relevant evidence and argument." Religious faith, at least as it is understood by many religious parents and as they would wish to see it promoted in schools, stands in tension with the "rational-critical principle" that underlies our conception of ethical autonomy (Callan, 1988). If public education policy aims to secure the conditions under which children may develop their autonomy, Callan argues, religious schools must be tightly regulated, perhaps even outlawed, and certainly should not be receiving public money.

Schooling all too easily slides into indoctrination because our "early beliefs, those we grow up with, especially, some might say, the beliefs we share with our parents or with those who bring us up, have a tendency to stick" (Gardner, 1988, p. 95), in the sense that we find it hard subsequently to subject these beliefs to rational scrutiny. Gardner takes seriously McLaughlin's concern that parents might threaten their child's future autonomy even by giving the child a religious upbringing *at home*:

> Given the pervasiveness and significance of the child's early experiences and in particular the powerful unintentional emotional and psychological pressures and influences that parents may exercise on their child, [one might worry that] the child will end its primary culture with a set of fixed religious beliefs that are very difficult to shake later. (McLaughlin, 1984, p. 80)

The particular problem with allowing religious parents to send their children to religious *schools*, however, is that these children will then be immersed in the same comprehensive ethical worldview at school as at home. Of course, the total immersion method might be judged appropriate for transmitting to children certain moral principles about which we think there can be no reasonable disagreement, but, as we discussed in chapter 4, it is a real cost to children if they fail to develop the capacities to find their own path in an ethical universe where no single path can be shown to be correct for everyone.

This critique of religious schools as inherently unsuitable to deliver education for autonomy translates into a positive vision of the school as "'detached' from local and parental control" (Levinson, 1999, p. 144) so as to "foster an atmosphere of reflection detached from the constitutive commitments of the other arenas of the child's life" (p. 61). The most important role that school can play in developing a child's future autonomy is to give her the necessary critical distance from her family's values for autonomous reflection to be possible. In typically forthright fashion, Bruce Ackerman (1980, pp. 155–56) questions whether liberals should even describe an institution as a "school" if it fails to serve this crucial function.

> Many school buildings are nothing more than an extension of the child's primary culture, with 'educators' interested only in weeding and pruning youngsters so that they will better accord to the parental design. In contrast, a liberal school has a different mission: to provide the child with access to the wide range of cultural materials that he may find useful in developing his own moral ideals and patterns of life.

Both Ackerman and Levinson think that the liberal state's policy of education for autonomy requires that "detached" schools be compulsory for all children, which amounts in practice to the abolition of religious schooling. Levinson (1999, p. 145) would require that all publicly funded schools be fully secular, and although she would apparently permit nominally religious private schools to operate, such "private schools would be subject to the same requirements and regulations as state schools [so that] there would in practice be little if anything to distinguish private schools from state schools."[2]

There is an important insight in Ackerman's and Levinson's vision of the fully detached liberal school, but their legitimate concern that schools might merely replicate the ethical environment of the home does not justify the radical conclusion that schools must be purged of *all* elements that support the values and beliefs of religious parents. Religious schools, just like the secular schools discussed in the previous chapter, must maintain some critical distance from the ethical commitments of parents and from majority opinion in the local community, but that requirement does not rule out religious schools altogether. Detachment is necessary, but it is also a matter of degree: as we have seen, complete ethical neutrality is a mirage, and most schools will inevitably tend disproportionately to reflect the values and beliefs of their particular constituency. My point here is that this limited congruence between the ethics of the school and those of the families it serves can be a matter of design, rather than merely a foreseeable and inevitable accident, without necessarily contradicting liberal purposes: education for autonomy need not be undermined if a school partially defines itself by emphasizing a particular religion in its curriculum and institu-

---

[2] Levinson never tells us in what ways (if any) private, religious schools might legitimately differ from public, secular schools: this omission surely reinforces her message that any legitimate differences would be slight. For this reason, I treat Levinson as calling for the abolition of religious schools.

tional ethos. As Eammon Callan (1997, p. 133) notes, "the essential demand is that schooling properly involves at some stage sympathetic and critical engagement with beliefs and ways of life at odds with the culture of the family or religious or ethnic group into which the child is born," and there is no reason why this demand could not be satisfied within a religiously affiliated school.

Callan's position on religious secondary schools as potential instruments of education for autonomy is more reasonable than that of Ackerman and Levinson, but it still has several flaws. First and foremost, it is distressingly vague. Callan (p. 177) maintains that common, secular schools are to be preferred "as a rule," but he has very little that is concrete to say about the nature and grounds of legitimate exceptions to that rule. Later in this chapter, I shall try to plug this important gap in the analysis by suggesting a number of hallmarks of permissible religious secondary schools. The most definite commitment Callan makes on this matter is to say that whatever the standards required of publicly funded schools, regulation of private religious secondary schools should be considerably less stringent. This softness on private schools is supposedly justified by the need to avoid what Callan (p. 189) calls "Jacobin liberalism, in which any lapse from the high demands of liberal virtue makes one fair game for political coercion." By contrast, Callan apparently endorses the view that there should be one rule for the poor and quite another for the rich. As I argued in chapter 2 in response to Gutmann's position, once the state has made a principled decision as to how we ought to balance competing interests in children's education, there is no justification for allowing parents with access to private means to buy their way out. This is scarcely "Jacobin liberalism"—in chapter 5, I defended the broad discretionary freedom of parents to direct their children's upbringing at home, even in many ways that do not serve the children's best interests, but the necessary counterbalance to that freedom is for the state to insist upon an appropriate education for autonomy during the hours of compulsory schooling.

The other great weakness of Callan's position is his unrealistic emphasis on the importance of achieving ethical diversity within the student body. I suspect Callan (p. 177) is right to say that the possibilities for ethical reflection and deliberation are significantly diminished by the absence of living representatives of and advocates for alternative views: "imaginary interlocutors are a pallid substitute for the real thing." But, as is well known, regional trends and residential patterns impose practical constraints on the state's capacity to ensure that all schools have an ethically diverse student body, and bussing schemes or systems of "controlled choice" that seek to transform the common school from myth to reality (Levinson, 1999, pp. 146–56) can only have limited success in eliminating this kind of unintended homogeneity that marks many secular public schools. So it is fatally impractical to argue, as Callan (1985, p. 118) does, that if "the very fact that a school caters to a religiously homogeneous clientele [inhibits] serious attention to alternative belief systems, regardless of the pedagogical practices that are adopted," such schools should not be allowed to operate, even if they genuinely diversified the ethical content of their curricula. As I shall soon propose, religious schools should be expected somewhat to diversify their student body where this is feasible in the light of local demographics and residential patterns, but actual diversity of membership cannot be a regulatory requirement of permissible religious secondary schools.

Before I proceed to offer my own hallmarks of permissible religious secondary schools, I want to consider the view advanced by Rob Reich (2002). Reich's insistence that religious schools must be carefully regulated but cannot be dismissed as incompatible with education for autonomy seems to me exactly right, but, as we shall see, the regulation implied by his view would be altogether less stringent than I propose, and the source of the disagreement lies in our different conceptions of autonomy and the grounds of its public justification in the liberal state. Like Ackerman, Levinson, and Callan, Reich (pp. 132–33) believes that "what facilitates the capacity for critical reflection is the introduction of and engagement with diverse and unfamiliar value orientations" because "exposure to and examination of other ways of life stimulates comparisons, illuminates contrasts, and encourages independence of thought." However, unlike Ackerman and Levinson, Reich (p. 141) shares my sense that the need for a degree of detachment between school and home cannot prescribe "any specific institutional arrangements of schooling [such as] closing down private and religious schools and forcing all children to attend integrated public schools." Reich astutely resists the temptation to overgeneralize, heeding McLaughlin's (1992, p. 115) warning that "it is rash . . to condone or condemn certain kinds of separate school solely on grounds of philosophical principle. Much depends on how the institutions actually operate and what their effects actually are on students and the broader community."

Although there is no justification for a general prohibition on religious secondary education, the arguments I have already canvassed do warrant "greater suspicion of educational arrangements that tend to reproduce the home environment of the child in the school, shielding students from exposure to and engagement with diversity" (Reich, 2002, p. 141), and religious schools are prime suspects in this respect. But, unlike Callan, Reich does not rely on diversity within the school's student body to provide the educational experience necessary to stimulate and develop autonomous reasoning among students. Instead, he puts his trust in features of the school that are more realistically under the control of public authorities: "the liberal state must regulate for autonomy by ensuring that the school, through its *curriculum* and *pedagogy*, does not aim solely to replicate and reinforce the worldview of the parents or cultural groups of the children who attend the school" (p. 197, my emphasis). It is too simple to judge that a school is frustrating children's development of autonomy merely because of its religious affiliation and the homogeneity of ethical opinion held by its students, parents, and even staff. The liberal state has no choice but to engage in the difficult task of looking closely at what goes on in the classroom to see whether a group of ethically like-minded students and teachers may nonetheless be engaged in meaningful, autonomy-promoting encounters with the ideas and perspectives of diverse ethical traditions. The result of this assessment of classroom practice would be that "certain kinds of homeschools and fundamentalist religious schools that consciously insulate children from the value diversity of a culturally plural state would be disallowed" (p. 200), but other institutions with similar membership would be permitted to operate.

Of course, the hard questions still remain after the principle of regulation has been accepted. What standards are to be required of religious schools? How and where is the line to be drawn between permissible and prohibited schools? As I noted above, Callan has little to say about translating the goal of cultivating autonomy through critical engagement with diversity into concrete standards for curricular content and pedagogical methods, and this is at least partly because of his emphasis on the ideal of a diverse student body. Reich offers a little more by way of meaningful practical criteria, but his standards turn out to be woefully inadequate. In a highly revealing passage, Reich (p. 198) argues that all schools must teach children about a plurality of religious doctrines but that schools are *not* required to teach that "all religious beliefs must be subject to rational scrutiny and deliberation." How are we to understand Reich's explicit disclaiming of this requirement, since he *does* require schools to cultivate children's capacity and inclination for "critical reflection" and "independence of thought"? It is initially tempting to try and explain away the above disclaimer, all the while insisting that Reich really is committed to the standard that all schools should teach children rationally to evaluate the various religious doctrines they encounter at school and outside. But careful attention to Reich's so-called minimalist conception of autonomy and his justification for adopting such a conception as a goal of public education policy reveals that there is no necessity for distinctively rational and ongoing reflection in the version of ethical independence that Reich would have all schools cultivate in students.

Reich's "minimalist conception of autonomy" (ch. 4) bears a striking resemblance to Gerald Dworkin's (1988) conception that I discussed and rejected in chapter 3 of this work. According to Reich (p. 101), in a passage where he acknowledges Dworkin's influence on his own view, "minimalist autonomy refers to the ability of persons to examine and evaluate their underlying commitments, values, desires, motivations, and beliefs. Humans are capable, that is, of forming second-order volitions about their first-order desires; they form preferences about their preferences." It is not insignificant that Reich, throughout his characterization of the type of second-order preferences that define the autonomous person, repeatedly uses the terms "independent" and "critical" but avoids the term "rational." Reich shares with Dworkin the belief that possessing "procedurally independent" second-order desires is necessary and sufficient for autonomy: all that matters is that my higher-order values were not simply implanted in me by others. I have already criticized this procedural independence condition in chapter 3: what I now want briefly to show is how the minimal nature of Reich's conception of autonomy translates into some limited and unpersuasive arguments for adopting autonomy as a public value and in turn implies minimal regulatory standards for religious schools.

Recall that, in chapter 4, I constructed a public justification for adopting autonomy as a goal of liberal education policy by appealing to the instrumental value of rational ethical reflection for individuals seeking to find and live a good life. This type of argument, resting as it does on the distinctive value of rational thought, is not available to Reich, and indeed he does not make any such claim. Rather, he tries (pp. 120–23) to justify treating autonomy as a universal value on the grounds that it is necessary to achieve *self-respect* and to *avoid servility*, both of which are supposedly necessary conditions of individual flourishing. I cannot embark on a detailed critical analysis of these claims, but let me sketch out the errors involved in each. A sizeable measure of self-respect may well be necessary for an individual to flourish, but Reich provides no reason to support the claim that being minimally autonomous, that is, possessing procedurally independent second-order desires, is necessary for a person to achieve self-respect. Why couldn't a person who was thoroughly indoctrinated into a particular religious faith, with second-order values implanted by her community to reinforce her first-order commitments, have self-respect? True, she hasn't shaped her own life, but what's wrong with that? Reich's unstated argument here must appeal in some way to the intrinsic value of living autonomously, but we have already seen in chapter 4 that such appeals are rightly judged inadmissible to liberal politics.

Recalling our discussion in chapter 3, it is not clear that minimal autonomy is sufficient to avoid servility: someone with a procedurally independent but irrevocable second-order commitment to obeying his priest is minimally autonomous but also, it seems to me, servile. Furthermore, a person need not be servile just because he lacks procedurally independent second-order commitments: someone whose parents instilled in him an unshakeable second-order commitment to rational scrutiny of his first-order values does not meet Reich's standards for minimal autonomy, but he is surely not servile. And, more generally, if one is concerned about individual flourishing, it is hard to see that the minimally autonomous person is necessarily any better off than the person who has been thoroughly indoctrinated into a religious ethic. If Reich's concern is that the indoctrinated person's life will go badly if the religious ethic in question is in fact wrong, the exercise of merely procedurally independent second-order preferences is not a reliable means by which that person can identify the flaws in his system of first-order commitments. The benefits to individual flourishing of reflecting upon one's first-order commitments lie in the rational nature of that ethical reflection, not in its mere independence from others. Deranged people may be minimally autonomous, according to Reich's standards, but there is no reason to think that they can exercise their procedurally independent second-order preferences to find and lead a good life for themselves. So, Reich's minimalist conception of autonomy not only lacks credibility as a publicly justifiable value but also, which is more important for our purposes here, issues in regulatory standards for religious schools that are far weaker than they should be.

HALLMARKS OF PERMISSIBLE RELIGIOUS SECONDARY SCHOOLS

Religious secondary schools must be carefully regulated by the liberal state to ensure that they do not threaten students' development of ethical autonomy. All the major theorists of education for autonomy discussed in the preceding part agree with this proposition, but none interprets and applies it adequately: Levinson and Ackerman would unjustifiably overregulate religious schools to the point where their religious character is scarcely recognizable; Callan unrealistically focuses on achieving a diverse student body and would make exceptions for private schools; Reich would not require that schools cultivate a conception of ethical autonomy with rational evaluation at its core. In this part, I sketch the hallmarks of a religious secondary school that would be compatible with education for autonomy as I have understood that ideal since chapter 3. In particular, I try to characterize acceptable pedagogy and reason-giving, I propose curricular requirements, and I suggest various ways in which religious schools should be expected to remain open to those beyond their community of faith. Of course, I cannot hope to do more than sketch these conditions, and not simply because of constraints of space. As Kevin McDonough (1998, p. 491) wisely counsels, "the business of determining how liberal principles that establish the legitimacy of moderate cultural identity schools translate into concrete policy in particular cases is inevitably an intricate, complex, and highly context-dependent undertaking." No general statement of conditions can replace the difficult contextual judgments that would need to be made by inspectors and educational professionals in particular cases. But I hope to say something that puts flesh on the bones of the view, as expressed by Brian Crittenden (1988, p. 149), that the educational goal of autonomy in a pluralist society requires, especially at the secondary level, that "*all* schools in such a society should encourage critical reflection on the values they uphold and engage in serious study of alternative value systems."

The first hallmark of an acceptable religious secondary school is a sincere commitment to the practice of rational justification wherein the reasons given are not exclusively religious in form and content. Members of staff, in their interactions with children in and out of the classroom, must give and receive secular as well as religious reasons for rules, actions, and academic claims. Schools must encourage rational deliberation *within* the faith as well as promoting the importance of secular perspectives from *outside* the faith, both those whose implications merely happen to be contrary to the religious view and those that directly challenge the grounds for belief in the tenets of the faith. The encouragement of rational deliberation within the faith should, I shall argue, also be a requirement for religious primary schools, and I shall have more to say about it in the next chapter. But only in secondary schools should it be mandatory for fully secular arguments to be given both to complement religious justifications and, even more importantly, to encourage children to reflect critically about the status of those religious justifications and about the underlying doctrinal principles more generally.

For example, Catholic schools teaching about the ethics of homosexuality or birth control should be required, as well as presenting the teachings of the Church, not only to analyze tensions and controversies within the faith on these questions but also to make time for the purely secular arguments on both sides of the debates. Similarly, courses of religious instruction must include the presentation (ideally by persons outside the faith, as I discuss in a related point below) of weighty skeptical perspectives on the faith as well as rational arguments within the faith about different possible interpretations and applications of accepted principles. Of course, this demand should not be applied at the level of each fifty-minute lesson, but there should be no course of study that systematically excludes nonreligious perspectives. In short, a religiously affiliated school can legitimately offer religious teachings and justifications, but not to the exclusion of secular reasons that both support and question the conclusions of those religious arguments.

Related to this pedagogical requirement that religious schools include secular reasoning in all their teaching is an important curricular requirement, namely, that significant parts of the school curriculum should be insulated from and independent of the religious ethos of the school. Christian fundamentalist schools can legitimately present the Creationist account to children in a class on Bible study (provided that the scientific critique is also taken seriously), but there should additionally be separate lessons in biology where the theory of evolution is taught without giving equal time to the rival biblical account of human origins. Some readers may think that this requirement is unfair given the pedagogical condition discussed in the previous paragraph: if religious reasoning must always be balanced by secular perspectives in the same course of study, why should there be specially insulated courses where secular science is taught without the competing fundamentalist religious view? The answer to this charge of unfairness appeals to the special importance of ensuring that children receive a thorough grounding in the methods of secular reasoning that are essential for autonomous reflection. In order to step wholly outside their familial religion and reflect critically on it, students need to understand the possibility and nature of a type of rational inquiry that makes no appeal to religious beliefs or values and that can therefore be used to make an independent assessment of such beliefs and values. The surest way to empower students with this understanding is to provide them with models of fully secular reasoning: the study of science might offer an especially good opportunity to practice and explore such a model. As discussed earlier, some courses should put religious and secular reasons into dialogue with each other, but if every course of study weaves in religious arguments and perspectives, students are never given a systematic training in the secular rational mode of thought they will need in order to make a truly autonomous evaluation of their inherited ethical (and other) beliefs and values.

Children from religious families are immersed in the religious worldview at home and, I shall argue in the next chapter, may legitimately be sent (at public expense) to religious primary schools where they will not be exposed to perspectives from outside their faith. At secondary school, therefore, the priority must be to develop children's capacities to think rationally outside of their family's ethical doctrine: children need to gain a firm grasp of the methods of secular, rational inquiry, and this cannot be reliably expected to happen if the entire school curriculum is infused with religious reasoning. A significant number of purely secular academic courses should be mandatory for all children in religious secondary schools, but there should be no courses that conversely employ only religious reasoning: the pedagogical condition that religious instruction and justification must always be balanced by secular discourse is distinct from the requirement that some academic disciplines be taught in a way that is fully independent of the school's religious affiliation.

So far, we have examined two hallmarks of permissible religious secondary schools: one focused on a balance of religious and secular reasoning in pedagogical methods of instruction and justification, the other on the need to preserve curricular space for purely secular academic study. The next requirement is also curricular: all religious secondary schools should be required to devote significant time to teaching their students about religious and ethical doctrines other than the religious tradition with which the school is affiliated. Since the purpose of this requirement is to give children a sense of the alternative ethical paths they might opt to follow, it is not automatically satisfied by the inclusion in the curriculum of a mandatory course in world religions, because of the very real possibility that these religions are being used as no more than "target-practice." McDonough (1998, p. 488) notes that "merely including the study of alien cultures" may be worse than useless if it means "teaching that the other cultures are rival, alien cultures and traditions to be rejected and resisted in favor of the traditions and values privileged by the culture of upbringing." So, as Callan (1985, p. 117) argues, schools should be required, in the name of autonomy, to present to children various religious doctrines, as well as the atheist position, "not just as aberrations from the one true faith or as sources of spiritual solace for other people but rather as belief systems among which the children themselves might come to find a more satisfactory alternative to their parents' religious convictions." What is crucial here is that schools should treat the possibility that some children will find the ethical alternatives "more satisfactory" not as a danger to be resisted but rather as the natural and not undesirable result of children's developing as autonomous persons.

No doubt this requirement of fair-minded exposure to other ethical doctrines, perhaps even more so than the other requirements I have suggested, would be a difficult and controversial one to adjudicate and enforce. But it should come as no great surprise that the dividing line between acceptable and unacceptable practices in secondary education cannot be drawn in ways that provide easily applied, clear-cut criteria that obviate the need for contextual, case-by-case judgments made by an accountable inspectorate. We must beware of the complacency of those, like Reich (2002, p. 53), who think that "it is a mystery how a teacher could simultaneously expose children to diversity yet not 'invite' them to use this knowledge of diverse values by turning an inquisitive, critical, or sceptical eye toward their own culture or set of values." Doubtless, some children are resourceful and independent-minded enough to frustrate their teacher's efforts to use examples of other ethical doctrines as mere cannon fodder, but we should not underestimate the capacity of educators to manipulate their young charges' responses to diversity by presenting other conceptions of the good in their least favorable colors, or even downright inaccurately.

In light of this very real danger, and the difficulties of discriminating between exposure to diversity that is likely to enhance autonomy and that which serves only to reinforce the appeal of the familiar faith, let me suggest a concrete example of good practice. Religious schools that invite representatives of other religious traditions to teach classes about those traditions can generally be assumed to be serving their students' interests in developing as autonomous persons. We might realistically envision an exchange program: a teacher from the Islamic school trades places with his counterpart from the nearby Sikh school one morning a week. Of course, this is not the only way in which religious schools might provide acceptable instruction about other religions, nor can we rule out the possibility that a school has deliberately selected the world's least competent and persuasive rabbi to teach the class on Judaism, but this example does provide a sense of one good way in which schools could discharge their responsibility to expose students to ethical diversity without simply using the other doctrines as cannon fodder.

The last hallmark of a permissible religious secondary school I want to suggest, in addition to the pedagogical and curricular conditions already discussed, concerns the openness of the school to those beyond its particular community of faith. We have just seen one example of such openness in the willingness of a school to invite a practitioner of another religious doctrine to teach students about that doctrine. But, I propose, there are several other important ways in which religious secondary schools could demonstrate the kind of outward-looking attitude that suggests a genuine commitment to developing children's autonomy by exposing them to a range of ethical alternatives. First, rather than merely inviting persons from outside the faith to teach occasional classes about their particular ethical beliefs, schools should actively seek to hire full-time teachers (and other staff) who subscribe to other religions or to none. Of course, religious schools might quite reasonably prefer that religious instruction and worship be provided by persons within the faith, perhaps qualified ministers or priests, but there is no reason why at least a sizeable minority of teachers could not come from outside the community of faith, especially given the requirement discussed above for significant space within the curriculum for purely secular teaching.

Religious schools should not limit their quest for a more diverse membership to their hiring practices: permissible religious secondary schools would also be expected to make themselves open and welcoming to children of other faiths and of no faith, although such schools could reasonably reserve a supermajority of places for children from within their community of faith. In this vein, McLaughlin (1987, p. 82) envisages religious schools aiming at "broadening the character of their intake to include a certain proportion of students who are not adherents of the particular religion in question." Of course, schools may find it hard to diversify their membership by attracting staff and students from outside their community of faith. Non-Jewish teachers may not wish to teach in a Jewish school, and agnostic parents may feel uneasy about sending their children to a Christian school (although the regulations I propose would precisely help to lessen these aversions by diluting the religious ethos of each school). Plus, of course, it will be hard to achieve a diverse student body in a region where the population is overwhelmingly of a single religion. For these reasons, we cannot follow Callan's lead by making actual diversity of membership a requirement of permissible religious secondary schools: in some areas, no such thing could be achieved without considerable coercion and extensive bussing schemes that are undesirable for a whole host of reasons.

But we can reasonably expect religious secondary schools to make sincere efforts to diversify their body of students and teachers, and perhaps also to find other ways to increase their students' exposure to ethical diversity if these efforts fail. For example, schools with a homogeneously Protestant student body might be expected to work actively to create joint programs with schools of other faiths or with no religious affiliation: such programs might bring children together regularly (or for short, intensive periods of time) to collaborate in athletics, drama, community service, or perhaps even to study an academic subject in which neither school could afford to employ a full-time teacher. Of course, these ideas are meant only as illustrations, but hopefully they are suggestive of the kinds of ways in which religious secondary schools might satisfy the requirement that they open themselves to those beyond their community of faith. There can be no exhaustive list or exact specification of the ways in which this requirement might be satisfied, but public regulatory authorities could reasonably be charged with the responsibility of enforcing the regulation in a way that is fair and appropriate given the particular circumstances of the school and region in question.

In summary, to be compatible with the goal of educating all children for autonomy, a religious secondary school would have to manifest a commitment to secular reason-giving inside and outside the class-room, balance religious instruction with critical perspectives on the faith, insulate significant parts of the academic curriculum from the religious ethos of the school, teach about other ethical doctrines in a way that makes children aware of viable alternatives to their family's faith, and demonstrate a sincere willingness to open the school to teachers and students outside the community of faith. It should be clear that these are demanding requirements, but also that schools could fulfill them while retaining their religious character: I am not advocating the kind of radical detachment of schools from parental and community values that Ackerman and Levinson mistakenly think necessary to cultivate children's autonomy. Religious secondary schools should be allowed to reserve a large majority of their places for students and teachers who belong to the community of faith, to emphasize religious justifications for school rules and structures so long as these are accompanied by secular reasons, and to run manda-tory classes of instruction in a particular religious doctrine, so long as these classes include some secular, critical perspectives by way of bal-ance. Of course, many religious organizations will be tempted to resist these requirements, but it is the duty of a liberal state to enforce them in order to guarantee all children a secondary education for autonomy.[3]

REGULATION AND ENTANGLEMENT

To some readers, the idea that the state should be involved in discrimi-nating among (proposed) religious schools will seem even more appall-ing than a blanket policy of funding all religious schools that enjoy suf-

---

[3] Devins (1992) catalogues the vigorous resistance that has greeted recent attempts to regulate religious schools in America, and he notes that several state legislatures have backed down rather than jail parents and alienate religious voters. Such resistance should certainly prompt us to reexamine the particular regulations under dispute, but if the reasoning withstands reexamination, we must not be shy of enforcing standards grounded in children's basic interests.

ficient parental support within a geographical area to make them viable and reasonably cost-effective. In some cases, opposition to my idea may rest on a stubborn refusal to abandon the notion that liberals must aspire to neutrality of effect on adherents of different conceptions of the good: either we must fund all religious secondary schools, or we must fund none. The response to this position is well-rehearsed: the liberal state endorses certain values, and, although it does not seek to impose a particular conception of the good life, it cannot simply abandon those values when they come into conflict with illiberal ways of life. As we saw in chapter 5, the liberal state should grant parents broad discretion to direct the upbringing of their children outside of the institutions of formal education, even in some ways that do not serve the children's best interests, but the sphere of formal education is the place where children's interest in developing autonomy must be respected.

But concerns about public regulation of religious schools need not rest on a misguided appeal to liberal neutrality. One can recognize the principle that liberal states may justifiably prohibit certain religious practices, such as female genital circumcision, while remaining concerned about a scheme that proposes greatly to expand the role of the state in making judgments on the acceptability of religious practices. The essence of such a position is the fear of excessive entanglement between politics and religion, even granted that some degree of entanglement will always be necessary. There is, after all, nothing especially radical about the basic idea that religious schools must be licensed and regulated by the liberal state: we could not permit the operation of schools that inflicted physical torture on students or declined to teach basic reading and writing, even if they did these things on grounds of sincere religious conviction and with full parental consent. But my proposal that the state should permit only those religious secondary schools whose practices are consistent with the goal of cultivating every child's personal autonomy clearly expands the scope of public regulation considerably.

It is an altogether different matter to judge the suitability of a school's methods to develop children's autonomy than it is to judge whether a school is torturing its children or refusing to teach them to read. But this is a judgment that will have to be made in liberal politics once the autonomy goal is adopted as part of public education policy. What is so disturbing about the prospect of the state making this kind of judgment, and is the problem so severe that we should renounce the autonomy goal despite the arguments of chapter 4? Concerns about entanglement can be broken into two separate claims: entanglement is bad for religions, and it is bad for liberal politics. Although I do not think we should be troubled by the plight of genuinely illiberal religions, I recognize that these two claims express valid concerns. Nonetheless, I shall argue that they are insufficient to justify abandoning the project of ensuring that all schools respect and further children's interest in developing as autonomous persons.

Entanglement between religion and politics, in the form of beefed-up public regulation of religious secondary schools of the sort I have proposed, might be thought to be bad for religion because it provides an incentive for religious groups to distort their doctrine merely in order to win the favor of the state. This is liable to destroy the integrity of religious groups, as they change the pedagogical practices and curricula in their schools to ensure that government inspectors will grant them the all-important certificate of public approval. Of course, we can distinguish two types of case here. In one type, a religious group desires to operate a school whose curriculum and pedagogical methods really would be seriously detrimental to children's development of ethical autonomy. In the second type, a different religious group desires to operate a school in a way that would, *ex hypothesis*, facilitate children's development of ethical autonomy, but the group fears that it will be unable to persuade the government of this fact and so considers changing the design of the school to one that more obviously coheres with the autonomy goal.[4]

I do not think we should worry in the slightest if groups of the first kind compromise or reform their doctrine so as to make their educational practices compatible with children's developing autonomy. Gutmann (1999, p. 121) discusses the case of Bob Jones University and notes approvingly that this private religious association, under pressure from public rules governing the funding of educational institutions, changed its *policy* against admitting black students *and* subsequently claimed also to have changed its *beliefs* on the issue. Similarly, Macedo (2000, p. 134), discussing the liberalization of the Catholic Church under Vatican II, argues that it is no bad thing if religions reform to qualify for public funds: "assimilation is not to be despised; it is rather to be embraced—if we assimilate in nonoppressive ways and towards justifiable values." Of course, both Gutmann and Macedo defend assimilation to purely civic values but, once we see that the autonomy goal is also publicly justifiable in liberal states, there is no reason not to extend their defense of assimilation to encompass this particular noncivic value. Furthermore, since the autonomy goal of public education policy is a matter of individual children's rights rather than the

---

[4] This is an ever-present danger, not least because of the tendency of courts and public officials, often without deliberate intent, to "favor the familiar over the unorthodox" in their assessments of religious practice (Greenawalt, 2000, p. 207).

needs of the political community for certain levels of civic virtue and skills in the citizenry as a whole, I shall argue that it is perfectly justifiable not only to deny funding but also to deny a license to prospective religious schools that refuse to reform their practices to make them compatible with this fundamental interest of all children.

The second case—the religious group whose proposed school design would actually facilitate children's future autonomy but which fears that the government will take a different view—connects to the claim that public regulation is bad for liberal politics. Neither likely outcome of this case seems altogether desirable. Either the religious group changes the school design, compromising its principles on purely strategic political grounds, or there is a complex, bitter, and protracted political dispute about the permissibility of the proposed school. In the first outcome, religious doctrine has been distorted for no good reason. In the second outcome, liberal politics becomes dominated by a sensitive issue with no likelihood of a clear resolution and every possibility of damaging the fragile trust between different religious and secular groups in society as passions become inflamed and accusations of bad faith begin to fly. McLaughlin (1987, p. 81) toys with the idea that "to avoid the invidious and highly controversial task of distinguishing religious faiths capable of establishing acceptable voluntary schools from those that are not, as a matter of public policy no voluntary schools should be supported." But this is not the only way, and perhaps not the best, to avoid the necessity of making these difficult and politically sensitive judgments. Perhaps it would be preferable simply to drop the autonomy goal from public education policy to avoid messy entanglement cases of this sort, which threaten to burden free exercise of religion or even to imperil the liberal state itself?

I think this is a serious objection, and I have no answer to it that will silence the critics. There are sure to be controversial and hard cases, some of which will never come to public light only because of the decision by religious groups to compromise their principles in order to avoid the political confrontation. The risks, to religious groups and even to the liberal state, are not illusory. But they must not be exaggerated, and above all I think they must be accepted as the necessary price for defending the interests of all children in developing as ethically autonomous persons. Some religious secondary schools pose a serious threat to children's development of ethical autonomy. We must not throw out the baby with the bath water by adopting a libertarian, hands-off approach to religious schools merely because we fear the consequences of trying to weed out the bad ones: we cannot allow religious groups to operate the kind of schools that simply indoctrinate children by immersing them in a comprehensive ethical view, stifling their potential to develop as autonomous persons who can employ their own rational faculties to try to find and lead the best lives for themselves.[5] Nor can we, in fairness to religious citizens, err the other way by insisting that all children attend fully secular secondary schools when we know full well that moderate religious secondary schools can satisfy the various goals of liberal education policy. It can be hoped, perhaps even expected, that most mainstream religious groups will propose schools that manifestly meet the requirements I have proposed. It may be appropriate for the regulatory process to give religious groups the benefit of any reasonable doubt about the suitability of their proposed or actual school to cultivate children's autonomy. But liberal states must take seriously their responsibilities as trustees of children's interests and so cannot duck the hard questions when they arise.

Conclusions and Policy Implications

Religious secondary schools of certain types are inadequate to cultivate autonomy in children, although suitably designed and regulated religious secondary schools are compatible with that goal. As I argued in chapters 4 and 5, the liberal democratic state can and should seek to cultivate autonomy in all children through its policies on mandatory formal education, even against the objections of religious parents. Therefore, the liberal democratic state has legitimate *noncivic* (paternalistic) reasons, grounded in the child's best interests, to take action against certain types of religious secondary schools. Furthermore, as we saw in chapter 1, religious schools that deny children exposure to ethical diversity and sufficient training in secular reasoning appear to provide an inferior preparation for citizenship, a conclusion that is obviously not unrelated to the arguments in this chapter.[6] Therefore, the liberal democratic state also looks to have legitimate *civic* grounds for

[5] Even if there exists an "absolute conflict" (Greenawalt, 2000, p. 228) between religious doctrine and the demands of education for autonomy, no relief should be granted to religious parents and educators whose proposed school would frustrate children's basic interest in developing as autonomous persons. The child's need to receive a formal education for autonomy must not be traded off against parental preferences, no matter how substantial the burden imposed on religious parents by the liberal state's education policy. As discussed in chapter 5, parents shoud have very considerable freedom to direct the upbringing of their child outside of schools, but this freedom is conditional on the child's being guaranteed a formal education for autonomy.

[6] Recall Callan's (1996, 1997) arguments (discussed in chapter 2) that the cultivation of ethical autonomy is one of the goals of liberal democratic *civic* education.

discriminating against narrowly religious schools. My conclusion is that the state is justified in making policy that reflects the general superiority of secular and moderately religious secondary schools over their narrowly religious counterparts.

But what should that policy be? As I argued in chapter 2, once the balance of legitimate interests—those of the child, the state, and the parents—has been found to count for or against a particular type of schooling, there is no justification for allowing wealthy parents to buy their way out of this normative conclusion. Parents have no right to frustrate their child's development of autonomy in the sphere of formal education, and the state appears to have a legitimate civic interest in children's attending secondary schools where they will be exposed to ethical diversity and taught secular reasoning. The policy implication of all this is that narrowly religious secondary schools, those that do not meet the requirements discussed earlier in this chapter, should not only be denied public funding, they should actually be prohibited.[7] To permit the operation of privately funded narrowly religious secondary schools is to grant undue weight to the parents' supposed right to direct their child's formal education while selling short the autonomy and civic goals of public education policy. If, as I maintain, the state is truly justified in refusing to fund narrowly religious secondary schools, then *for those exact same reasons*, the state is entitled, indeed obligated, to prohibit the operation of such schools altogether.

This would certainly represent a radical change in policy for most liberal democratic states, which have tended to regard the largely unconstrained freedom of parents to buy their children a private religious education as a fundamental right (see, for example, *Pierce v. Society of Sisters*, 1925). I am led to this radicalism by taking seriously the thought, expressed by Barry (2001, pp. 204–5) but not taken as seriously by him as by me, that "what goes on in private schools not in receipt of public funding is just as much a matter of public concern as what goes on in those that are." But the extent of my radicalism should not be overstated. I suspect that narrowly religious secondary schools currently operate in almost all liberal democratic states, and my proposal is indeed that these schools should not be allowed to continue in their current form. (They could, of course, escape the noose by adopting the best practices I discuss, though some schools might be

---

[7] To be precise, attendance at a private narrowly religious secondary school or home school equivalent should not be considered to satisfy the requirements of mandatory formal education: parents should not be prohibited from sending their teenage children to a private Sunday school or after-school program of religious instruction—such decisions lie within the sphere where substantial discretion is rightly accorded to parents.

changed beyond recognition by these reforms. That would be all well and good.) But moderate religious secondary schools—those that show the hallmarks I outlined—should be permitted to operate and should satisfy the desires of many religious parents. Furthermore, the state should be willing to fund such moderate religious secondary schools, given that they have been shown to be both autonomy-promoting and effective instruments of civic education. My argument here, as in chapter 2, is that we should substantially close the gap between the types of schools that are permitted and the types that are eligible for public funding. To do otherwise is either to grant rich parents the right to buy their way out of requirements designed to advance the best interests of children and the state or arbitrarily to deny poor parents the opportunity to give their children an education in the faith that nonetheless coheres with the civic and autonomy goals of education. Neither of these options is acceptable in a liberal state committed to defending the basic interests of all its members while promoting their freedom to live according to their various conceptions of the good.

Chapter 8

THE ROLE OF RELIGIOUS PRIMARY SCHOOLS

IN THE PREVIOUS CHAPTER, I argued that the need for all schools to cultivate children's autonomy justifies subjecting religious secondary schools to extensive regulation, including curricular requirements, expectations for pedagogy and the justification of rules, and requirements of openness to those beyond the school's particular community of faith. In this chapter, I ask whether the same arguments and conclusions hold in the case of primary schools, and I argue that they do not. The liberal case for detaching children's educational environment from the ethics of their religious parents and communities is much less persuasive as a criticism of religious primary schools, which actually have the potential to play an important positive role in preparing young children from religious families for an autonomous future. As instruments designed to meet children's developmental needs in the first phase of formal education for autonomy, religious primary schools should be regulated differently from and altogether less extensively than their secondary counterparts, but some significant regulation is still needed to ensure that the foundations of autonomy are satisfactorily laid. At the end of this chapter, I sketch the necessary regulations by setting out the hallmarks of permissible religious primary schools and explaining how and why these differ from those for secondary schools discussed in the previous chapter.

AGE-SENSITIVE EDUCATION

Readers will recall that the regulations I proposed in the previous chapter are justified by the need to ensure that all secondary schools both adequately expose children to ethical diversity and provide them with the skills and inclination to respond in a critical-rational manner to such diversity. Children of religious parents need to attend secondary schools that encourage students to achieve a degree of critical distance from the familial religion if they are to have a fair chance of developing as autonomous persons, although Levinson's and Ackerman's arguments for compulsory attendance at fully secular, common schools overstate this case. My goal in this chapter is to demonstrate that religious primary schools, unlike religious secondary schools, are potentially *superior* to their secular counterparts because of their special suitability to lay the foundations for future autonomy in children from religious families. Interestingly, the roots of this argument are to be found in the work of both Ackerman and Levinson, but neither sees the full significance of their own observations about the importance of providing schools that are sensitive to the particular developmental needs of children of different ages, especially preadolescents.

For all their paeans to the detached, liberal school, Ackerman and Levinson both recognize that the development of autonomy requires more than just being exposed to ethical diversity and learning the critical thinking skills to rationally evaluate these different positions. As I argued in chapter 3, autonomous choice is impossible, in fact an incoherent ideal, unless individuals possess a relatively secure provisional identity to situate their choice between ethical positions, a choice that is always underdetermined by pure reason. So, as Levinson (1999, p. 56) concedes, "membership in a community and embeddedness within a cultural and normative framework is a primary need of individuals—and an essential prerequisite for autonomy. One cannot act autonomously if one has no firm structure of beliefs on which to act." Similarly, Ackerman (1980, p. 141) observes, in a much quoted phrase, that "while an infant may learn English or Urdu or both, there are limits to the cultural diversity he can confront without losing a sense of the meanings that the noises and motions might ultimately signify." So, both Ackerman and Levinson acknowledge that a person's autonomous reflection must be grounded in a coherent (if provisional) ethical-cultural identity.

What are the implications for schools of recognizing children's need for cultural coherence as a prerequisite for the development of autonomy? According to Levinson (p. 144), "while children's development of autonomy may be the school's ultimate educational aim, it should help foster different skills and capacities at different times." Liberal schools must educate "in an age-sensitive and age-appropriate manner. Very young children, it is true, may well experience confusion and distress if confronted with a plethora of choices too early, or with teachers who tell them that their way of life embodies only one possibility among many" (p. 95). But, Levinson insists, the necessary age-sensitive and age-appropriate education can perfectly well be supplied in detached schools—there is no need to provide a religiously homogeneous and supportive environment even for very young children. Similarly, Ackerman (p. 157) urges that, for the sake of children's cultural coherence, "the early stages of a liberal curriculum will content themselves with the elaboration of life options relatively close to those with which the child is already familiar," but he never takes seriously the idea that, especially for the children of devoutly religious parents, this might require a separate religious elementary school.

My thesis in this chapter is that the significance of cultural coherence as a prerequisite for autonomy provides one of several reasons to believe that religious primary schools are an important part of the best sequence of educational institutions to cultivate ethical autonomy in the children of religious parents.[1] Ackerman and Levinson both err by insisting that children's need for cultural coherence is always satisfactorily accommodated by modifying the curriculum and pedagogy of secular, detached schools, rather than by making provision for religious schooling. Levinson (p. 95) is right to say that "the early grades . . . are not the appropriate context in which to teach radical doubt or critical thinking skills"—and, as we shall see, this is true not only because of concerns for cultural coherence—but she fails to see that the same reasons that tell against teaching young children to be skeptics also yield a powerful case for providing religious primary schools to consolidate the child's grasp of her primary culture and begin the practice of ethical reasoning within it, long before she is cognitively equipped to engage in fully fledged autonomous reflection. In the rest of the chapter, I develop this case in four separate arguments before considering what regulations are nonetheless appropriate to ensure that a religious primary education does not retard or stifle the child's development as an autonomous person.

Primary Culture and Identity

The first argument in favor of religious primary schools as instruments of education for autonomy appeals to the importance of consolidating a young child's primary culture by designing the school experience to harmonize with and reinforce the ethical messages she receives at home.[2] If cultural coherence is an important step on the road to per-

---

[1] As I discussed in the introduction, my arguments about religious schools and families should, in principle, generalize to nonreligious comprehensive ethical doctrines. The development of autonomy in children whose parents subscribe to such nonreligious doctrines would be best served by primary schools that reflect the familial values, although without a critical mass of like-minded parents in a local area it might be impractical for such schools to operate privately and unreasonably burdensome on the public purse for the state to fund them. I focus on religious doctrines in large part because they often do have the requisite local concentration of believers to make an affiliated school practical and cost-effective.

[2] De Jong and Snik (2002) seem to appeal to something similar to my argument from identity and primary culture in their argument for public funding of religious primary schools.

sonal autonomy, as Ackerman and Levinson admit, then there is value in positively promoting such coherence. In this spirit, Coons and Sugarman (1999, pp. 82–83) recommend "binding the younger child's home values to his formal education as a means of promoting emotional security and appreciation for the role of personal values." As we shall soon discuss, certain types of religious primary education are at odds with the goal of eventually developing the child's ethical autonomy, but most forms of religious instruction that include the ideas of rational justification and reasonable disagreement can be defended as ways of consolidating the young child's provisional sense of identity with which he will later set out on the road to autonomy. Children need a point of departure for that journey, and, as we saw in chapter 3, it is obviously not something that they can choose for themselves. Here I emphasize that the child's provisional ethical identity should be secure and stable, for all that it is provisional. As Burtt (1996, p. 425) argues, "the effort to provide a consistent moral and religious environment for a child represents an important way of building the psychological and cognitive resources the child will need to choose and lead a good life as an adult."

Of course, many children's homes sadly do not provide a stable and well-ordered ethical environment of any kind: for these children, no primary school, religious or otherwise, will enable them to enjoy the kind of consistent and coherent ethical upbringing that best lays the foundations for future development of autonomy. As discussed in chapter 5, there are important reasons of principle, as well as practical arguments that are perhaps even weightier, not to grant the liberal state the power to intervene extensively and routinely in the lives of families, whether to give children a more coherent ethical upbringing or for the sake of other noble-sounding goals. Therefore, there is unfortunately only so much that liberal states can do through education policy to help lay the foundations for autonomy in children who are being raised in homes that lack a consistent ethical environment. Of course, a good school may provide for such children the only example of what it means to live by a coherent set of ethical principles, but those principles could perfectly well be nonreligious, so it is not these children whose developmental needs warrant public support of religious primary schools. But the situation is otherwise for children who do grow up in a strongly religious family, and for whom the threat to the coherence of their ethical upbringing lies precisely in the possibility that their primary school will actively or passively undermine the principles espoused and practiced at home. As McLaughlin (1985, p. 122) notes, "religious elements are not essential to the coherence of primary cultures for children in general, but they may nevertheless be crucial to those whose parents are themselves religious"—the issue is one of consonance between home and school. It is for these children from religious families that religious primary schools have the potential to play an important positive role in the first stage of education for autonomy.

For the young child of devoutly religious parents, a school with a secular curriculum, diverse membership, and not a whisper of religious reasons in its pedagogical methods of motivation and justification can be a profoundly disorientating place. To send a six-year-old each day from a religious home to a "detached" school "places the strongest educational influences in the child's life at cross purposes and sows confusion and discord rather than coherence and stability" (Gilles, 1996, p. 969). In his more recent work, Callan (1997, p. 158) also recognizes this danger associated with premature exposure to ethical diversity: "if the attempt were to leave children feeling merely confused, demeaned, or frightened, then some real harm might be done." Notice that this problem is not solved merely by designing the school's curriculum in an age-sensitive but still secular way, as Levinson would propose: it is often precisely the total absence of familiar and reassuring religious language and cues and the presence of a large majority of children from families with very different ethical doctrines that threaten to disturb the young child's fragile sense of self. The problem is especially acute for children from strongly religious families because they will be dramatically outnumbered among their peers by children from families that are less devout, are altogether secular, or subscribe to a different religious doctrine. This might be the predicament, for example, of the relatively few young orthodox Jewish children scattered across a city.

The importance for eventual autonomy of children's establishing a secure and stable provisional ethical identity lies significantly in their learning the nature and value of personal commitments and how to make such commitments. As McDonough (1998, p. 477) puts it, before children can start to reflect autonomously on their conception of the good, they must "learn what it is like to have a conception of the good in the first place." And Galston (2002, p. 105) rightly notes how important it is for future autonomy that children should grow up "knowing what it means to live within a coherent framework of value and belief." It will be instructive to think of this issue in the developmental psychology framework established by James Marcia, following the work of Erikson (see, for example, Erikson, 1968). Marcia (1980, p. 161) defines four identity statuses "in terms of the presence or absence of a decision-making period (crisis) and the extent of personal investment (commitment) in two areas: occupation and ideology."[3] Failure to at-

---

[3] In the case of children, we are typically more interested in the ideology question.

tain ethical autonomy, in my terms, can come about in two ways. The familiar liberal worry is that children will fall into Marcia's (p. 161) category of "Foreclosures," persons whose commitments "have been parentally chosen rather than self-chosen." But scoring equally "low on various measures of self-directedness" (p. 164) are so-called Identity Diffusions, persons who lack "ideological direction, regardless of whether or not they may have experienced a decision-making period" (p. 161). The identity-diffused person "is easily influenced by others and changes her beliefs often" (Miller, 1989, p. 167) precisely because she has not developed the ability to make personal commitments. Whereas Foreclosures typically report strong parental pressure to conform to family values, Identity Diffusions frequently describe themselves as feeling "detached" from their parents (Marcia, 1980, p. 171). Our efforts to avoid Foreclosure must not disrupt the coherence of the child's primary culture to the extent that she develops into an Identity Diffusion, lacking an understanding of the nature and value of personal commitments.

As I discussed in chapter 3, any attractive conception of personal autonomy must incorporate the capacity to undertake ethical commitments that are lasting, serious, and partly constitutive of one's identity, although truly autonomous persons cannot regard any of their beliefs or values as being entirely beyond review. It should also be noted that this capacity for structuring one's life according to serious ethical commitments is not something whose development we can take for granted in children's development. Whether or not one agrees with Galston (1989, p. 101) that "the greatest threat to children in modern liberal societies is not that they will believe in something too deeply, but that they will believe in nothing very deeply at all," it is surely true that a sense of apathy, lack of purpose, and the inability to find adequate reasons for plotting a determinate life course are not uncommon psychological symptoms in modern societies. This may well be connected with the conceptual observation, made in chapter 3, that pluralism, whether conceived as meta-ethical fact or limitation of human reason, means that many ethical choices are fundamentally underdetermined by reason. A secure grounding in a coherent primary culture is an important way to avoid the kind of listlessness that can all too easily inhibit autonomy just as much as lack of critical reflection. So we should not be too concerned with Callan's (1985, p. 116) observation that a thoroughly religious upbringing may leave certain ethical options "less eligible" to the teenage child or young adult: this loss of eligibility may simply be the price of having a sufficiently substantive provisional identity to be able to grasp the nature and value of personal commitment. Even Gardner (1988, p. 97), for all his worries about the threat to autonomy posed by the "stickiness" of early beliefs, takes seriously the thought that "to function effectively people require a set of ideas which occupy a position of some permanence."

REASONING WITHIN AN ETHICAL FRAMEWORK

A second reason to believe that religious primary schools may form part of the best educational program to cultivate autonomy in the children of religious parents rests on the idea that ethical reasoning and reflection begin and are best learned within a framework of provisional commitments (Crittenden, 1988, pp. 136–37). The best theoretical defense of this claim lies in the work of Thiessen (1987), who builds upon but significantly departs from the analysis offered by Hirst in his *Moral Education in a Secular Society* (1974). Hirst differentiated and analyzed several concepts of education, including education as "transmission of beliefs" and education as "development of critical rationality." Thiessen's argument is that these two concepts should be reinterpreted as two phases of liberal education, and that the transition from the first phase to the second should be gradual. Initially, ethical reasoning takes the limited form of considering how to apply or interpret fairly concrete principles within a particular ethical system that is transmitted to children but not itself justified to them in rational terms. Later, the child is exposed to alternative principles and ethical systems, but this first exposure is "still from the vantage point of the tradition into which he/she was first initiated" (Thiessen, 1987, p. 229). Only later still are children typically ready for and able to profit from critical reflection on the very framework of principles and commitments within which their ethical reasoning capacities were first developed.

The idea that ethical reasoning is best taught at first within a fairly well-defined ethical system is justified by appeal to the young child's limited cognitive capacities and social or emotional maturity. It is important not to overwhelm young children with the sheer complexity and enormity of ethical disagreement in the world, or even within the confines of a local community in a modern, multicultural, multireligious society. Confronted by the full extent of ethical diversity, young children are unlikely to be able to grasp its magnitude without giving up altogether on the idea of reasoning about ethical issues. As we saw in chapter 6, this is a difficult task for adolescents even with their more advanced reasoning capacities: secondary education must be carefully designed if it is successfully to build upon the achievements of the primary phase to cultivate true autonomy in students. For the moment, it suffices to observe that a religious primary school can be the ideal venue in which to encourage an early, limited form of ethical reasoning in the young child of religious parents. The religiously grounded curriculum and pedagogy as well as the high degree of homogeneity in the ethical commitments different children bring from home provide a natural framework within which students can practice ethical dialogue and reflection. "While conflict under some conditions can stimulate growth, the quality of the moral dialogue, particularly in the early years, may rest on a relative compatibility of view among the children. Interchange employing a common and familiar set of values may be the most complex kind of moral engagement possible for young children" (Coons and Sugarman, 1999, p. 84).

It is important to recognize at this stage that not all forms of religious primary education give children an opportunity to begin the development of their ethical reasoning capacities. Parents who desire to raise their child in a way that would endanger her future capacity for autonomy should be denied the right to access a formal education that satisfies that desire, even at the price of risking the coherence of the child's provisional identity. For the sake of their future autonomy, some children need to be rescued from their parents, at least during school hours. But what types of formal religious primary education should be rejected by liberal states on the grounds that they would compromise the long-term goal of cultivating students' autonomy? I return to this important question shortly when I outline the hallmarks of permissible religious primary education and contrast these requirements with the more extensive regulations I have already proposed for secondary schools.

Of course, if ethical reasoning begins within an unquestioned framework of principles and commitments, it cannot end there if it is to merit the title of "autonomous" reasoning. So we should beware of those, like Stephen Gilles (1996, p. 949), who see the value of learning to reason within a religious tradition but do not insist that children should ever be encouraged to reflect on the merits of that tradition versus possible alternatives. "Many people think a child gradually achieves true autonomy by making choices and acting well within a belief system that the child's parents adhere to and instruct the child to accept as true." Cultivating autonomy in children is not simply a matter of teaching the skill of critical reasoning, which can take place wholly within an unexamined doctrine, but rather of initiating children into the practice of using that skill to assess one's ethical conduct and values, including (eventually) one's deepest commitments. So, Gardner (1988, p. 96) is quite right to worry that, all too often, religious beliefs constitute "the frameworks within which inquiry and assessment take place, and, as a result, they remain immune to, or above, our reflections and decisions." And McLaughlin (1984, p. 80) appropriately recognizes the specific danger that "autonomy might be seen as limited in scope (its exercise being confined to details within a religious faith rather than its fundamental basis)." Therefore, although the state can and should support some religious primary schools as providing the best first stage on certain children's developmental path to autonomy, we must not forget the need for a satisfactory second stage at which children reflect critically upon the religious tradition within which they initially learned to reason about ethics. The arguments of this chapter do not undermine but rather give new urgency to the conclusions of the previous chapter, namely, that religious secondary schools must be tightly regulated to ensure that all children are provided with the means and the opportunity to undergo that second stage and emerge from their required education as autonomous persons.

Cognitive Development and Autonomous Reflection

So far, I have argued that religious primary schools of a suitable type may positively advance the cultivation of ethical autonomy in the children of religious parents by consolidating their primary culture and providing a suitable environment in which to begin the practice of ethical reasoning in the limited form of which young children are capable. But both these arguments are premised on the notion that religious institutions are suitable only for an early stage of education for autonomy, and one might wonder whether that stage really lasts until the end of formal primary education. Is it not possible that consolidation of the primary culture and reasoning within an ethical framework are indeed both important characteristics of the early stage of education for autonomy, but that this stage ends much earlier than I imply—perhaps it even ends before formal primary schooling begins? My goal in this third argument is to show that there is a good reason in cognitive developmental theory to draw the line at the end of primary education: only by the age of eleven or twelve have most children developed the cognitive capacities necessary to engage in a recognizable form of autonomous reasoning. Before this age, it would therefore be futile to try to move children beyond the limited practice of reason-giving within a fixed ethical framework that, for children of religious parents, is best taught within a religious school.

The father of modern cognitive developmental psychology, Jean Piaget (1962/1999), argued that the development of intelligence passes through four distinct stages, beginning before the child's acquisition of language with the "sensori-motor stage" and culminating at the age of eleven or twelve years with the stage of "formal operations." Much criticism of Piaget's theory has focused on the apparent rigidity of the stage model, implying as it does a series of abrupt changes from one type of intelligent thought and behavior to another. But it is worth noting that this idea of rigid stages may be less important to Piaget's thought than has often been assumed. "In his last years, Piaget put less emphasis on stages. He began to view development as less steplike, with longer transition periods between stages" (Miller, 1989, p. 99). The value of Piaget's insight for our purposes does not depend on there being a sudden change in all children's intellectual capacities over the summer vacation between the last year at primary school and the first at secondary school: the institutional design of children's formal education will inevitably involve drawing lines and imposing stages in a way that fails fully to capture the nuances of individual children's continuous development. Given the inevitability of drawing such lines, Piaget's theory offers a strong reason to believe that schools designed directly to foster distinctively autonomous reflection will serve little purpose for children before they reach the age of eleven or twelve. To see this reason, we need to understand more about the stages of cognitive development and their connection to ethical autonomy.

At around the age of eleven or twelve, children become capable of "formal deduction, i.e., reasoning from premises that are merely assumed and not supplied by immediate belief," an operation that requires "a sort of detachment from one's own point of view or from the point of view of the moment" (Piaget, 1928/1976, p. 71). Once children reach this stage of formal operations, "thought has become truly logical, abstract, and hypothetical" (Miller, 1989, p. 60). Of course, this claim sounds absurd if it is understood to entail mastery: very few twelve-year-olds exhibit consistently logical thought or operate comfortably at high levels of rational abstraction. Piaget's claim is rather more modest: formal thought, imperfect but recognizable as such, is possible for most children of twelve in a way that cannot be said for most ten-year-olds. Therefore, when children are about twelve, it makes sense for a system of formal education to begin assigning tasks and encouraging behavior that require formal operations. Although he may not use the capability reliably, at around the time he enters secondary school, "the child becomes capable of reasoning not only on the basis of objects, but also on the basis of hypotheses, or of propositions" (Piaget 1962/1999, p. 41).

The significance of formal thought for autonomous ethical reflection should be immediately apparent, given the account of the latter developed in chapters 3 and 4. Autonomous reflection requires an agent to detach herself from some of her existing beliefs and values to seriously consider the merits of an alternative ethical perspective. To see and evaluate the appeal of a doctrine not one's own, one must be able to see what would be entailed by holding a belief or value that one does not actually hold: this involves "reasoning in a hypothetico-deductive manner" (Piaget 1950, p. 148), which is the essence of formal operational thought. Indeed, Piaget sometimes refers to formal operations as "reflective thought" because of the way in which this activity of the mind liberates the person from his concrete circumstances: "with formal operations there is even more than reality involved, since the world of the possible becomes available for construction and since thought becomes free from the real world" (1950, p. 151). In a passage that is particularly revealing for our purposes, Piaget (1928/1976, p. 194) departs from his more typical discussions of elementary scientific method and propositional logic and offers an example of distinctively formal thought that bears a striking resemblance to the autonomous ethical reflection that I have described. "The individual adopts a certain rule as a hypothesis, to see whether by applying it he reaches a state of moral satisfaction, and especially whether he can remain true to himself and avoid contradiction."

Lawrence Kohlberg famously used a Piagetian approach to cognitive development to analyze the development of moral reasoning in children and young adults, arguing that the capacity for formal thought is necessary for persons to reach moral autonomy. Although Kohlberg's explicitly Kantian concern with moral autonomy differs in important respects from my focus on ethical autonomy,[4] there is a clear and instructive analogy between the two concepts in terms of the kind of cognitive capacities that are required for an agent to engage in rational-critical evaluation of the values in which she has been raised. For Kohlberg (1987, p. 283), the achievement of moral autonomy is defined by the transition from conventional to postconventional moral reasoning, where "the term conventional means conforming to and upholding the rules and expectations and conventions of society or authority just because they are society's rules, expectations, or conventions." Directly analogous to Kohlberg's conventional person is Marcia's "Foreclosure," the agent who established a secure ethical identity in her primary culture but lacks ethical autonomy because she still passively and uncritically accepts that ethical doctrine in which she was raised. The ethically autonomous person, like Kohlberg's (p. 283) postconventional person, is one who, by rational reflection, "has differentiated his or her values from the rules and expectations of others and defines these values in terms that may sometimes conflict with those of soci-

---

[4] As discussed in chapter 3.

ety." As Marcia (1980, pp. 180–81) has proposed, both Kohlbergian postconventional moral reasoning and the ethical reflection necessary to autonomously shape one's identity are possible only in subjects whose cognitive development has reached the level at which formal thought is possible.

Cognitive developmental psychology supports both the general notion that education for autonomy should proceed in stages, because younger children lack the resources to practice the critical reflection that partially constitutes the ideal of ethical autonomy, and the specific claim that the first stage, during which the child consolidates his ethical identity as a member of his primary culture and begins to reason within that culture, should extend until the age of eleven or twelve, when the child completes his primary education. As Dearden (1968, p. 181) puts it, "Cartesian doubt, the taking out of one's beliefs and examining of them to establish which are good and which to be rejected, is not normally a feature of the primary school child," so it would be futile to design primary education to enable and encourage the child to make a "choice of ideal: the kind of person that he thinks he ought to be." Primary education must operate within the constraints of young children's developmental level, and it should make a virtue out of a necessity by working both to give students a secure ethical identity within their primary culture and to begin the practice of ethical reasoning within the framework of that culture. Religious primary schools, subject to certain pedagogical requirements that I shall soon elaborate, can be excellent tools for this first stage of education for autonomy.

Maintaining the Option of Autonomous Religious Belief

I have argued that primary school is not the place to expose children to broad ethical diversity and try to teach them to think critically about their family's values and beliefs. To adopt these goals for primary education is to make unrealistic demands upon young children's cognitive faculties and to miss the opportunity to lay important foundations for future autonomy by teaching children both to understand and value personal commitment and to reason within an ethical system. Furthermore, I want to argue, religious primary schools may have another important advantage over secular schools in terms of children's ultimate development as autonomous persons. According to this fourth argument, the systematic religious instruction and supportive atmosphere of faith in a religious primary school are the best means to ensure that the children of religious parents will have an adequate understanding of their family's religion so that it can be the object of an informed choice in their future as autonomous agents. As Shelley Burtt (1994, p. 66) argues, "given the difficulty of nurturing and protecting genuine religious faith . . . schools that claim a commitment to furthering liberal principles regarding the importance of autonomous choice should show particular sensitivity when formulating policies that might have the effect of denying certain choices to their charges." An important premise, strangely neglected by Burtt, to this argument for religious schools on grounds of autonomy is the idea that not all options are equally valuable for an autonomous person: in particular, I suggest, it is of special importance that children be able to make an informed choice about their parents' ethical doctrine once those children have developed their ethical autonomy. As I discussed in chapter 3, it is often a natural expression of one's autonomy to endorse, reflectively and rationally, many elements of the ethical system in which one was raised, and we should do everything we can to ensure that a robust education for autonomy does not preclude its beneficiary from exercising that autonomy to endorse the religious faith of her family.

If children are to have the option of making an autonomous choice to accept the religious beliefs and values of their parents, they must be informed as to the nature of those beliefs and values. But it can be argued that it is difficult, perhaps even impossible, truly to understand and evaluate the option of living according to a particular religious doctrine without experiencing such a life. If we emphasize "the significance of *practice* to religious meaning and understanding" (McLaughlin, 1984, p. 82), we must recognize that children will be much more likely to develop an informed opinion of their parents' religious doctrine if they are immersed in that doctrine as participants during their early years. Of course, even without the help of a religious school, parents can give their children a significant taste of life in accordance with their religious beliefs by taking the children to acts of collective worship, reading to them from religious texts at home, and requiring them to participate regularly in a variety of religious rituals, including prayer. But if children of religious parents attend a secular primary school, the religious nature of their upbringing is necessarily compromised, or at least substantially diluted: teachers will invoke exclusively secular reasons and explanations, there will be no collective acts of worship or supportive references to the familial religion, and the children will mix with peers who mostly do not share or even understand their religious beliefs. If an upbringing in the faith enhances one's understanding of a religious tradition, then religious primary schools can significantly enhance children's future ability to make autonomous choices about their parents' deepest beliefs and values.

Religious primary schools may also make a special contribution to children's understanding of their parents' religion, besides just ensuring that the religious character of their upbringing is not disrupted for six hours a day. At least some of the teachers at religious schools are likely to be qualified to provide religious instruction in a way that most parents are not. Try as they might, many religious parents will lack the knowledge and skills to provide high-quality religious teaching to their children, and such parents might quite naturally desire that the task could be entrusted to an expert. So, Brighouse (1998, p. 733) misses a crucial element when he observes, quite rightly as far as he goes, that "a child cannot be autonomous either in her acceptance or rejection of a religious view unless she experiences somewhat enthusiastic advocacy." Enthusiasm is important, but *competence* in an instructor is even more vital if we are preparing children to make rational, autonomous decisions about their lives. So, when McLaughlin (1985, p. 121) argues that a religious upbringing can be justified in the name of autonomy by the "aim of ensuring a significant engagement with the beliefs, so that their subsequent assessment—and perhaps rejection—will be based on appropriate understanding and acquaintance," we should emphasize that the ideas of "significant engagement" and "appropriate understanding" should not merely be quantitative measures of the child's exposure to religious ideas but rather judgments about the *quality* of the instruction and the child's resulting understanding.

It might be objected that, for the children of devoutly religious parents, primary school is the one sphere in which they can understand "from the inside" what it means *not* to lead a religious life: where is the autonomy gain if the child's informed understanding of a religious tradition is purchased at the price of an adequate grasp of all other choiceworthy options? As we saw in the last chapter, this would indeed be a powerful objection to allowing both the primary and secondary phases of education to take place in religious schools. But it does not discredit the autonomy argument for religious primary schools, and for two reasons. First, primary schools can legitimately focus on consolidating the child's grasp of her primary culture because they will, according to my argument, be followed in the sequence of formal education by schools that will be required to expose adolescents to a range of alternative ethical options in an environment where secular reasoning is practiced and encouraged. Second, the option of religious faith is particularly fragile in most contemporary, pluralist, liberal democratic societies, whose mainstream culture is overwhelmingly secular. In this spirit, McLaughlin (1985, p. 126) suggests that we expand children's range of options by giving them "a substantial exposure to a domain of experience, a tradition of thought and response, a

view of and a way of life which tends to be rather stifled in the general
conditions of the wider society and which is not therefore as available
as it might be for the autonomous consideration of young people."
Does this mean that we should require all children to attend a religious
school, regardless of the ethical convictions of their parents, on the
grounds that we would thereby increase the number of valuable options among which these children might ultimately exercise their ethical autonomy? We would only be led to this conclusion, I suggest, if
we thought that the option of a religious life was a particularly important option for *all* children to have, but I do not make that claim,
and I do not think that any liberal state could justify making it. My
more limited claim is that the option of making an autonomous choice
to live according to religion X is an option of special value to the children of parents who subscribe to religion X.

Again, it should be noted that not all forms of religious primary education would enhance the future autonomy of recipients by providing
them with a more informed basis on which to endorse or reject the
principles of the faith. An authoritarian religious school—one that
merely emphasized obedience to priests, teachers, and religious pre-
cepts without offering some substantive and rational explanation or
justification for these demands—would not equip children to make a
future autonomous decision about the religion in question, assuming
that there are such reasons available within the doctrine and that the
school simply neglected to furnish them to students. Such a school
would also fail to develop in children the primitive ethical reasoning
skills that subsequent formal education seeks to enlarge into the practice of autonomous reflection. So my conclusions here, like my proposals for policy toward secondary schools, are somewhat double-edged:
liberal democratic states certainly cannot justify a general refusal to
fund religious primary schools on the grounds that such schools are
contrary to the goal of cultivating children's autonomy, but nor can
they commit to funding any and all religious primary schools without
first inquiring into their pedagogical methods. Certain types of religious primary school are superior to common, secular schools for the
purpose of preparing children from religious families for future autonomy—these types of religious primary school should be eligible for
public funding.[5] But other types would seriously retard children's de-

---

[5] When I argue for public funding of religious schools, I am not proposing that the
government should run religious schools itself—the state has no authority to interpret
religious doctrine, although it can and must constrain the freedom of other groups to
teach religious doctrine to children in a manner that threatens their development of autonomy and/or the virtues and capacities of citizenship.

velopment of autonomy and should not be funded or even permitted. Liberal states need criteria by which to distinguish autonomy-friendly religious primary schools from those that should be prohibited: it is to this question that I now turn.

HALLMARKS OF PERMISSIBLE RELIGIOUS PRIMARY SCHOOLS

Given the fact that primary school children are not yet developmentally capable of reasoning in a truly autonomous fashion, we must be realistic about the expectations we have of primary schools in terms of their contribution to fulfilling the eventual autonomy goal of education. The requirements I proposed in the last chapter were designed to ensure that secondary schools provide the conditions in which adolescents can begin the practice of genuinely autonomous ethical reflection, but this cannot be the goal for preadolescent children's formal education, which aims instead to lay the foundations upon which secondary schools can build. Indeed, religious primary schools modeled on the ideal of the religious secondary school might well do considerable harm to the prospects for autonomy of a child from a religious family by failing to consolidate the child's primary culture and identity and introducing perspectives and forms of reasoning that the child is not yet ready to comprehend. But this does not mean that "anything goes" at the primary stage, just that requirements for religious primary schools must be tailored to the particular developmental needs and capacities of young children. As Callan (1997, p. 179) rightly points out, "a separate schooling of even brief duration which works against the necessary ends of common education is something no state could rightly sponsor," and, as I have argued against Callan and Gutmann, there is good reason to believe that schools that are incompatible with the proper goals of liberal democratic education policy should actually be prohibited, not merely denied public funding. All primary schools must lay the foundations for the development of autonomy that will be the direct goal of secondary education. In this section, I want to translate this statement into a set of hallmarks of the permissible religious primary school.

A first key point to make is that religious primary schools should not be required, for the sake of cultivating autonomy,[6] to expose children to multiple ethical doctrines or, therefore, to encourage critical engage-

---

[6] I leave open the possibility, discussed in chapter 1 and reiterated in the conclusion to this chapter, that some degree of exposure to ethical diversity at primary school might justifiably be required on civic grounds.

ment with doctrines other than that around which the school is constructed. These requirements are appropriate for secondary schools as the sites where actual autonomous reflection can realistically begin, but they are useless and possibly harmful for preadolescent children, as discussed earlier. In practice, this means that the obligation to balance religious content with secular and other ethical perspectives in the curriculum should not apply to religious primary schools, nor should the requirement of openness to those beyond the community of faith. The temptation to extend these regulations to primary schools derives from the mistaken tendency to regard primary schools as miniature secondary schools rather than accepting that the same ultimate end may imply quite different means in different phases of children's education and development. Even de Jong and Snik (2002, p. 584), who see the distinctive role that religious primary schools can play in laying the foundations for autonomy, err in this way by applying standards appropriate for secondary education to primary schools. "There should be no indoctrination and no segregation. Moreover, in denominational schools alternative views should be brought to the fore, children should not be shielded from diversity, and debate must be tolerated and even encouraged." As we shall see, the prohibition on indoctrination and the requirement of debate are warranted, but the requirements for exposure to ethical doctrines beyond those around which the school is based are altogether too strong. Roughly speaking, religious primary schools should be subject to certain requirements on acceptable pedagogy, but the autonomy goal does not justify the kind of curricular regulations or expectations of openness to which secondary schools should be held.

Let me make one more general point before I examine in more detail the pedagogical hallmarks of a permissible religious primary school. Some theorists make the mistake of insisting that religious primary schools must *aim* at the child's eventual autonomy. For example, de Jong and Snik (p. 583) would require schools whose "aim it is to provide the child with an initial and stable conception of the good as the starting point for autonomous reflection." And McLaughlin (1987, p. 77) insists that each religious school should "have to include a clear commitment to the development of autonomy as part of its aims." Of course, an explicit commitment of this type could never be sufficient to satisfy state regulations: the right aims, even if sincerely held, obviously do not guarantee that appropriate means are chosen or that those means are competently executed. But, I would argue, it should not even be a necessary requirement that religious primary schools explicitly aim at the eventual autonomy of children, although inspectors might naturally be more suspicious of those that did not. "The actual effects of schools may diverge from, and even conflict with, the educational aims to which they aspire. For example, a community whose cultural identity schools explicitly aspire to permanent cultural survival may in fact provide students with the cultural rootedness that allows them to develop an autonomous identity" (McDonough, 1998, p. 484). Of course, to say that our primary concern is with effects, not aims, also serves as a timely reminder of the limitations of purely philosophical analysis in this field. As discussed in the previous chapter, the suitability of particular types of school, curriculum, or pedagogical method for the goal of developing children's autonomy is, at least in principle, an empirical question, but the barriers to meaningful empirical investigation are formidable, and I hope that the arguments of these two chapters have shown that valuable progress can be made by careful theoretical analysis.

What are the hallmarks of acceptable pedagogy in a religious primary school? As Dearden argues in *The Philosophy of Primary Education* (1968, p. 178), we should be deeply suspicious of schools that consistently eschew the practice of giving reasons to their students, whether for ideas taught in class or for exercises of discipline, and deny those same students the opportunity to give and request reasons. "From the premise that moral education is at first largely a matter of having to do what is insisted upon by others, it by no means follows that it must therefore be authoritarian in character." Schools can and should give reasons for the ethical ideas they teach and for their exercises of authority even before children are in a position fully to grasp these reasons, although we should add to Dearden's account that, at primary school, it suffices to give reasons that are valid only within the ethical framework of the school. The practice of reason-giving by teachers stimulates the reasoning capacities of even very young children by "drawing attention to the basis on which people can determine for themselves what to think and do" (Dearden, 1972, p. 464). Through their commitment to reason-giving, permissible religious primary schools will exemplify the principles of "rational authority" rather than "authoritarianism" (Dearden, 1968, p. 170).

But what does this distinction mean in pedagogical practice? First, it means that teachers should typically invoke religious authority indirectly, reasoning inferentially and interpretively from accepted values and principles, rather than by immediate appeal to the claims or commands of a text or divine entity. "Why? Because God (or the Bible) says so" is a prime example of such an unmediated appeal to religious authority: the problem with this kind of authoritarian justification is that it treats as virtues only "unquestioning obedience, conscientious compliance and deference" (Dearden, 1968, p. 170) rather than encouraging the child's instincts and capacities for a primitive form of ethical reasoning. Primary school pedagogy that effectively lays the foundations for children's future autonomy must divert attention from the authoritative status of particular principles, persons, and texts toward the rational process of interpreting and applying the words and ideas of these authorities.[7] At a minimum, this helps children to understand the notion of ethical consistency and how it is derived from the application of unvarying principles: rational authority means the rule of ethical law, not rule by ethical decrees issued by teachers or priests. It should also help to encourage the kind of questioning that is an essential part of the autonomous person's approach to ethical issues: "a child will be encouraged to be critical only if he finds that both he and his teacher can be at any time called upon to defend what they say— to produce, in relation to it, the relevant kind of ground" (Passmore, 1972, p. 420).[8]

Of course, the "relevant kind of ground" in a religious primary school can be a principle or value within the accepted religious doctrine and need not itself be justified in a way that would be acceptable to someone outside the faith. Drawing the distinction between reasons within a narrowly defined religious doctrine, on the one hand, and direct appeals to an authority, on the other, will sometimes be controversial and difficult, but the distinction is meaningful: there is a real difference between offering children reasons that explicitly draw upon interpretations of biblical passages and meeting children's demands for justification with a flat "because the Bible says so." In any case, permissible religious primary schools will employ pedagogical techniques and assign classroom activities that clearly show a commitment to the first conception of justification, namely, the practice of reasoning interpretively to particular applications from general values and beliefs. "The crucial principle seems to be: wherever possible and as soon as possible, substitute problems for exercises. By a problem I mean a situation where the student cannot at once decide what rule to apply or how it applies, by an exercise a situation in which this is at once obvious" (Passmore, 1972, p. 428). Even before children are ready

[7] Notice that diverting attention from an authoritative text does not mean denying the authority of that text. As I have argued throughout this chapter, there is positive value in consolidating young children's commitment to ethical principles such as those found in religious texts. My point here is that children must not be taught that belief in the authority of a text obviates the need for reasoning about how to interpret and apply that text—otherwise, primary schools will fail to develop the primitive ethical reasoning skills I discussed in the second argument above.

[8] See also Matthews (1980) on the natural way in which young children ask questions and the importance for cognitive development of taking these questions seriously.

to subject received ethical principles to criticism, working through such problems can help children develop the skills of and inclination for primitive ethical reasoning, which involves "the application of [rules] to circumstances which cannot be wholly predicted in advance" (Passmore, 1972, p. 428; see also Thiessen, 1987, discussed earlier in this chapter).

In order for the regime to be one of rational authority rather than authoritarianism, it is also necessary for a religious primary school to admit the existence of hard cases, conflicts, and tensions within its religious doctrine. Children should be exposed to, and ideally engaged in, reasoning about the various possible resolutions of these difficulties. So on this point, religious primary and secondary schools should be subject to the same requirement, namely, that they draw children's attention to those issues where reasonable disagreement exists within the faith. "The teacher should certainly place special emphasis, so far as he can, on problems to which the answer is not known, or is a matter of controversy—only in that way can he prepare his pupils for the future. . . . He will hope to teach them in what way the questions which puzzle them ought to be discussed, what sort of evidence is relevant to their solution" (Passmore, 1972, p. 429). It is important to be clear what I am not claiming here. Religious primary schools are certainly not required to teach that there are no right answers to ethical questions, or even always to abstain from presenting an official view on the best answer to disputed questions within their faith. What is important is that the school's orthodoxy not be presented in a way that suppresses or replaces the kind of discussion that teaches children the reasonableness of disagreement on the question. Children benefit from having a stable and coherent ethical upbringing, but their prospects for developing autonomy are not well served if they are taught that reason always selects a unique right answer to tough ethical questions.

Religious primary schools might even adopt Kant's (1784/1983, p. 42) maxim, attributed to Frederick the Great—"argue as much as you want and about what you want, but obey!"—except that schools would have to positively encourage the argument, not merely tolerate it. The point here is that one can lay the foundations for children's future autonomy while still insisting on the temporary settlement of disagreements for practical purposes by an acknowledged ethical authority. This approach would not be acceptable for religious secondary schools because the full realization of ethical autonomy, as I have understood the concept, cannot include an unconditional obligation to obey a particular ethical authority regardless of the outcome of one's ethical reflections. But since primary school children are only practicing some of the skills they will later need to live autonomous lives, they can legitimately be required, in the final instance, to conform to the ethical norms of the school authorities, provided that these are backed by reasons as discussed above. And, of course, those reasons will necessarily be inconclusive because we are talking about areas where reasonable disagreement exists. Nonetheless, religious primary school teachers do not threaten children's future autonomy by insisting that they conform to a particular interpretation of religious doctrine while admitting the reasonableness of other views: Passmore (1972, p. 430) characterizes this, in rather extreme terms, as a "frank admission ... that a particular rule [is] purely arbitrary, not defensible in itself, although perhaps defensible as a rule in the game."

In summary, religious primary schools should be free to design their curricula and to select students and teachers in such a way as to immerse children in a particular religious tradition, but the pedagogy of such schools should be regulated to ensure that children develop the primitive reasoning capacities and inclinations that are the first step on the road to ethical autonomy. In particular, teachers should exercise rational authority by structuring most justifications as reasoned inferences from explicit principles and values, asking and encouraging questions that invite rational analysis rather than recitation of dogma, and highlighting hard cases within the religious doctrine where reasonable disagreement exists even among the faithful. Needless to say, effective public regulation of pedagogical methods is an even more formidable task than those I assigned to the state in the previous chapter—regulation of curricula and enforcement of policies requiring openness to those beyond the community of faith. But systems of teacher training and (re)certification, parental feedback, and school inspections could and should all be designed to help ensure that religious primary schools serve to consolidate children's primary ethical culture without failing to lay the appropriate foundations for their future development into autonomous persons.

Conclusion

The goal of this chapter was to show that religious schools that deliberately shield children from diverse ethical perspectives and secular reasoning, although inadequate for pursuing the autonomy goal in secondary education, may have a valuable positive role to play for certain children at the primary level. I have argued that our sophisticated conception of autonomy, conjoined with insights from developmental psychology and observations of the predominantly secular character of most contemporary liberal democratic societies, justifies treating primary schooling separately from secondary education as the first of two developmental stages on children's path to autonomy. Before children have the cognitive capacity to engage in authentically autonomous rational reflection, their interest in developing autonomy may be best served by consolidating their sense of identity within a coherent primary culture and beginning to teach the practice of ethical reasoning within the framework provided by that secure cultural identity. For the children of religious parents, a religious primary school may well be the ideal institutional environment in which to achieve these first-stage goals, provided that such schools are committed to the principle of rational authority in ethics—and public regulation of pedagogical methods would be needed to ensure that this condition is satisfied. Religious primary schools that satisfy this condition also offer another advantage in terms of the child's future autonomy: persons who have received consistent support and competent instruction in the religious doctrine of their parents are ultimately more likely to be able to make an informed choice on the important question of whether to endorse, modify, or reject their familial culture of upbringing.

In chapter 2, when I was still operating under the political liberal's assumption that the liberal state may not take a position on the value of autonomy for individual lives, I asked whether the civic reasons to oppose narrowly religious schools would always be sufficient to outweigh the claims of certain religious parents who prefer schools that do not tend to develop children's ethical autonomy. I concluded that the civic reasons would not always be sufficient because the principle of political primacy does not apply. One might therefore have supposed, at the end of chapter 2, that the availability of a public justification for adopting autonomy as a goal of public education policy would license the state to prohibit narrowly religious schools altogether.[9] As we saw in the previous chapter, I think this is the correct conclusion with respect to secondary education. And, I have argued, the same form of argument does indeed justify the state in prohibiting the operation of those religious primary schools that would be obstacles to children's future development as autonomous persons.

But now that we have delved more deeply into the conception of autonomy that liberal states can legitimately endorse and identified the best educational institutions to promote its development, it turns out that parents who want a nonauthoritarian religious primary school for their child will find an enlightened liberal state in agreement with them. Parents and state may agree that such a school best furthers the

---

[9] Here I assume the soundness of the civic case against narrowly religious schools, discussed in chapter 1.

important noncivic interests of children, even if they disagree on what exactly those noncivic interests are. At the level of primary education, the path to eventual autonomy need not diverge from the path preferred by parents who are hostile to autonomy, although disagreements about secondary schooling will remind us that these are indeed two different paths that merely happen to coincide for parts of their lengths. Certain children's interests in developing autonomy are best served by a religious primary education that shields students from ethical diversity and secular perspectives, provided that reasoning within the faith is practiced and encouraged. Furthermore, given that ethical autonomy is not only instrumentally valuable to individuals but also a virtue of citizens in liberal democratic regimes (as discussed in chapter 2), nonauthoritarian religious primary schools may turn out to be the best instruments of *civic* education for the children of religious parents. But, of course, the cultivation of ethical autonomy does not exhaust the civic goals of education. Religious primary schools that are perfectly appropriate to provide the first stage in an education for autonomy but that nonetheless foster intolerance and lack of respect for other religions are not ideal instruments of civic education: public regulation should seek to correct the civic shortcomings of these schools without, as far as possible, erasing those features that are especially suitable to lay the foundations for children's future development of autonomy.

Conclusion

QUESTIONS ABOUT public funding and regulation of religious schools are on the agenda in liberal democratic countries around the world—and for good reason. Even in societies where levels of religious belief are relatively low, there are significant numbers of parents who strongly desire that their children should attend a religious school. Many such parents cannot afford or otherwise access private schools, and even those who have the financial means often claim that the government ought to foot the bill, just as it routinely does for secular schooling. At the same time, citizens and policymakers in many liberal democratic states are concerned about the civic costs of religious education: schools that are segregated along religious lines may not be effective in teaching the virtues of tolerance and mutual respect and the capacities for deliberation that are so important in citizens of pluralist liberal democracies. Others are uneasy about religious education not (only) because of its perceived inadequacies as an instrument of civic education, but (also) because they believe it threatens to retard or stifle children's development as ethically autonomous persons. There are strong emotions and powerful arguments in play on all sides of the debate, but sometimes the only point of agreement among the parties is a common recognition that the stakes are high.

So, the questions are firmly on the political agenda, but how should they be resolved? I hope to have shown that the first step toward resolution must be a searching inquiry into the principles that should govern liberal education policy: before we can judge whether a particular type of religious school should be permitted and/or funded by the state, we need to develop and defend a normative account of the goals of public funding and regulation of schools. Given the widespread disagreement about educational goals that characterizes most pluralist societies, we have a formidable challenge to identify those goals that can justifiably be adopted by the state and imposed on all families. Meeting this challenge requires deciding on the correct division of authority between parents and the state in the education and upbringing of children, which in turn depends in part upon identifying and deciding how to balance the legitimate but competing claims and interests of parents, children, and other citizens. These are the fundamental issues of political philosophy with which I have been concerned throughout this work; I hope to have convinced you, at the very least, that one cannot take an intelligent stand on the policy questions without doing some serious philosophy.

In chapters 6 through 8, I tried to demonstrate that theoretical arguments are not only necessary to address the policy questions but also, and perhaps more surprisingly, sufficient to reach some moderately specific and determinate answers to those questions. The goals that should be common to all schooling in the liberal state—cultivation of children's capacities and inclinations for autonomy and good citizenship—are scarcely amenable to measurement by the techniques of social science, but theoretical and conceptual analysis can help us to identify the types of educational institutions that are likely to foster autonomy and good citizenship. I presented the conclusions of this analysis in the form of hallmarks of permissible religious primary and secondary schools, schools that are compatible with the proper goals of liberal education policy. All religious schools must teach children the skills of ethical reasoning, and religious secondary schools must expose students fair-mindedly to a variety of ethical doctrines other than the religious tradition with which the school is affiliated. Religious schools that fail to meet these requirements should be prohibited, but there is a flip side to my position that is friendlier toward religious schools, at least compared to the policy we currently find in America. I argue that liberal states should not merely permit but also fund religious schools that satisfy these regulations, out of fairness to religious parents and in recognition of the particular suitability of religious primary schools to provide the first stage of education for autonomy for children from religious families.

In the remainder of this conclusion, I shall not reiterate my claims about the particular regulations that are necessary to ensure that religious primary and secondary schools are compatible with the proper goals of liberal education policy. Instead, I want to review the main normative theoretical claims that I have made and reflect briefly on their broader significance, that is, their implications for issues other than religious schooling. My goal in broadening the discussion at this late stage is not to provide any definitive answers, but merely to suggest ways in which the arguments and perspectives in this book might change our understanding not only of educational theory and practice but also of liberal politics more generally.

Let me begin by suggesting two broad lessons that should be learned in the sphere of education. First, there is an urgent need to expand our conception of educational goals beyond scholastic achievement and to fight the excessive focus on children's performance on standardized tests. It has become an orthodoxy in many countries that schools are to be evaluated and ranked primarily, and often exclusively, on the basis of students' test scores. Critics of the prevailing evaluative standards rarely challenge the assumption that scholastic achievement is the right metric: they argue merely that the particular tests being used are not the best way to measure scholastic achievement; or they demand that school rankings should control for the socioeconomic status of the student body to ensure that we are actually assessing schools rather than simply proving once again that kids with educated and affluent parents perform well on tests. In the United States, constitutional issues aside, too much of the debate about school vouchers focuses on the narrow question of whether private religious schools enable children to achieve higher test scores.

Of course, scholastic achievement matters, both for its own sake and for economic reasons, and we ought to find better ways to assess schools' success in promoting such achievement by their students. But the greatest danger is not that we will use the wrong measure of schools' contributions to children's academic achievement, but rather that we will neglect entirely the vital roles that schools should play in pursuing other educational goals, especially those whose realization is extremely difficult to measure in any precise way. Political philosophers and educational theorists spend a great deal of time talking about the civic functions of education and the role that schools can play in cultivating children's autonomy, but these goals need to have a more prominent place on the agendas of policymakers and educational professionals. There is nothing wrong with the principle that schools should be held accountable for their performance, but if performance is defined and measured narrowly, then schools have an almost irresistible incentive to adopt a similarly narrow conception of their goals. As it stands, this dominant but impoverished conception of education's purposes translates into schools that often both fail to cultivate children's autonomy and threaten our collective pursuit of liberal democratic justice.

The second lesson to be learned regarding education is that serious attention must be given to the status and role of private and home schools in liberal democratic societies. For too long, liberals have been content to accept an educational system in which wealthy parents can send their children to a private school of a type that the state refuses to provide for poorer families. The principle to which I am objecting is not, I hasten to add, the one that permits wealthy parents to spend ten times as much money on their child's education as the state spends per capita in the public schools.[1] My concern is rather with cases in

---

[1] Perhaps it is objectionable on other grounds for the state to permit unlimited spending on private education, but that is not my subject here.

which it would be no more expensive for the state to provide a school of the type that it routinely permits the private sector to operate, but the state nonetheless refuses to do so. One of two things is wrong in these cases. If the type of school that runs privately and that poor parents want for their children is suitable to pursue the various goals of education in a liberal democratic society, then the state acts unfairly toward poor families by refusing to provide public funding for their children to attend such a school. This is an unreasonable restriction on parents' freedoms to direct the upbringing of their children. Again, I am assuming that the poor parents are not asking for any more public money than is currently being spent upon their children's education: they just want that money diverted to pay for a particular type of schooling that, *ex hypothesis*, the state deems suitable to advance the proper goals of education. Alternatively, if the state refuses to fund children's attendance at such a school because schools of this type do *not* meet reasonable public requirements, then that same reason should suffice to prohibit the operation of private or home schools of this type. Put simply, private and home schools must not offer an escape route for wealthy parents who want to buy their way out of educational requirements that strike the proper balance between the parents' legitimate interests, the needs of the child, and the value of sustaining and improving the liberal democratic regime for the benefit of citizens in current and future generations.

But let us now leave aside questions of educational theory and policy altogether to ask about the broader significance of my arguments for liberal politics. I have proposed answers to two major questions in contemporary liberal thought—one about the relationship between autonomy and liberal politics, the other about the status of civic goals and values when they conflict with the private values of citizens—and in each case the answer has important implications, both for public policy beyond the sphere of education and for our understanding of liberal political theory. I cannot do more than gesture toward these implications as I review the normative theoretical content of the answers I have offered, but I nonetheless hope that my gestures will point the way for further research.

In chapters 3 through 5, I aimed to restore the value of individual autonomy to its rightful place at the heart of liberal political philosophy. There were two key moves in the argument: rejecting a series of caricatures of autonomy that make the idea of ongoing rational ethical reflection sound incoherent or deeply undesirable, and distinguishing claims about the intrinsic value of autonomy (which are rightly judged inadmissible to liberal politics) from those about autonomy's instrumental value (which the state can and should endorse). In short, my conclusion is that liberalism can and should be based around the value of autonomy without thereby becoming a perfectionist political theory, that is, without taking a substantive position on the nature of the good life for man. But it is worth pausing to consider why I have gone to such lengths to distinguish my account of the central place of autonomy in liberal theory from more familiar, perfectionist accounts. I want to suggest that the controversial nature of liberalism's claims, although perhaps not diminished, is nonetheless importantly refocused by my nonperfectionist approach.

The liberal state must not be drawn into arguments about the nature of the good life, but I say this not because of any general requirement that the liberal state remain agnostic on controversial matters. It is often necessary for the state to take a position that many citizens vehemently reject. But where controversy concerns the substantive merits of competing ethical views, it is neither necessary nor permissible for the state to take a position. Society's ongoing debates about the nature of the good life would be both distorted and deadened by the intervention of a player with the state's authority and coercive power. It is a bedrock principle of liberalism that, as long as they do not harm others, citizens have the right to make and live by their own ethical judgments, whether these judgments are right or wrong, wise or foolish. If autonomy is to be regarded as a component of the good life, this is a judgment to be made not by the state but by individual citizens in their private lives. Liberal perfectionism is a contradiction in terms: on this point the Rawlsian political liberals are correct.

But my claim that the liberal state rightly takes no substantive position on the nature of the good life does not entail the false conclusion that liberal politics should not aim at, among other things, equipping citizens to live a good life. We should reject the austere libertarian position according to which the only role of the state is to enforce contracts and protect citizens from harm by others. Nonlibertarian liberals, who are often grouped together under the dubious name of "egalitarian liberals," are united in the belief that the state has a legitimate and important positive role in ensuring that citizens possess the various means to a good life. In John Rawls' influential formulation of this goal (1971/1999 p. 79), the "primary goods" with whose distribution the state rightly concerns itself include income and wealth because money is an all-purpose means to the pursuit of the good life, no matter what one's conception of the good may be. Leaving aside the question of exactly what distribution of the primary goods is required by justice, one way to understand my defense of autonomy's instrumental value would be as a proposal to add autonomy to the list of primary goods. That list already includes the negative freedom to revise one's ethical commitments, but without autonomy it does not include the capacity or disposition to use that freedom in a way that is likely to improve those commitments. I hope, therefore, that my argument for the instrumental value of autonomy will be understood as, among other things, a contribution to the general debate within political philosophy about the proper list of goods whose availability to citizens is properly a matter of liberal public concern.

The liberal state must aim to equip its citizens to find and lead a good life without, as far as possible, biasing their choices among substantive conceptions of the good. From a liberal perspective, it is not hard to see the objection to putting the authority of the state behind Aristotle's advice (1984, p. 225) that pregnant women should make regular visits to the temple because walking there will be good exercise![2] The liberal state rightly seeks to promote citizens' health, subject to the constraints imposed by antipaternalism, because health is instrumentally valuable for the pursuit of the good life,[3] but the health benefits of a brisk walk do not depend upon there being a house of God at one's destination. Of course, the successful promotion of any instrumentally valuable good will necessarily affect individuals' substantive ethical choices. Public health campaigns that publicize the risks of smoking and support people who are trying to quit the habit will, if successful, reduce the number of people whose idea of a good life involves a pack of cigarettes each day. Similarly, as we have seen, successful promotion of autonomy will reduce the number of people who belief in Creationism. Neutrality of effect is a futile goal. But the liberal state should affect a citizen's ethical choices only by providing her with better tools—information and the skills, inclinations, and opportunities to use it—with which to decide for herself how to live her life. And so, as I argued in chapters 7 and 8, the fact that certain types of religious school are inimical to the goal of education for autonomy does not license the liberal state to discriminate against other religious schools whose curriculum, pedagogy, and membership are compatible with that goal.

Unlike perfectionist defenses of autonomy, my position maintains a clear distinction between the values and ethical beliefs that constitute a person's conception of the good, on the one hand, and the manner in which she arrives at and holds that conception of the good, on the other hand. In so doing, I reject Alasdair MacIntyre's (1981) view that the good life is properly understood as *consisting in* the ongoing quest

---

[2] Of course, the "car culture" in America has already done much to defeat the force of this advice!

[3] There are also civic reasons for the state to take an interest in the health of its citizens.

for one's ethical beliefs and values; there is a certain poetry in this view but, I argue, it ultimately rests on conceptual confusion.[4] Indeed, my defense of the admissibility to liberal politics of claims about autonomy's instrumental value also casts doubt on the weaker claim that autonomy itself can properly be understood as being part of a person's conception of the good. If autonomy is conceptualized, as I argue it should be, simply as ongoing rational scrutiny of oneself and one's ethical beliefs and values, then it is no more than a bare method or procedure. By this I mean that an agent's commitment to practice autonomous reflection on an ongoing basis does not constitute acceptance of a substantive ethical value. Autonomy has instrumental value, most notably because of its epistemological utility, and it can be understood as a way of taking full moral responsibility for one's conception of the good,[5] but it lacks the substance of a value that might feature in a person's conception of the good.

One might perhaps find a type of satisfaction in practicing autonomous reflection, but only because one expects thereby to achieve good results and/or to assume full responsibility for one's beliefs and values: these types of satisfaction do not appeal to any intrinsic value of autonomy. The value of autonomous reflection might be understood to be intrinsic if autonomy were conceptualized as self-creation *ex nihilo*, but in chapter 3 I rejected this view as incoherent, arguing instead that autonomous reflection strives to reach outcomes that are faithful to a preexisting self, internally coherent, and consistent with the evidence of the external world. Mill's ideal of individuality, also discussed in chapter 3, is a potential bearer of intrinsic ethical value precisely because, unlike my conception of autonomy, it celebrates certain substantive ethical choices, those that are original in that they challenge customary practices and reduce the individual's conformity to social conventions. But, I suggest, autonomy as I have understood it is not something to which we can meaningfully attach intrinsic ethical value. If I am right, all coherent perfectionist accounts of autonomy's value must, like Mill's, be operating with a conception of autonomy that is different from and "thicker" than mine.

My nonperfectionist defense of autonomy will not be accepted by all citizens; in particular, it will be rejected by people who maintain that unreflective faith and/or uncritical obedience to authority are better routes to the good life. It is hard to estimate how many such opponents truly exist in any particular liberal democratic society. But I think

[4] I am grateful to Marilyn Friedman for pointing out the inconsistency between MacIntyre and myself on this point.
[5] I explored this argument for autonomy's value in chapter 4.

it is an appreciable advantage of my nonperfectionism that it does not alienate those religious believers who accept autonomy's instrumental value, who believe that the exercise of autonomy has led them to true religious beliefs, but who deny that the autonomous manner in which they hold those true beliefs is any part of the goodness of the life they now lead. Such citizens believe that autonomy has been an important tool in their lives so far, and they acknowledge the wisdom of keeping that tool at hand for the rest of their lives, but they insist that autonomy is nothing more than a tool, and I can see no reason why the liberal state should contradict them on this point. Again, it will be hard to know how numerous these citizens are relative to the die-hard opponents of autonomy, and I certainly do not believe that rival versions of liberalism should be judged by weight of numbers in a popularity contest, but I think it is important to observe that there is a category of citizens for whom the switch from a perfectionist to a nonperfectionist defense of autonomy's value makes the difference between an argument they cannot accept and one that they can (and sometimes do) accept.

Let us now consider a putative counterexample that is designed to show that the nonperfectionism of my defense of autonomy is actually a weakness and not a strength.[6] A monk has taken the traditional vows of poverty, chastity, and obedience. He understands these vows to be irrevocable, life-long commitments. Since he has consciously and explicitly renounced the prospect of reevaluating these vows at any time in the future, the monk is, at least with regard to these major ethical commitments, a paradigmatic example of a nonautonomous person. But, it might be argued, unless one takes the perfectionist view that autonomy is a necessary component of the best life for any person, it is hard to see that the liberal state should find fault with the choices that this monk has made. He is, by conventional standards and in the estimations of many, living a noble and admirable life of discipline and humility. If the liberal state were to succeed fully in its quest to promote autonomy, no one would take monastic vows and there would be, in a sense, no more monks. Can we accept a liberal theory with these implications?

The first response to this challenge is, of course, to make clear that the liberal state makes no judgment about the substantive content of the monk's vows. It is not the role of the state to determine whether chastity is the right principle by which this person should govern his sexual capacities. As far as the state in concerned, this monk is to be judged no differently from a man who has taken a vow to have consen-

---

[6] I am grateful to Larry May for suggesting this example.

sual sex twice a week. In both cases, the liberal state says merely that it is unwise to foreclose the possibility of reexamining one's circumstances and the grounds for one's ethical commitments. The world changes and human judgments are fallible. Ethical commitments have value, but they should be revocable. To qualify as autonomous the monk would not have to expose himself to daily temptation—fast cars to make vivid the opportunity cost of the vow of poverty, scantily clad beauties to remind him of the pleasures of the flesh—but he would have to periodically revisit and reaffirm his grounds for a life of poverty and chastity. It might be empirically difficult to determine whether a monthly ritual in the monastery at which monks renew their vows represents a genuine opportunity for autonomous reflection or rather an institutional device for reinforcing commitment. But that difficulty does not disturb the principle: the liberal state recommends ongoing ethical reflection to all of its citizens, including poor, chaste monks.

But, the challenge continues, there can be wisdom in the strategy of precommitment. We are all prone to err, and we may abandon important ethical commitments in a moment of weakness if we allow ourselves to reevaluate them. Following Jon Elster (2000), we might look to the story of Ulysses for an example of a prudent and successful strategy of irrevocable precommitment. Ulysses binds himself to the mast of his ship to avoid succumbing to the lure of the Sirens' song. If Ulysses was right to do this, as he surely was, then why could one not similarly approve of the monk's vows? The answer is that metaphorically binding oneself to the mast is a good strategy only when one reasonably and reliably expects one's capacity for rational thought and action to decline significantly in the future. This is precisely the scenario that Ulysses confronts: he has good grounds for believing that the song of the Sirens will attract him in a way that bypasses his rational faculties. His strategy of precommitment is therefore not a renunciation of autonomy, but rather a recognition that his autonomy will not be operational while the Sirens are singing to him. The monk, *ex hypothesis*, has no good reason to believe that his capacity for autonomous judgment will decline precipitously in the short or medium term. If he did have such a reason then he, like Ulysses, would actually be manifesting his autonomy by taking steps to ensure that the rational judgments he makes now will continue to govern his actions even after his capacity for such rationality has been compromised.

So, it is no embarrassment to the nonperfectionist defense of autonomy that it entails disapproval of the practice of taking irrevocable vows. Without judging the content of particular ethical commitments—something that the liberal state is indeed bound not to do—the state rightly urges all its citizens to remain open-minded about their conceptions of the good in light of human fallibility, the changing world, and our potential to learn both from experience and from the views of others. And, of course, the liberal state does not deny the *right* of adults to make vows and other binding contracts with regard to their conception of the good; it merely declares that it is unwise to exercise the right. Adults are ultimately free to make their own mistakes both in their substantive ethical choices as well as in their second-order decisions about how to make those first-order choices. As we turn our attention now more directly to issues of public policy, the case of the monk reminds us that the position I advocate not only is nonperfectionist but also retains a strong liberal opposition to paternalism—the state should endorse autonomy and require schools to promote it, but it must not coerce adults who wish to live nonautonomous lives. It might seem, therefore, that I have placed autonomy at the heart not of liberal politics but only of liberal education policy—this would still be an important conclusion, but its implications would be quite narrowly circumscribed.

However, it would be a mistake to infer from my antipaternalism that the value of autonomy should not figure prominently in the liberal state's relationship with those of its citizens who are over the age of majority but do not yet have children. Although the liberal state may not coerce adult citizens into developing or exercising autonomy, this is not to say that its policies and priorities may not be importantly influenced by its recognition of the value of autonomy. In particular, I suggest, liberal public policy should be guided by the goal of maximizing *opportunities* for all citizens to develop and exercise their ethical autonomy. What might this mean in practice? Liberal states should support institutions and programs that expose people to ethical difference and foster deliberation, encouraging citizens to interact open-mindedly and to learn about alternative systems of value and belief. Only in schools will such interaction be mandatory, but there are many other institutions and venues in civil society that the liberal state should create as (or convert into) spaces that stimulate and support ethical dialogue and autonomous reflection.

A few examples will give the flavor of this proposal. The state should sponsor the arts and the media in ways that increase the availability and visibility of cultural forms that challenge our ethical assumptions and prompt us to reflect. Whether through direct state provision or by offering incentives to the private sector, public spaces—shopping malls, parks, town squares—should be designed and operated in ways that combat patterns of segregation and trends toward privatization of citizens' ethical lives. Adult education should be seen as a legitimate and worthwhile use of public funding not only because of its potential to provide individual and social economic benefits through imparting vocational skills but also because it can open up new opportunities for citizens to encounter and rationally debate unfamiliar ideas. With a broader conception of the purposes of adult education, we should see a broader range of subjects being taught in institutions that receive tax dollars. There should also be public support for associations in civil society whose members come from multiple religious and ethnic communities and that therefore help to break down patterns of de facto segregation. Theorists of civic engagement have recently urged the revitalization of social networks that "are outward looking and encompass people across diverse social cleavages," thereby building up so-called bridging social capital (Putnam, 2000, p. 22). I suggest that the liberal state might promote these networks not only because of the civic value of increased social capital, but also because of the benefits of this type of interaction to citizens' personal autonomy.

It should now be apparent that public endorsement of the value of autonomy would also have important implications for the debate over affirmative action in higher education and beyond. Affirmative action programs, originally conceived and justified as providing long-overdue opportunities to members of minority groups that have faced (and often continue to face) systematic discrimination, are now increasingly framed in terms of the benefits that accrue to *all* of an organization's members from the achievement of a more representative work force or student body. In recent debates this latter claim has often been called the "diversity argument" for affirmative action, and its force is significantly increased once the promotion of individual autonomy becomes a public priority. The conceptual and strategic importance of the diversity argument is that it emphasizes affirmative action's benefits to members of majority groups, who had previously been presented simply as the losing parties whose sacrifice is, according to supporters of affirmative action, morally required. A focus on the value of autonomy promises to turn this picture on its head. As we saw in chapter 5, it is often cultural majorities rather than minorities whose autonomy is most likely to be undermined by insufficient exposure to diverse ethical perspectives. And it is important to remember that affirmative action is not limited to university admissions: liberal states might also help to increase diversity in the workplace by sponsoring exchange schemes that give people a chance to live and work in a different country or region, or by providing incentives for employers to expand their recruitment activities among underrepresented religious and ethnic groups.

I do not, of course, intend to prescribe the details of particular strategies that states should employ to promote autonomy, but merely to illustrate the claim that there are many ways in which liberal states might act to promote opportunities for citizens to develop and exercise their ethical autonomy without coercing those adult citizens who choose not to live autonomously. Public recognition of the value of autonomy should profoundly shape the liberal state's response to the challenges and opportunities of a multicultural society. One important subset of those "multicultural issues" involves the desire of certain members of minority cultural groups for state assistance in preserving institutions that support their cultural identity in the face of strong social and economic pressures for members to assimilate to the dominant culture. Autonomy is not well served by policies that facilitate cultural self-segregation of adults, especially when individuals already face significant pressure not to stray from the group. But, I should add, not all types of interaction between members of different cultures are equally likely to generate autonomy benefits for participants: the state should selectively sponsor projects that provide opportunities for all participants to have their voices properly heard, in the hope that their ideas will be judged rationally and on their merits. A debate or panel discussion featuring representatives of different cultural groups would be a better candidate event for public funding than would a shouting match or, dare I say, a rugby match.

Should we worry that some ethical traditions will become extinct without special treatment by the state? The liberal state quite properly provides financial support to certain arts organizations that would not otherwise survive in a marketplace whose currency is simultaneously ideas and money, but the justification of this use of public funds must be premised on a claim that these cultural forms deserve privileged status, that they are higher or special in some way other than merely being different from their more commercially successful competitors. If this claim is correct, there may be a compelling case for public subsidies that enable broader access to an important cultural form that is otherwise available only to a few. Typically there is no analogous argument to be made on behalf of state support for endangered minority cultures because those cultures have no claim to privileged status.

Autonomy is enhanced by the availability in society of a diverse range of options (Raz, 1986, p. 373) but, as Rawls (1993/1996, pp. 36–37) posits, this condition of pluralism can be expected to persist under a liberal regime without the need for state intervention to buttress minority ways of life. The fact that some cultures disappear from a society does not diminish the autonomy of its members as long as the extinct cultures are replaced by others as viable objects of autonomous choice.

Even the appearance of a homogeneous dominant culture can be misleading; on closer inspection, one often finds significant and evolving differences behind a veneer of uniformity. John Stuart Mill (1859/1989, p. 64) rightly observed that we all benefit from exposure to people whose ways of life are very different from our own, but it is important to recall that he uses this claim in defense only of liberty and toleration and not to argue that those who practice "experiments in living" deserve special support from the public purse.

Once autonomy is enshrined as a public value, I argue that there can be no serious objection to taxing opponents of autonomy to support autonomy-promoting programs; antipaternalism requires only that the state should not coerce adults into living autonomously (even assuming that such a goal could be achieved coercively). It should also be noted that a set of policies designed to maximize adults' opportunities to develop and exercise autonomy does not make redundant the paternalistic policy of promoting autonomy in schools. If people are not taught as children to practice and value autonomy, they are less likely as adults to be willing and able to take advantage of the opportunities provided by voluntary associations and other institutions of civil society. School days are the time for paternalism, and a state that adopts autonomy as a public value should insist that the cultivation of autonomy is one of the paternalistic goals of schooling.

Restoring autonomy to the heart of liberal political philosophy should also change the way we think about free speech. We have already seen, in chapter 2, that the distinctive value of the particular individual rights and freedoms to which liberals are committed cannot be demonstrated without appealing to the value of enabling individuals to exercise ethical autonomy. And once we recognize that the normative force of liberal rights is grounded in the value of ethical autonomy, we are led to interpret and defend those rights in ways that Rawlsian political liberals might not. For example, the politically liberal state values and protects free speech because of its central importance for democratic political life and because self-expression may be an important part of an individual's pursuit of his conception of the good. But the politically liberal state cannot give such a clear account of the value of free speech to the listener, who may be persuaded to change his beliefs and values as a result of the arguments he hears. A state that endorses the value of autonomy, by contrast, protects free nonpolitical speech for the sake of both speaker and audience: free speech rights are valuable because they safeguard the deliberative exchange of ideas that stimulates autonomous ethical reflection.

Autonomy and political liberals may well agree about the degree of support and protection the state should give to political speech, but a state that endorses autonomy has a reason to support and protect nonpolitical speech that the politically liberal state does not. Notice, however, that this additional reason to value and protect nonpolitical speech would not, at least in principle, apply equally to all forms of speech but would weigh more heavily to the extent that the speech enables listeners to develop and exercise their autonomy. So, when free speech rights conflict with other important values, the autonomy liberal may have more robust grounds for upholding the former, but the evidentiary base that is needed to resolve the conflict will also be broader once we reject the strict content-neutrality that characterizes the free speech jurisprudence of political liberalism.

Finally, I want to add a couple of thoughts to my observations in chapter 2 about the implications for liberal political theory and practice of abandoning the principle of political primacy, according to which legitimate civic goals presumptively outweigh all competing claims of value. The civic values promoted and defended by liberal democratic governments are important, to be sure, but they must nonetheless be balanced against the reasonable concerns of individuals and families who would be burdened by policies that aim at realizing civic goods. Political primacy appears defensible only if we swallow the alarmist rhetoric of survival, according to which any deviation from civically optimal policies threatens to wreck the liberal democratic enterprise to which we rightly attach great value. Once we recognize that the existence of a liberal democratic regime is a matter of degrees of health and flourishing, depending in complex ways on the level and distribution of civic virtues and capacities in the citizenry, there is no reason to accept the proposition that an improved liberal democracy is always worth the cost along other dimensions of value.

The requirements of liberal public justification, although stringent, do not prevent the state from appealing to noncivic values, but these appeals must be transparent and explicit: noncivic values must not be smuggled into a hazy conception of the civic good in the way that Gutmann and Macedo seem to sneak the paternalistic grounds for cultivating children's ethical autonomy into an argument that supposedly appeals only to civic educational values. The key point here is that we must recognize both the limits on what can legitimately be regarded as a liberal democratic civic value and the limited justificatory force of appeals to those values. Recognition of these twin limits on the invocation of civic values in the sphere of public justification has obvious implications for all policymaking, not just for education policy. Public justifications grounded only in supposedly civic values must be subjected to careful scrutiny (by citizens, legislators, and courts). Even if there is found to be a genuine and legitimate state interest at stake, it cannot be presumed that this interest will be decisive against compet-ing noncivic values. These noncivic values are not sufficiently pro-tected by courts, whose role is only to adjudicate on particular requests for exemptions and accommodations in light of the burdens imposed by laws justified by legitimate state interests. Legislators and the citi-zens to whom they are accountable must weigh the noncivic costs of proposed laws before they are voted onto the books, rather than shifting the responsibility to individuals to bring costly lawsuits and then to courts to decide when and how to grant accommodations. No doubt there are particular circumstances that cannot be anticipated and provided for by general legislation, but the rejection of political pri-macy entails that policymakers should make a good faith effort to weigh and respond to concerns grounded in noncivic values as part of the legislative process.

BIBLIOGRAPHY

Ackerman, B. 1980. *Social Justice in the Liberal State*. New Haven: Yale University Press.

Appiah, K. A. 1996. "Culture, Subculture, Multiculturalism: Educational Options." In R. Fullinwider, *Public Education in a Multicultural Society*. Cambridge: Cambridge University Press.

Aristotle, 1984. *The Politics*. Trans. C. Lord. Chicago: University of Chicago Press.

———. 1985. *Nicomachean Ethics*. Trans. T. Irwin. Indianapolis: Hackett.

Arneson, R., and I. Shapiro. 1996. "Democratic Paternalism and Religious Freedom: A Critique of Wisconsin v. Yoder." In I. Shapiro and R. Hardin, *Political Order: NOMOS 39*. New York: New York University Press.

Arons, S. 1983. *Compelling Belief: The Culture of American Schooling*. New York: McGraw-Hill New Press.

Aviram, A. 1995. "Autonomy and Commitment: Compatible Ideals." *Journal of Philosophy of Education* 29/1.

Barry, B. 2001. *Culture and Equality*. Cambridge: Harvard University Press.

Bates, S. 1994. *Battleground: One Mother's Crusade, the Religious Right, and the Struggle for Our Schools*. New York: Henry Holt.

Bridges, D. 1984. "Non-paternalistic Arguments in Support of Parents' Rights." *Journal of Philosophy of Education* 18/1.

Brighouse, H. 1998. "Civic Education and Liberal Legitimacy." *Ethics* 108.

Burtt, S. 1994. "Religious Parents, Secular Schools." *Review of Politics* 56.

———. 1996. "In Defense of Yoder." In I. Shapiro, and R. Hardin, *Political Order: NOMOS 39*. New York: New York University Press.

Callan, E. 1985. "McLaughlin on Parental Rights." *Journal of Philosophy of Education* 19/1.

———. 1988. "Faith, Worship, and Reason in Religious Upbringing." *Journal of Philosophy of Education* 22/2.

———. 1994. "Autonomy and Alienation." *Journal of Philosophy of Education* 28/1.

———. 1996. "Political Liberalism and Political Education." *Review of Politics* 58/1.

———. 1997. *Creating Citizens*. Oxford: Clarendon Press.

Carter, S. 1987. "Evolution, Creationism, and Treating Religion as a Hobby." *Duke Law Journal*, no. 6.

———. 1993. *Culture of Disbelief: How American Law and Politics Trivialize Religious Devotion*. New York: Anchor Books.

Charney, E. 2000. "Taking Pluralism Seriously." Ph.D. dissertation, Harvard University.

Coleman, J. 2002. "Answering Susan: Liberalism, Civic Education, and Status of Younger Persons." D. Archard, and C. M. MacLeod, *The Moral and Political Status of Children.* Oxford: Oxford University Press.

Coons, J. E., and S. D. Sugarman. 1999. *Education by Choice: The Case for Family Control.* Troy, NY: Educator's International Press.

Crittenden, B. 1988. *Parents, the State, and the Right to Educate.* Melbourne: Melbourne University Press.

Crowder, G. 1994. "Pluralism and Liberalism." *Political Studies* 42.

de Jong, J., and G. Snik. 2002. "Why Should States Fund Denominational Schools?" *Journal of Philosophy of Education* 36/4.

Dearden, R. F. 1968. *The Philosophy of Primary Education.* London: Routledge & Kegan Paul.

———. 1972. "Autonomy and Education." In R. F. Dearden, P. H. Hirst, and R. S. Peters, *Education and the Development of Reason.* London: Routledge & Kegan Paul.

———. 1975. "Autonomy as an Educational Ideal I." In S. C. Brown, *Philosophers Discuss Education.* London: Macmillan.

Dent, G. W. 1988. "Religious Children, Secular Schools." *Southern California Law Review* 61.

Devins, N. 1992. "Fundamentalist Christian Educators v. State." *George Washington Law Review* 60.

Dworkin, G. 1988. *The Theory and Practice of Autonomy.* Cambridge: Cambridge University Press.

Dworkin, R. 2000. *Sovereign Virtue: The Theory and Practice of Equality.* Cambridge: Harvard University Press.

Elster, J. 2000. *Ulysses Unbound: Studies in Rationality, Precommitment, and Constraints.* Cambridge: Cambridge University Press.

Erikson, E. 1968. *Identity: Youth and Crisis.* New York: Norton.

Feinberg, J. 1980. "A Child's Right to an Open Future." In W. Aiken and H. LaFollette, *Whose Child?* Totowa, NJ: Rowman & Littlefield.

———. 1989. "Autonomy." In J. Christman, *The Inner Citadel.* New York: Oxford University Press.

Feinberg, W. 1995. "Liberalism and the Aims of Multicultural Education." In Y. Tamir, *Democratic Education in a Multicultural State.* Oxford: Blackwell.

Fried, C. 1978. *Right and Wrong.* Cambridge: Harvard University Press.

Friedman, M. 1955. "The Role of Government in Education." In R. Solo, *Economics and the Public Interest.* New Brunswick: Rutgers University Press.

———. 1962. *Capitalism and Freedom.* Chicago: University of Chicago Press.

Fullinwider, R. 1996. "Multicultural Education: Concepts, Policies, and Controversies." In *Public Education in a Multicultural Society.* Cambridge: Cambridge University Press.

Galston, W. 1989. "Civic Education in the Liberal State." In N. Rosenblum, *Liberalism and the Moral Life.* Cambridge: Harvard University Press.

———. 1995. "Two Concepts of Liberalism." *Ethics* 105/3.

———. 1999a. "Value Pluralism and Liberal Political Theory." *American Political Science Review* 93/4.

―――. 1999b. "Diversity, Toleration, and Deliberative Democracy: Religious Minorities and Public Schooling." In S. Macedo, *Deliberative Politics*. New York: Oxford University Press.

―――. 2002. *Liberal Pluralism*. Cambridge: Cambridge University Press.

Gardner, P. 1988. "Religious Upbringing and the Liberal Ideal of Religious Autonomy." *Journal of Philosophy of Education* 22/1.

Gaus, G. F. 1996. *Justificatory Liberalism*. New York: Oxford University Press.

Gilles, S. 1996. "On Educating Children: A Parentalist Manifesto." *University of Chicago Law Review* 63.

Gray, J. 1996. *Isaiah Berlin*. Princeton: Princeton University Press.

Greenawalt, K. 2000. "Five Questions about Religion Judges Are Afraid to Ask." In N. Rosenblum, *Obligations of Citizenship and Demands of Faith*. Princeton: Princeton University Press.

Gutmann, A. 1995. "Civic Education and Social Diversity." *Ethics* 105.

―――. 1996. "Challenges of Multiculturalism in Democratic Education." In R. Fullinwider, *Public Education in a Multicultural Society*. Cambridge: Cambridge University Press.

―――. 1999. *Democratic Education*. Princeton: Princeton University Press.

Gutmann, A., and D. Thompson. 1996. *Democracy and Disagreement*. Cambridge: Belknap, Harvard University Press.

Hampton, J. 1998. *The Authority of Reason*. Cambridge: Cambridge University Press.

Hand, M. 2002. "Religious Upbringing Reconsidered" in *Journal of Philosophy of Education* 36/4.

Hill, T. E. 1991. *Autonomy and Self-respect*. Cambridge: Cambridge University Press.

Hirst, P. H. 1974. *Moral Education in a Secular Society*. London: University of London Press.

Illich, I. 1971. *Deschooling Society*. New York: Harper & Row.

Kant, I. 1784/1983. "An Answer to the Question: What Is Enlightenment?" In *Perpetual Peace and Other Essays*. Trans. T. Humphrey, Indianapolis: Hackett.

―――. 1785/1993. *Groundwork for the Metaphysics of Morals*. Trans. J. Ellington. Indianapolis: Hackett.

Kohlberg, L. 1971. "Stages of Moral Development as a Basis for Moral Education." In C. M. Beck, B. S. Crittenden, and E. V. Sullivan, *Moral Education: Interdisciplinary Approaches*. New York: Newman.

―――. 1987. "Development as the Aim of Education." In *Child Psychology and Childhood Education*. New York: Longman.

Kukathas, C. 1992a. "Are There Any Cultural Rights?" *Political Theory* 20/1.

―――. 1992b. "Cultural Rights Again: A Rejoinder to Kymlicka." *Political Theory* 20/4.

Kymlicka, W. 1989. *Liberalism, Community, and Culture*. Oxford: Clarendon Press.

―――. 1995. *Multicultural Citizenship*. Oxford: Oxford University Press.

Levinson, M. 1999. *The Demands of Liberal Education*. Oxford: Oxford University Press.

Lindley, R. 1986. *Autonomy*. London: Macmillan.

Lomasky, L. E. 1987. *Persons, Rights, and the Moral Community*. Oxford: Oxford University Press.

Macedo, S. 1990. *Liberal Virtues: Citizenship, Virtue, and Community in Liberal Constitutionalism*. Oxford: Clarendon Press.

———. 2000. *Diversity and Distrust*. Cambridge: Harvard University Press.

MacIntyre, A. 1981. *After Virtue*. Notre Dame: University of Notre Dame Press.

Marcia, J. E. 1980. "Identity in Adolescence." In J. Adelson, *Handbook of Adolescent Psychology*. New York: John Wiley & Sons.

Matthews, G. B. 1980. *Philosophy and the Young Child*. Cambridge: Harvard University Press.

McConnell, M. 1991a. "Multiculturalism, Majoritarianism, and Educational Choice." *Chicago Legal Forum*.

———. 1991b. "Selective Funding Problem." *Harvard Law Review* 104.

McDonough, K. 1998. "Can the Liberal State Support Cultural Identity Schools?" *American Journal of Education* 106/4.

McLaughlin, T. H. 1984. "Parental Rights and the Religious Upbringing of Children." *Journal of Philosophy of Education* 18/1.

———. 1985. "Religion, Upbringing, and Liberal Values: A Rejoinder to Eamonn Callan." *Journal of Philosophy of Education* 19/1.

———. 1987. " 'Education for All' and Religious Schools." In G. Haydon, *Education for a Pluralist Society: Philosophical Perspectives on the Swann Report*. London: Institute of Education.

———. 1992. "The Ethics of Separate Schools." In M. Leicester and M. Taylor, *Ethics, Ethnicity, and Education*. London: Kogan Page.

Mendus, S. 1995. "Toleration and Recognition: Education in a Multicultural Society." In Y. Tamir, *Democratic Education in a Multicultural State*. Oxford: Blackwell.

Mill, J. S. 1859/1989. *On Liberty*. Cambridge: Cambridge University Press.

Miller, P. H. 1989. *Theories of Developmental Psychology*. New York: W. H. Freeman & Co.

Mozert v. Hawkins County Board of Education. 1987. (827 F 2d 1058--6th Circuit)

Nagel, T. 1986. *The View from Nowhere*. New York: Oxford University Press.

———. 1987. "Moral Conflict and Political Legitimacy." *Philosophy and Public Affairs* 16/3.

Newey, G. 1997. "Metaphysics Postponed: Liberalism, Pluralism, and Neutrality." *Political Studies* 45.

Passmore, J. 1972. "On Teaching to Be Critical." In R. F. Dearden, P. H. Hirst, and R. S. Peters, *Education and the Development of Reason*. London: Routledge & Kegan Paul.

Piaget, J. 1950. *The Psychology of Intelligence*. Trans. M. Piercey and D. E. Berlyne. London: Routledge & Kegan Paul.

———. 1928/1976. *Judgment and Reasoning in the Child*. Trans. M. Warden. New York: Harcourt, Brace, & Co.

———. 1962/1999. "The Stages of the Intellectual Development of the Child." In D. Muir and A. Slater, *The Blackwell Reader in Developmental Psychology*. Oxford: Blackwell.

Pierce v. Society of Sisters. 1925. (268 U.S. 510)

Putnam, R. D. 2000. *Bowling Alone: The Collapse and Revival of American Community*. New York: Simon and Schuster.

Rawls, J. 1971/1999. *A Theory of Justice*. Cambridge: Belknap, Harvard University Press.

———. 1993/1996. *Political Liberalism*. New York: Columbia University Press.

———. 1999. "The Idea of Public Reason Revisited." In *Collected Papers*. Cambridge: Harvard University Press.

Raz, J. 1986. *The Morality of Freedom*. Oxford: Clarendon Press.

———. 1994. "Facing Diversity: The Case of Epistemic Abstinence." In *Ethics in the Public Domain*. Oxford: Clarendon Press.

Reich, R. 2002. *Bridging Liberalism and Multiculturalism in American Education*. Chicago: University of Chicago Press.

Riesman, D. 1969. *The Lonely Crowd*. New Haven: Yale University Press.

Rorty, R. 1989. "The Contingency of a Liberal Community." In *Contingency, Irony, and Solidarity*. Cambridge: Cambridge University Press.

———. 1991. "The Priority of Democracy to Philosophy." In *Philosophical Papers*. Cambridge: Cambridge University Press.

Sandel, M. 1982. *Liberalism and the Limits of Justice*. Cambridge: Cambridge University Press.

Sartre, J. P. 1943/1992. *Being and Nothingness*. New York: Washington Square Press.

Scheffler, I. 1973. "Moral Education and the Democratic Ideal." In *Reason and Teaching*. London: Routledge & Kegan Paul.

Schumpeter, J. A. 1950. *Capitalism, Socialism, and Democracy*. New York: Harper.

Short, G. 2002. "Faith-based Schools: A Threat to Social Cohesion?" *Journal of Philosophy of Education* 36/4.

Stolzenberg, N. 1993. "He Drew a Circle That Shut Me Out." *Harvard Law Review* 106.

Strike, K. A. 1996. "Must Liberal Citizens Be Reasonable?" *Review of Politics* 58/1.

Tamir, Y. 1995. "Two Concepts of Multiculturalism." In *Democratic Education in a Multicultural State*. Oxford: Blackwell.

Taylor, C. 1985. "What Is Human Agency?" In *Human Agency and Language: Philosophical Papers*, vol. 1. Cambridge: Cambridge University Press.

Telfer, E. 1975. "Autonomy as an Educational Ideal II." In S. C. Brown, *Philosophers Discuss Education*. London: Macmillan.

Thiessen, E. J. 1987. "Two Concepts or Two Phases of Liberal Education?" *Journal of Philosophy of Education* 21/2.

Verba, S., K. L. Schlozman, and H. E. Brady. 1995. *Voice and Equality: Civic Voluntarism in American Politics*. Cambridge: Harvard University Press.

Waldron, J. 1989. "Autonomy and Perfectionism in Raz's Morality of Freedom." *Southern California Law Review* 62.

Walzer, M. 1983. *Spheres of Justice*. New York: Basic Books.

———. 1995. "Education, Democratic Citizenship, and Multiculturalism." In Y. Tamir, *Democratic Education in a Multicultural State*. Oxford: Blackwell.

White, J. P. 1982. *The Aims of Education Re-stated*. London: Routledge & Kegan Paul.

Wisconsin v. Yoder. 1972. (406 U.S. 205)

Wolfe, A. 1998. *One Nation, After All*. New York: Viking.

Wringe, C. 1995. "Educational Rights in Multicultural Democarcies." In Y. Tamir, *Democratic Education in a Multicultural State*. Oxford: Blackwell.

Zelman v. Simmons-Harris. 2002. (536 U.S. 639)

INDEX

Ackerman, Bruce, 77, 93, 164, 183–84
adult education, 214–15
affirmative action, 215
Amish, the, 45–46, 106, 115n, 116. See also *Wisconsin v. Yoder*
Appiah, Kwame Anthony, 20, 32
Aristotle, 17, 19–20, 31–32, 39, 210
Arneson, Richard, 77, 92, 98–99, 111
Arons, Stephen, 131, 148, 150
atheism, 172. See also secular humanism
autonomy: abstinence about value of, 4, 7–8, 11, 15, 22, 46–49, 55, 59, 92, 98, 203; and civic education, 7, 26, 46, 54–58, 69, 130–31; and commitment, 74–76, 186–87, 212–14; and common schools, 45, 49, 54; definition of, 23; degrees of, 58–59, 75; exercise v. development of, 154; and identity, 77, 80, 82–84, 87, 94, 98, 183–86, 192–93; instrumental value of, 8, 96–106, 110–11, 127, 134, 211–12; intrinsic value of, 88–93, 95, 127, 134, 168, 211; in liberalism, 23, 61–62, 93; measurement of, 6, 162; moral v. ethical, 67–68, 74n, 90n, 94, 143n, 192; and availability of options, 128, 145, 194, 196, 216; parental opposition to, 41, 45–46, 49, 54, 57–59, 108–9, 122, 124, 204, 211–12; as a primary good, 209–10; promoting v. enabling, 105, 133–34, 189; and public policy implications, 214–18; and radical choice, 76, 82–83, 85; role of reason in, 69, 77, 80, 85–86, 95, 99, 105, 109, 188, 199–201; and religious faith, 128, 144–45; role of schools in education for, 158, 160–61; v. second-order thought, 69–72, 168–69; v. substance of belief 80, 107, 128. See also Callan, Eamonn; Galston, William; Gutmann, Amy; Macedo, Stephen; Rawls, John; Raz, Joseph
Aviram, Aharon, 75, 85, 95, 134

Barry, Brian, 26, 47, 52, 73, 106, 115–16, 128, 133, 143, 180
Bates, Stephen, 125–26
Berlin, Isaiah, 76

Bob Jones University, 177
Brady, Henry, 30
Bridges, David, 119–21
Brighouse, Harry, 20, 96, 104, 130, 133, 159–60, 195
burdens of judgment, 21, 36, 38, 55–56, 60, 131, 145
Burtt, Shelley, 113, 118, 158–59, 185, 194
Bussing, 165, 174. See also diversity, exposure to

Callan, Eamonn, 29, 120–22, 162–63; on autonomy, 75, 82, 89, 96–97, 128, 144; on autonomy as a civic value, 26n4, 55–59, 88n, 131, 179n6; on civic education, 18, 28, 32, 38; on education for autonomy, 143, 146, 160, 165–67, 172, 174, 186–87, 197
Carter, Stephen, 125
Catholic schools, 29, 170
Charney, Evan, 70, 92
childhood, definition of, 135
children, authority over, 4, 113–14, 136, 205. See also paternalism
citizenship: measurement of, 6, 30; as power, 27
civic education, 7, 15, 21, 24, 28–29, 179, 197n, 204; and autonomy, 7, 26, 46, 54–58, 69, 130–31; in common schools, 32–33; definition of, 3; in a liberal democracy, 17–20, 31, 43, 60, 148n; and obedience, 37; as public good, 16, 39, 52, 125; dimensions of success of, 43. See also Callan, Eamonn; Galston, William; Gutmann, Amy; Macedo, Stephen
Coleman, Joseph, 135n7
commitment, 74–76, 186–87, 212–14
comprehensive doctrine, 21–22, 26–29, 31–32, 34–35, 52, 56, 61, 82, 91, 184n1; consistency within, 100–102; definition of, 2n2
conception of the good. See comprehensive doctrine
constitutionalism, 2, 6, 42, 144
Coons, John, 50, 79, 135, 149, 154, 158, 185, 189

creationism, 34, 81–82, 102, 145n, 171, 210
Crittenden, Brian, 141, 152, 158–59, 170, 188
Crowder, George, 60
culture: primary, 77–80, 115, 122, 163–64, 183–85, 187, 192–93, 195; traditional, 9, 124–29, 216
curriculum, 167, 171–72, 198; hidden, 31

De Jong, Johan, 184n2, 198
Dearden, R. F., 76, 83, 95, 102, 154, 193, 199
deliberation, 37, 52–54
Dent, George, 43–45, 143, 147
developmental psychology, 77, 83n, 135n7, 157, 186–87, 190–93
Devins, Neal, 120, 175n
Dewey, John, 128
diversity, exposure to, 124, 165–66, 174; and civic education, 32, 39; and education for autonomy, 75, 145–46, 150, 155; management of, 158–62, 172–73, 183, 186, 188, 197–98
Dworkin, Gerald, 70–75, 77, 168
Dworkin, Ronald, 70, 94

education: adult, 214–15; for autonomy (see autonomy, and civic education; autonomy, and common schools; autonomy, exercise v. development of; autonomy, parental opposition to; autonomy, promoting v. enabling; autonomy, role of schools in education for); civic (see civic education); mandatory, 46–47, 152–53, 161, 165; as a primary good, 27, 47–48, 53
Elster, Jon, 213
entanglement, 10, 175–79
epistemology, 8–9, 100, 104, 106. See also autonomy, instrumental value of
Erikson, Erik, 186
evolution. See creationism
existentialism, 76. See also autonomy, and radical choice

faith, 128, 144–45
Feinberg, Joel, 69, 77, 95–96, 117, 153
Feinberg, Walter, 79
free speech, 217–18

freedom, 4–5, 115–16, 135. See also paternalism
Fried, Charles, 114–16, 118
Friedman, Milton, 16
Fullinwider, Robert, 18
fundamentalism, 29, 124–26, 144, 171

Galston, William, 60–61; on autonomy, 91–92, 98, 158–60, 186–87; on civic education, 18, 20–21, 26, 36–37, 130; on offensive v. defensive reasons, 52–54; on parents, 119, 122; on political pluralism, 44–45, 125
Gardner, Peter, 79, 163, 187, 189
Gaus, Gerald, 55, 108–10
Gilles, Stephen, 103–4, 158–59, 186, 189
Gray, John, 60, 76
Greenawalt, Kent, 177n, 179n5
Gutmann, Amy, 27–28, 31, 118n2, 123, 151, 177; on autonomy, 25–26, 54–55, 103, 155; on civic education, 15, 19–20, 30, 33–35, 37, 125, 130–31; on nonrepression and nondiscrimination, 17, 24, 26; on political primacy, 41–48; on private schools, 50–51

Hampton, Jean, 109–10
hidden curriculum, 31
Hill, Thomas, 72, 86
Hirst, Paul, 188
home schools, 9, 123n, 161n, 207–8
Hume, David, 17

identity, 77, 80, 82–84, 87, 94, 98, 183–86, 192–93
Illich, Ivan, 10, 151–53
incommensurability, 82–84. See also pluralism
indoctrination, 125, 127, 162–63, 168–69; by parents, 107, 117, 122; in schools, 4, 148–50, 153, 178, 198
Islamia Primary School, 1

Kant, Immanuel, 17, 67–68, 91, 201
Kohlberg, Lawrence, 192–93
Kukathas, Chandran, 115–16, 118, 126–27, 129
Kymlicka, Will, 61–62, 100, 129

Levinson, Meira, 39, 62, 77, 82, 151, 153, 155, 160, 163–65, 183–84, 186

libertarianism, 16, 115, 178, 209
Lindley, Richard, 85
Lomasky, Loren, 61

Macedo, Stephen, 30–31, 117, 177; on au-
    tonomy, 24–25, 57, 63, 85, 93, 104; on
    civic education, 15, 18, 20–22, 28, 34–35,
    39, 52, 130–31; on political primacy,
    42–49, 54
MacIntyre, Alasdair, 76, 83–85, 87, 210
Marcia, James, 186–87, 192–93
Matthews, Gareth, 200n8
McConnell, Michael, 17, 117, 142–43,
    147, 149
McDonough, Kevin, 170, 172, 186, 199
McLaughlin, Terence, 161, 163, 166, 174,
    178, 185, 190, 194–95, 198
Mendus, Susan, 91
Mill, John Stuart, 10, 88–91, 98–99, 111,
    117–18, 147–49, 211, 217
Miller, Patricia, 187, 191
Mozert v. Hawkins, 124–26, 141

Nagel, Thomas, 55, 71
neutrality, 93, 126, 209–10, 212; in justifi-
    cation, 22, 103–4, 176; in schools, 10,
    142–43, 145–46, 164; and the value of
    autonomy, 106–7, 111 (*see also* auton-
    omy, abstinence about value of)
Newey, Glen, 60

parents, 9, 113–15, 118–23, 150. *See also*
    autonomy, parental opposition to;
    paternalism
Passmore, John, 200–202
paternalism, 7, 9, 47–48, 69, 88, 119, 128,
    134–35, 153–55, 179; of adults, 209–10,
    214, 217; by state v. parents, 107–9, 117
    (*see also* children, authority over; parents)
patriotism, 18, 28–29
pedagogy, 167, 170–72, 196, 198–202
perfectionism, 209–12. *See also* neutrality
Piaget, Jean, 190–92
Pierce v. Society of Sisters, 180
Plato, 17
pluralism, 68, 125; and autonomous
    choice, 82–84; political implications of,
    36, 60–61, 91–92, 110; and rational re-
    flection, 78–79, 86, 96, 99, 187
political liberalism, 7, 24, 42, 46–47, 49,
    54, 91–93, 217–18; and public justifica-

tion, 22, 103. *See also* autonomy, absti-
    nence about value of; political primacy;
    public reason
political primacy, 7, 44–45, 48–49, 57–59,
    62, 106, 125; definition of, 3–4, 41–42;
    implications of rejecting, 49–54, 218–19.
    See also Gutmann, Amy; Macedo, Ste-
    phen; political liberalism
primary goods, 27, 47–48, 53, 209–10
psychology, developmental, 77, 83n,
    135n7, 157, 186–87, 190–93
public justification 21–22, 33–34, 55, 88,
    95–96, 103, 107–10, 218
public reason, 22, 33–34, 52–53
Putnam, Robert, 215

Rawls, John, 2n2, 15, 21–22, 28–29, 35,
    38n, 42, 54, 57–58, 60, 92, 216; on auton-
    omy, 46, 62, 81, 97–98; on burdens of
    judgment, 21, 36, 38, 55–56, 60, 131;
    145; on primary goods, 27, 47, 209; on
    public reason, 22, 33–34, 52–53; on
    reflective equilibrium, 5, 101–2
Raz, Joseph, 54, 56n; on concept of auton-
    omy, 68–69, 75–76, 82, 84; on autonomy
    and availability of options, 128, 145,
    216; on value of autonomy, 90, 102–3
reciprocity, 18–19, 21–22, 28, 32, 35–36, 39,
    52, 55–57, 60. *See also* public justifica-
    tion; public reason
reflective equilibrium, 5, 101–2
Reich, Rob, 46n, 79, 147, 154, 160, 162,
    166–69, 173
relativism, 142–43, 146–47
Religious Freedom Restoration Act, 43n
religious instruction, 193–96
religious schools: for civic education, 36;
    differences among, 29–31; primary,
    182–204; prohibition of, 164, 167, 178,
    180, 197; public funding of, 12, 50, 196;
    secondary, 157–81
representative government, 18
responsibility, 93–96
Riesman, David, 70
Rorty, Richard , 95

Sandel, Michael, 81, 100–101
Sartre, Jean-Paul, 76
Scalia, Antonin, 42
Scheffler, Israel, 37
school choice, 154. *See also* vouchers

schools: as authoritarian institutions, 151–53, 196, 199; Catholic, 29, 170; common, 32–33, 45, 49, 54; as democratic institutions, 32–33; detached, 150, 155, 163–64, 182–83, 186; funding v. permitting, 50–51, 53, 181, 208; home, 9, 123n, 161n, 207–8; primary, 182–204; private, 5, 50–52, 165, 180, 207–8; public control and regulation of, 10–11, 52, 117–18, 122, 147–51, 161n, 163, 165, 168–69, 175–79; religious (*see* religious schools); secondary, 157–81; secular, 141–47
Schumpeter, Joseph, 19n
science , 171. *See also* creationism
secular humanism, 141, 144. *See also* atheism
secular reasons, 34, 170–72. *See also* public reason
Shapiro, Ian, 77, 92, 98–99, 111
Shlozman, Kay, 30
Snik, Ger, 184n2, 198
social capital, 215
Stolzenberg, Nomi, 107, 125–26, 129, 144n
Strike, Kenneth, 35–37
subjectivism, 142–43, 146
Sugarman, Stephen, 50, 79, 135, 149, 154, 158, 185, 189

Tamir, Yael, 61, 90
Taylor, Charles, 83–85, 87, 95
teachers, 151–53
Telfer, Elizabeth, 81
tests, standardized, 206–7
Thiessen, Elmer, 188, 201
Thompson, Dennis, 125, 148n, 153n
toleration, 36, 38

Values Clarification, 142–43, 146–47
Vatican II, 177
Verba, Sidney, 30
vouchers, 1–2, 35, 117, 207. *See also* school choice

Waldron, Jeremy, 79
Walzer, Michael, 40, 50
welfare , 47
White, John, 134
Wisconsin v. Yoder, 45–46, 106, 124–25. *See also* Amish, the
Wolfe, Alan, 35n
Wringe, Colin, 78

Zelman v. Simmons-Harris, 2n1